STRATEGIC MANAGEMENT OF TEAMS

STRATEGIC MANAGEMENT OF TEAMS

DAVID I. CLELAND

Ernest E. Roth Professor & Professor of Engineering Management, University of Pittsburgh, Pittsburgh, Pennsylvania

JOHN WILEY & SONS, INC.
NEW YORK / CHICHESTER / BRISBANE / TORONTO / SINGAPORE

Library of Congress Cataloging-in-Publication Data:
Cleland, David I.
    Strategic management of teams / David I. Cleland.
        p.   cm.
    Includes index.
    ISBN 0-471-12058-8 (cloth : alk. paper)
    1. Self-directed work groups. 2. Organizational change.
3. Strategic planning. 4. Reengineering (Management) I. Title.
    HD66.C57   1996
    658.4'036—dc20   95–35708
                                                    CIP

Printed in the United States of America

10 9 8 7 6 5 4 3 2 1

CONTENTS

PREFACE

The traditional model of organizational design is an endangered species. Organizations have used reengineering, downsizing, empowerment, and restructuring strategies to reduce the number of middle managers and decentralize authority and responsibility, and they have used alternative teams as key elements in the strategic management of an enterprise. Computer technology, information systems, and enhanced means of communicating have significantly increased the awareness and competencies of people in organizations. The use of teams has become recognized as an effective way to manage change in organizations, from product, service, and process development to benchmarking and reengineering efforts. Teams have become key organizational elements in the design and execution of strategic management initiatives for an enterprise.

Team management is an idea whose time has come. Teams are becoming a key and distinct element of an organizational design in which effective cross-functional and cross-organizational work have become the norm for dealing with the inevitable changes that face all organizations. The use of teams has modified both the theory and practice of management. The ability to serve as a contributing member of teams and to provide leadership of teams has become recognized as a core competency that managers, managers-to-be, and professionals at all levels and disciplines will need to develop. The traditional command-and-control managers are anachronisms in contemporary organizations and are being replaced by managers and leaders who follow a consensus-and-consent philosophy in their organizations and with key stakeholders outside the organization's boundaries.

Change has become a way of life in contemporary organizations. The key challenge facing all enterprises—industrial, military, educational, governmental, medical, agricultural, and so forth—is the ability to anticipate change and assemble and organize resources to develop competitive strategies that will increase the chances for survival in what is becoming an increasingly unforgiving global marketplace. The inevitability of change—sometimes sudden and radical—poses a particular challenge for today's managers and leaders: how to manage strategically so the change can be dealt with and work to the advantage of the enterprise.

The basic theme of this book is that alternative types of teams are a necessary organizational design to manage change within organizations, and that the outcome of the use of teams consists of building blocks in the design and execution of product, service, and process strategy. The effective use of teams as elements of organizational strategy will result in improvement of competitive capabilities reflected in product, service, and process changes. Developmental efforts by an organization today provide the vehicle through which people can be given the opportunity to excel in creating something that has not previously existed but is needed to improve competitive capabilities in the marketplace. In so doing, people gain valuable learning and contribute meaningful value to the enterprise.

According to *Business Week* magazine, the formation and use of teams is an art form for corporate America. Getting people to work together on alternative teams has become a critical management skill. An editorial in *Business Week* noted that "those companies that learn the secrets of creating cross-functional teams are winning the battle for global market share and profits. Those that don't are losing out."[1]

BOOK USERS

This book is written for use in senior undergraduate or graduate programs within universities and colleges that provide management curriculum in the areas of business, engineering, education, public health, public administration, and law. The book should also have wide appeal for training programs in the user communities—such as industry, hospitals, educational institutions, the military, and governmental bodies. Any person that considers using any or all of the alternative teams described in this book will find valuable orientation to and guidance on designing and implementing a team-driven organization culture. Directors and instructors in executive development programs and continuing education training initiatives courses will find that this book provides a comprehensive overview of why, how, and when teams should become part of management philosophies and techniques for dealing with change.

In recent years there has been a flood of how-to books on the management of teams. All of these books have provided general guidance on how teams should be used, but they have offered limited guidance on the purposes for

[1] *Business Week,* November 1, 1993, p. 160.

which teams can be used—such as benchmarking, reengineering, concurrent engineering, production teams, and other sundry uses. None of the existing books provide guidance on how teams can be used as elements of strategic management or offer insight on both the positive and negative sides of teams.

This book is a primer on how responsiveness to change in contemporary organizations can be facilitated through the strategic management of teams. More specifically, the book deals with teams in the following contexts:

- Alternative uses to which teams can be put in dealing with product, service, and process change in the enterprise
- How teams can be used by managers to bring about a cross-functional and cross-organizational focus in planning for, and using resources in, the enterprise
- How teams can be used to facilitate greater participation of all people in the enterprise in designing, developing, and implementing technical, social, management, and leadership strategies, leading to enhanced competitiveness
- How organizational cultures are changing as a result of the use of teams as initiatives of strategic management
- Alternative types of teams and how to go about preparing teams and organizations for the use of teams
- Positive and negative results of using teams and how to adopt practical, on-the-job team development strategies

ORGANIZATION OF THIS BOOK

This book is adaptable for different uses. Each of the chapters can stand alone for a particular aspect of the use of teams yet is also a building block in considering the design and development of strategy for using teams as instruments of corporate purposes. Taken together, the chapters present a strategy for how teams can contribute to the long-term survival of an enterprise in a world of changing global competition. A description of the book sections and chapters follows.

Part I. SETTING THE STAGE: This part presents the concept and practice of strategic management as the major responsibility of senior managers in the enterprise. A roadway for strategic management is suggested in which teams play a vital role in dealing with change in the enterprise.

Part II. DEVELOPING THE PLAYERS: This part (chapters 2–5) addresses how to prepare an organization and the players for the new roles that teams will play in the management of change.

Part III. USING TEAMS: This part (chapters 6–12) discusses the alternative types of teams, including under what conditions they should be used.

Part IV. NEW DIMENSIONS: This part (chapters 13–14) discusses the negative side of teams and describes the results that teams have accomplished for organizations. These results are drawn from the literature and from the author's conversations, consultations, and correspondence with practitioners who have tried using teams and have realized both positive and negative consequences.

ACKNOWLEDGMENTS

My deep appreciation goes to my students and clients with whom I had the opportunity to discuss and debate the use of alternative teams in contemporary organizations. Much was learned about the strategic management of teams through a careful perusal of the literature, particularly as to how and when teams were used as instruments of corporate strategy. My appreciation thus also goes to the editors and authors of those journals that provide extraordinary insight into the use of teams in modern organizations.

I thank Dr. Harvey Wolfe, chairman of the Industrial Engineering Department, and Dr. H. K. Chang, dean of the School of Engineering, University of Pittsburgh, who provided the environment and resources that made the writing of this book possible.

Finally, a special note of thanks to my secretary of many years, Claire Zubritzky, whose administrative assistance and support during the preparation of the manuscript were well above and beyond what could have been expected. Her constructive criticism, encouragement, and empathy contributed greatly to this book. I thank her for her continued willingness to share her expertise in helping me in my professorial career.

Dr. David I. Cleland

Pittsburgh, Pennsylvania
March 21, 1995

PART I
SETTING THE STAGE

1

THE CONCEPT
AND PROCESS OF
STRATEGIC MANAGEMENT

There is nothing more difficult to take in hand, more perilous to conduct, or more uncertain in its success, than to take the lead in the introduction of a new order of things.

THE PRINCE, NICOLO MACHIAVELLI (1469–1527)

Selecting and setting the future direction of an enterprise is increasingly becoming the key challenge facing managers today. This is true not only for those companies that are having difficulties, but also for those that are enjoying success. When an enterprise encounters difficulties—particularly after it has enjoyed success—the reasons are usually the failure to anticipate market and competitive changes and the failure to develop suitable competitive products and organizational processes, which will position the company to regain success. Strategic sluggishness, satisfaction with a successful status quo, pride, bureaucratic organizational and management philosophies, and other cultural characteristics discourage and stifle creativity and innovation in an enterprise. People are not encouraged to seek continuous improvement in their own work and in their contributions to product and process developments that will make the enterprise competitive.

Organizations seldom encounter difficulties without working at it, in the sense of having managers who "work at" creating (perhaps unknowingly) the conditions conducive to failure. Even when confronted with a major crisis in the markets being served, company officials often refuse to accept a major competitive challenge in the marketplace. For example, in 1888, the CEO of

Zeis, upon seeing the new Kodak Brownie camera, stated, "It's a stupid fad and will be gone in three years."[1]

At IBM, senior executives finally accepted the personal computer (PC) as a reality and set up two competing project teams to design a simpler PC than existed in the market. Within a couple of years, IBM had become the world's PC manufacturer and set the standard for the industry. Yet a few years later, IBM was in trouble in both the mainframe and the PC business. Around the same time, Sears, Eastern Airlines, and other once innovative and successful companies encountered strategic difficulties. What happened? Many of their strategic failures were caused by the absence of a way of thinking about the strategic management of the enterprise.

This chapter discusses how to think about the strategic management of an enterprise and how to manage that enterprise as if its future mattered.

KEEPING THE BALANCE

For an enterprise, the essence of strategic management is to maintain balance in using resources to face major challenges. The key is balancing operational competence, strategic effectiveness, and functional excellence (Figure 1–1).

Operational competence concerns the ability to use resources to provide customers with quality products and/or services, which are delivered on time and provide value for customers. Operational competence requires the ability to use resources in a cost-effective manner to produce and deliver products and/or services that exceed what competitors are offering. Resources must be used efficiently in the organizational processes required to produce, finance, market, and provide after-sales services. The final measure of operational competence is profit or, in the case of a not-for-profit entity, greater value to the customers than was required to produce and deliver the products and/or services. Doing things right is fundamental to maintaining operational competence.

Strategic effectiveness is the ability to assess what may be possible and probable in future products and/or services and organizational processes to support future purposes. Strategic effectiveness is concerned with doing the right things to get an enterprise ready for its future. Senior managers, who have the most direct responsibility for the future of the enterprise, must develop fluency in evaluating risks and uncertainties and provide leadership that will motivate employees to examine opportunities for the enterprise's future. Product and/or service and process development teams are crucial in preparing for the future. Such teams provide focus for using resources to

---

[1] Peter F. Drucker, "The Theory of the Business," *Harvard Business Review,* September–October 1994, p. 97.

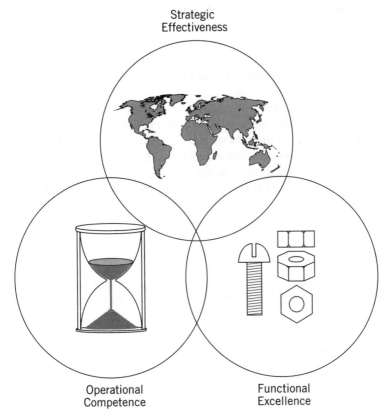

Strategic
Effectiveness

Operational
Competence

Functional
Excellence

Figure 1–1. Balance must be achieved and maintained among strategic management challenges.

prepare the enterprise for its future, and they provide the best way to integrate the many functions needed to flesh out the destiny of the enterprise.

Functional excellence means state-of-the-art use of resources in the disciplines that support the enterprise's organizational processes: research and development, engineering, manufacturing, marketing, finance, and after-sales service. Functional excellence includes ongoing improvement in employees' capabilities so they can provide the personal services that are required to support future enterprise purposes. Providing efficient, quality services to support enterprise products and/or services and processes is critical and determines the enterprise's profitability.

The bottom line of strategic management is to maintain balance among strategic effectiveness, operational competence, and functional excellence. The following roadmap for strategic management can help chart the course for the enterprise.

A ROADMAP FOR STRATEGIC MANAGEMENT

A roadmap is a representation of a route of travel to a desired destination. It provides a summary of where one wants to go, preliminary destinations along the route of travel that serve as checkpoints to measure progress, and the journey's endpoint.

Strategic managers require roadmaps to prepare the organization for its future. Those people who work with the leader in developing a future direction for the enterprise, as well as those people who will follow the leader, also require a roadmap to understand where they are going and how they will get there. A roadmap that outlines a general route for the future of the enterprise contains several key checkpoints on the road to the final destination:

- Foresight
- Competitive assessment
- Organizational strengths and weaknesses
- Benchmarking
- Strategic performance standards
- Functional expertise
- Vision quest
- Stakeholder interfaces
- Market needs
- Product and/or service and process development
- Feedback

A brief description of these checkpoints follows.

Foresight: The orderly development and anticipation of the possible and probable changes in the markets in which the organization would like to provide products and services. Performance in the desired markets will be affected by changes in the political, social, economic, legal, and technological forces in such markets. Foresight includes consideration of both existing markets and those markets likely to develop.

The purpose of foresight, as the act of looking forward with concern or prudence, is to predict events and forces likely to affect the enterprise's business. Nothing is more important to the organization than its future—assuming, of course, that it has demonstrated operational competence in providing current quality products and/or services to its customers. Effective foresight can give the enterprise an opportunity to get its products and/or services to the future first and stake out a leadership position. Foresight is based on deep insights into those forces and events that have a good chance of changing competitive practices. The deep insight needed to develop credible foresight comes after in-depth study of the real or potential systems changes found in technological, social, economic, legal, political, and competitive events that will change the game in the marketplace. The future is found in these systems changes.

One company appointed "headlight" teams to evaluate a preliminary set of industry discontinuities or drivers (developed by senior management) that were likely to affect the company. The teams evaluated each industry discontinuity in depth, seeking to discover (1) how the trend might influence current customers and current economies in the company, (2) the dynamics of the trends, (3) probable accelerating and decelerating factors, and (4) which companies were likely to gain or lose from the trends. As tentative answers began to emerge, they were studied in more depth in company workshops involving business units and corporate managers. At the conclusion of the headlight teams' initiative, senior managers felt that the company had developed the most penetrating insight into industry changes.[2]

When successful, the objective of adequate foresight is to satisfy customers' current needs for existing products and services and then to develop organizational processes that lead customers where they may not know they want to go. As one CEO said "We plan to lead the public with new products rather than ask them what they want." Many of today's products were developed by companies that had foresight into the probable desires of customers (although these customers were lacking foresight about these products), such as minivans, cellular telephones, fax machines, multivalve automobile engines, compact disk players, onboard car navigation systems, global satellite positioning receivers, automated teller machines, and the Home Shopping Network. For companies today, the challenge is to come up with future products and services not yet envisioned by existing customers—and do it before the competitors get there. This is too big of a job for managers working in the context of traditional organizational structure alone. Means must be developed for using teams that have the freedom to work in cross-functional and cross-organizational contexts to find out what is going on and what is likely to happen. Competing for the future is a big job, and one in which everyone can play a useful part—as long as they are properly organized and motivated.

Competitive Assessment: A rigorous examination and evaluation of the strengths, weaknesses, and probable strategies of competitors in their

---

[2] Gary Hamel and C. D. Prahalad, "Seeing the Future First," *Fortune,* September 5, 1994, pp. 64–70.

products and/or services, organizational processes, and market performance.

Organizational strengths and weaknesses: Assessment of the strengths and weaknesses of the enterprise, particularly regarding the ability to deliver competitive products and/or services through the use of effective organizational processes.

Benchmarking: Review of the performance of competitors and other organizations that are considered the best in the industry, to determine what operational and strategic abilities enable them to perform so well.

Strategic performance standards: Identification, development, and dissemination of the elements required to establish strategic performance standards and guide the use of resources in the enterprise. These standards include the organizational mission, objectives, goals, strategies, and design; individual and collective roles; leader and follower style; supporting systems; and the quality and quantity of organizational resources.

Functional expertise: The ability to develop and maintain centers of excellence in the disciplines needed to support operational and strategic initiatives.

Vision quest: The ability to envision what the future should be for the enterprise—that is, the general direction the enterprise should follow to become what organizational leaders want it to be.

Stakeholder interfaces: Discovery, development, and maintenance of common boundaries with those people and organizations that have a vested interest in the products and/or services and processes provided by the enterprise. Customers and suppliers are the principal stakeholders with whom close working relationships need to be maintained.

Market needs: Assessment of the probabilities and possibilities of the marketplace, including the potential for products and/or services for markets that do not currently exist.

Product and/or service and process development: The use of project teams to focus cross-functional and cross-organizational resources to conceptualize, design, develop, and initiate continuous improvements in existing products and/or services and organizational processes, as well as the development of new initiatives in such products and/or services and processes.

Feedback: Ongoing insight into how well the strategic roadmap elements are being developed and implemented in positioning the organization for its future purposes.

Figure 1–2 shows a model of this strategic roadmap. The effective use of this model requires alternative types of teams to focus resources for operational and strategic purposes.

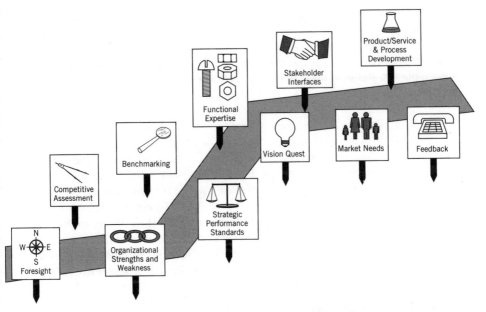

Figure 1–2. Roadmap for strategic management.

THE TEAM LINKAGES

Strategic management is necessary because of the inevitable changes that face all organizations today. Response to many of these changes can be brought about through the use of alternative teams, such as

- Reengineering teams
- Crisis management teams
- Product and process development teams
- Self-directed production teams
- Task forces
- Benchmarking teams
- Facilities construction teams
- Quality teams
- General-purpose project teams
- Audit teams
- Plural executive teams
- New business development teams

Teams are the common denominator of organizational change—a medium for cross-functional and cross-organizational integration of resources to accomplish a specific purpose. One way of classifying teams by their type, output, and time frame is indicated in Table 1–1.

A brief description of these teams follows. In subsequent chapters, a more complete description of these teams will be given and the principal role such teams play in the development and execution of organizational strategy will be discussed.

1. *Reengineering teams.* These teams are used to bring about a fundamental rethinking and radical redesign of business processes to achieve extraordinary improvements in critical contemporary measures of performance, such as cost, quality, service, and speed. Reengineering teams, when used properly, can bring about a fundamental rethinking and radical redesign of business processes. Today, much attention is focused on the use of reengineering teams, and their ability to produce real results is questioned. Michael Hammer, the guru of the reengineering movement whose definition of reengineering has been paraphrased in this paragraph, openly admits that 70 percent of such efforts fail.[3]

TABLE 1–1   Classification of Teams

Type	Output/Contribution	Time Frame
Reengineering teams	Handle business process changes	Ad hoc
Crisis management teams	Manage organizational crises	Ad hoc
Product and process development teams	Handle concurrent product and process development	Ad hoc
Self-directed production teams	Manage and execute production work	Ongoing
Task forces and problem solving teams	Evaluate/resolve organizational problems/opportunities	Ad hoc
Benchmarking teams	Evaluate competitors/best-in-the-industry performance	Ongoing
Facilities construction project teams	Design/develop/construct facilities/equipment	Ad hoc
Quality teams	Develop/implement total quality initiatives	Ongoing
General-purpose project teams	Develop/implement new initiatives in the enterprise	Ad hoc
Audit teams	Evaluate organizational efficiency and effectiveness	Ad hoc
Plural executive teams	Integrate senior-level management decisions	Ongoing
New business development teams	Develop new business ventures	Ad hoc

---

[3] Reported by Michael Rothschild, "Want to Grow? Watch Your Language," *Forbes ASAP,* October 25, 1993, p. 19.

2. *Crisis management teams.* Teams that deal with any crisis that may arise in the organization's activities.

3. *Product/process development teams.* Concurrent design and development of organizational products and/or services and processes (manufacturing, marketing, purchasing, after-sales services, engineering, and so on), resulting in products and/or services of higher quality with lower costs and leading to earlier commercialization and greater profitability.

4. *Self-directed production teams.* Improved quality and productivity in manufacturing and production operations through the use of self-directed teams that manage themselves.

5. *Task forces.* Ad hoc groups used to solve short-term organizational problems or exploit opportunities for the enterprise.

6. *Benchmarking teams.* The ongoing strategy of measuring organizational products and/or services and processes against the most formidable competitors and industry leaders, resulting in the design of improved performance standards that will lead to improved performance. The use of teams to facilitate the benchmarking process will be described in this book, as well as types of benchmarking, benchmarking philosophies, the major steps that are involved, information sources, and the incorporation of benchmarks in key strategic performance standards.

7. *Facilities construction project teams.* Teams that integrate organizational resources to design, engineer, and build facilities and equipment and initiate products and/or services that create enterprise support strategies. The use of such teams has reached a level of maturity in many organizations, such as in construction, defense, engineering, research and development, and governmental and military organizations.

8. *Quality teams.* Total quality management accomplished through the use of quality teams (quality circles) that utilize cross-functional organizational designs to integrate quality improvement efforts.

9. *General-purpose project teams.* Used to design and develop a wide variety of ad hoc initiatives in the enterprise to improve organizational performance. Facilities layout, order entry procedures, training programs, union–management cooperation, company relocation, and productivity improvements are examples of such teams.

10. *Audit teams.* Teams that evaluate the competency of organizations, programs, projects, and functions to deliver quality products and processes. Projects in the public domain are often audited to ascertain the prudency with which public funds have been utilized.

11. *Plural executive teams.* Senior-level executives who work together in a strategic management context in the design and execution of major strategies to prepare the enterprise for its long-range future. The use of such teams provides for a top-level synergy in the strategic management of the enterprise. When the plural executive team members main-

tain surveillance over the operation of other teams in the company, they glean insight regarding how well the company is preparing for and dealing with inevitable changes in organizational products and/or services, processes, and resources.

12. *New business development teams.* Teams that are used to explore the design and development of new business ventures for the enterprise. Such teams arise out of the strategic planning efforts of the company. The work of such teams involves assessment and development of new business areas, in contrast to teams dedicated to a specific program or project within a new business area.

REVISITING STRATEGIC PERFORMANCE STANDARDS[4]

Key checkpoints on the strategic roadmap are those performance standards presented on page 8. A summary of these standards, with real-world examples, follows. Managers and leaders should note that these checkpoints, properly established and used, provide extraordinary insight into how new the enterprise is performing, both operationally and strategically. These standards include

- Mission
- Objectives
- Goals
- Strategies
- Organizational design
- Individual and collective roles
- Leader and follower style
- Supporting systems
- Quality and quantity of organizational resources

Figure 1–3 provides a model of these strategic performance standards. A description follows.

ORGANIZATIONAL MISSION AND VISION

One must first understand the concept of vision, because a vision for the enterprise sets the stage for all of the performance standards that follow.

[4] Material on the strategic performance standards is stated in a somewhat different context in my book, *Project Management—Strategic Design and Implementation*, McGraw-Hill, New York, 1994.

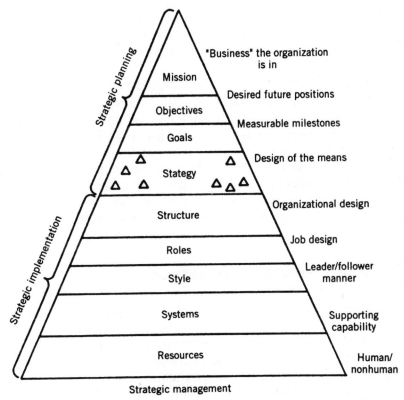

Figure 1–3. The strategic context of organizational planning. (From David I. Cleland, *Project Management: Strategic Design and Implementation,* 2d ed., McGraw-Hill, New York, 1994, p. 238. Reproduced with permission.)

Vision, is the art of seeing things invisible to others. Senior managers who have foresight, competence, and discernment have the opportunity to develop a suitable vision for the strategic direction of the enterprise, along with the supporting products and processes.

A vision is a dream of what the future should be—the general direction in which the enterprise should travel to be what its leaders want it to be. A review of the visions held by a few organizations provides insight into how such visions offer a dream for the future:

- "[Our company] in its chosen lines of business, will grow with new opportunities and be the leader in an ever-changing global market."
- "[Ours will be] a corporation that will look large but have the dynamics of small teams."
- "PP&L will be the energy supplier of choice." (1992 annual report, Pennsylvania Power & Light Company)

- "[Our company has] a vision for growth based on critical mass in large product categories, geographic diversity, brand leadership, and marketing innovation." (1994 annual report, H. J. Heinz Company)

How important is vision for an organization? If the current focus on the development of vision statements for organizations is any indication, then a vision statement that has been developed through a participative process of the members, has been accepted by all, and then is disseminated throughout the organization is important in that it provides a sense of direction for organizational stakeholders. One study that benchmarked the performance of business teams found compelling evidence concerning the importance of a vision for high-performance teams. Team members stated that the most important factor for high performance was a clear and elevating vision.[5]

BACK TO THE ORGANIZATIONAL MISSION

An organization's mission is the final strategic performance standard for the enterprise. All organizational activity must be judged according to how well such activity ultimately contributes to the mission—the business the organization is in. A mission statement provides the final performance criterion for the enterprise. It is a declaration of a broad, enduring intent that an organization pursues—the overall strategic purpose toward which all organizational resources are directed and committed. A mission statement also provides a symbol around which all organizational effort is focused. The following are mission statements of a few contemporary organizations:

- "To be the number one aerospace company in the world and among the premier industrial concerns in terms of quality, profitability, and growth." (1993 annual report, The Boeing Company)
- "Our mission is to develop, manufacture, market, sell, and distribute a broad line of high-quality generic drug products at competitive prices."
- "[Our mission is to] Provide Western Pennsylvania small and medium-sized manufacturers with the tools necessary to compete in the global marketplace." (Manufacturing Assistance Center, University of Pittsburgh 1994)

Sometimes a mission statement is written in a proactive sense, such as the one developed by Procordia:

---

[5] Larson Carl and Frank LaFasto, *What Must Go Right/What Can Go Wrong*, Sage, Newbury Park, Calif., 1989.

The company shall develop as an industrial corporation focusing on its core areas and striving to generate superior long-term value for all interested parties. Procordia aims to achieve a sustained high level of profitability, with a balance of risks, by developing and restructuring companies with a strong position in the areas of health care and branded consumer products.[6]

Sometimes the mission statement is intermingled with the strategy for an organization, as in the case of Procordia.

On a more sobering note, an executive in the automobile industry noted what can go wrong in the development of a mission statement: "A bunch of guys take off their ties and coats, go into a motel room for three days, and put a bunch of friggin' words on a piece of paper—and then go back to business as usual."[7]

THE OBJECTIVES

Organizational objectives are ongoing, enduring end purposes that must be achieved in the long term to ensure accomplishment of the mission. These objectives are usually stated in quantitative or qualitative terms—or a combination thereof—and are the performance criteria to be achieved and measured in the use of organizational resources. For example, a computer company defines one of its objectives as "leading the state of the art of technology in its product lines." Other examples of objectives are as follows:

- "Provide customers with quality goods, and make the goods available when and where customers want them." (Wal-Mart)
- "Meet or exceed the state of the art of competitors in machining capability." (machine tool builder)
- "Achieve and sustain a minimum return of shareholders' equity of 20 percent." (annual review, Engelhard Corporation)
- "Implement a more responsible special events management program to adequately meet FBI counterterrorism responsibilities." (Federal Bureau of Investigation, U.S. Department of Justice)

Objectives, when attained, provide strong evidence that progress is being made to accomplish the organizational mission. To determine if the objectives of an enterprise are being attained, the goals of the organization must be reviewed.

---

[6] *Procordia Annual Report,* 1992, p. 3.
[7] *Fortune,* May 16, 1994, p. 18.

THE GOALS

A goal is a milestone whose specificity can be measured (on time-based points) that the organization intends to meet as it pursues its objectives. When properly selected and attained, goals provide specific insight into how well the strategic management system is preparing the enterprise for its future. For example, one company stated one of its goals as follows: "We intend by the end of 1984 to complete the transition begun in 1983 from a predominantly R&D service company to an industrial manufacturer."[8] In project management, the completion of a project work package on time and within budget means that one of the project goals has been completed. As progress on all of the work packages is realized, insight is provided into how well the project's objectives are being attained. The following are examples of organizational goals:

- "Attain financial performance capability of 15 percent return on investment by the end of 1992." (electronics company)
- Conceptualize, design, build, and put in operation an automated factory on a green-field site by the middle of 1993." (auto parts manufacturer)

Goals and objectives are often intermingled in definition and in use. However, it is important to keep in mind that an objective describes an enduring, ongoing end purpose, whereas a goal is a specific milestone. If a company chooses to use an objective as a specific milestone and a goal as an ongoing purpose, there will be no problem as long as the meaning and use are consistent.

In the strategic management of an enterprise, executives often find it easy to define an objective and win acceptance of it. However, when dealing with a goal in the strategic management sense, time-based measurement is involved. Many executives are uncomfortable with making a commitment to a goal since performance toward that goal can be measured in specific terms. Failure to reach a goal in the strategic management of the enterprise can be the basis for criticism or an unfavorable performance rating. Nevertheless, a goal can provide a specific, effective criterion with which to measure progress in the strategic management of the enterprise, and it can be an ongoing test of whether the organizational strategy is working.

THE STRATEGY

A strategy determines how resources will be used to accomplish the organizational goals, objectives, and mission. The means include action plans, policies, procedures, resource allocation schemas, organizational design, motivational

---

[8] *Genex Corporation, 1983 Annual Report*, p. 3.

techniques, leadership processes, evaluation and control systems, and the use of teams as building blocks in the design and execution of strategies. Reengineering, benchmarking, new product and/or service and process development, facilities and equipment construction and purchase, recapitalization, and the use of information systems are a few of the means to implement organizational strategies. In modern organizations, most of these efforts are carried out using teams. Such teams provide for integration of organizational resources across organizational boundaries to accomplish tasks that will prepare the organization for its future. A key part of any strategy is the team-driven initiatives toward the creation of a plan for the organization's future. Organizational strategies can be narrow or broad, depending on the means available and how such means will be employed to prepare the organization for competition and the future. Examples of current organizational strategies are as follows:

- "Concentrate on improved earnings from Kodak's core photography business and build a future with digital technologies, such as all-electronic cameras, thermal printers, and image-storage devices" (Kodak Company). The CEO of Kodak, George Fisher, has formed ten teams to examine strategic issues in the company, such as R&D productivity and cycle-time improvement.
- "Develop interlocking computer/information support systems augmented by a private satellite-communication system to video link all stores, distribution centers, the truck fleet, and corporate headquarters." (Wal-Mart)
- "Establish and maintain a distinct competitive advantage by maximizing the productivity and efficiency of all operations." (drug company)
- "[Achieve] Global expansion through agreement with British Airways, one of the world's most successful international airlines." (USAir Group, Inc.)
- "Develop a culture that emphasizes quality improvement, cross-functional training, and understanding the needs of customers as the keys to success in this highly competitive market." (The Boeing Company)

The turnaround strategy initiated by CEO Jack Smith of General Motors has been as follows: (1) Establish a vision for the entire company; (2) clear performance standards at each level of the organization; (3) construct pragmatic strategies that do not require "rocket science"; (4) focus on the customers—they are the ultimate arbiters of success or failure; and (5) develop the capability to execute by reorganizing people and reallocating assets. General Motors' reorganization strategy is being executed on the production floor, where the company is moving away from traditional assembly lines into smaller units known as cells, in which workers have more opportunity to design work processes and develop strategies to improve output.[9]

[9] Alex Taylor III, "GM's $11,000,000,000 Turnaround," *Fortune,* October 17, 1994, pp. 54–74.

Strategies also include those policies that guide the thinking of the decision makers in the enterprise. "Thou shalt not kill a new product idea" is a well-known policy of the 3M Company—a policy that has helped facilitate the suggestion of new ideas from everyone in the company, from senior managers to workers in the factories. Texas Instruments' policy is that "we seek to create a working environment where all individuals are motivated to participate in the achievement of TI goals through the pursuit of their personal goals to the maximum possible." Procedures are elements of strategy as well (e.g., guidance on budgeting, grievances, and billing instructions). In more specific terms, rules are elements of strategy as well (e.g., rules against smoking, drinking, or the use of drugs in the workplace).

Other elements of strategy include functional and project plans of action developed within the enterprise. Employee training programs, inventory management techniques, and executive development initiatives are additional examples of strategies. Whatever form the strategy takes, the end purpose is to utilize resources to prepare the organization for its future.

ORGANIZATIONAL DESIGN

The organizational design of the enterprise is the alignment of the functions to be performed to accomplish desired purposes—along with the assignment of people to relevant positions accompanied with appropriate authority and responsibility. Organizational designs are undergoing significant changes from traditional models. These changes include downsizing, restructuring, employee empowerment, closer working relationships with suppliers and customers, reduction of staff, and the use of improved information systems to facilitate better communication in working with organizational stakeholders.

In modern organizations teams are used to manage a wide variety of strategic and operational initiatives, and they have had an impact on the success of companies. For example, "the ability to organize employees in innovative and flexible ways and the enthusiasm with which so many American companies have deployed self-managing teams is why U.S. industry is looking so competitive."[10]

Markets and the basis of competition are changing. These changes have affected the way resources are used in the enterprise and how people are organized to do the work to sustain current operations, develop ways of improving existing products, develop new products, and change the organizational processes to support strategic initiatives in the enterprise. Teams are being used increasingly to develop organizational initiatives that will lead to positive results.

[10] Rahul Jacob, "Corporate Reputations," *Fortune,* March 6, 1995, pp. 54–64.

TEAM RESULTS

A brief summary of team results follows. (Chapter 14 provides a more detailed description of team results.)

- Replacement of a traditionally decentralized purchasing system with a centralized unit. (H. J. Heinz Company)
- Benchmarking or "best practices" assessment to determine the basis of competitors' successes. (General Electric Company)
- Boost in productivity up to 40 percent. (Federal Express and IDS)
- Design, development, manufacture, test, and creation of an integrated logistics support for a new, faster aircraft of higher quality and lower cost than achieved using previous traditional development methods. (The Boeing Company)
- Integration of teams of management and union officials in eleven hospitals (this produced "stunning results").
- Teams that design and execute R&D projects, farming out the technical details to commercial labs that replace former in-house R&D laboratories. (Lyondell Petrochemical Company)
- Redesign of an assembly line to make a typewriter, down from more than eight hours under previous methods. (Lexmark International, Inc.)
- A center manufacturing team with responsibility for the entire order process of a product, from the first customer contact to invoicing. This reduced order cycle time by more than 90 percent. (Asea Brown Boveri)
- A total of 1003 workers mustered into 168 special teams dedicated to improving quality, cutting costs, and reducing cycle time. (Motorola Corporation)
- A team of lawyers and engineers (not the most natural bedfellows), which trimmed the standard invention disclosure form from fifteen pages to two and whittled down the backlog without adding staff. (Motorola Corporation)
- Consolidation of a spare parts distribution center, in which over 2600 orders for spare parts are received daily, with a promise to get parts moving to customers within four hours. (The Boeing Company)
- Development of a new diesel car engine that is expected to meet strict emissions standards and to attain 48 mpg (miles per gallon) in town and 55 mpg on the highway. (Honda Motor Company)
- Technology assessment teams to review current and emerging technologies. (IBM Corporation)
- Use of teams to develop key processes and product decisions. (Goodyear Company)

- Transformation of the company's approach to manufacturing from a single facility to focused factories dedicated to a narrow, newly developed product line. (Copeland Corporation)
- Teamwork between designers and manufacturing, which trimmed 33 percent off assembly time for the newest models of vehicles. (General Motors Corporation)
- Shut down of traditional factory and initiation of new factory without any lost production time. (H. J. Heinz Company)
- Use of small teams to develop products faster than the company's formal product development organization. (Hewlett-Packard Company)
- Installation of cross-unit teams to encourage cooperation among otherwise independent businesses. In addition, a team that includes the heads of four major business groups runs the company from day to day. (AT&T)
- Flow of most innovative ideas for new products from interdisciplinary teams, which focus on specific product lines with a success rate of more than 365 new products a year. (Rubbermaid Company)
- Use of workplace safety teams to reduce accidents and lower workers' compensation costs. (mandated by several state legislatures)
- Use of teams of doctors, nurses, administrators, and medical technicians to challenge every step in treating patients and root out steps that add costs without improving results. (Henry Ford Hospital)
- Use of teams with sales reps, engineers, technicians, and production managers to serve customers and win new accounts. (Dupont, Digital Equipment, Data General, and Tandem Computers)
- Use of "skunk works" or a special team isolated from organizational bureaucracy to revamp the Mustang auto development effort, which looked too expensive. (Ford Motor Company)

There are many changes affecting contemporary organizations that have both operational and strategic import (e.g., fundamental changes in the nature of jobs).

JOBS ARE CHANGING

One of the more exciting and provocative changes in organization designs is that traditional jobs are changing from fixed specific areas of responsibility to a team effort, in which individual responsibilities are less certain. Manufacturing (production) is being changed from standard product output to an increasingly customized output. The use of part-time and temporary workers is increasing, as is the use of consultants and contract workers. The organization of people is being transformed from specific job responsibilities into cooperative efforts by team members, who work together to produce output.

Although traditional jobs remain in the modern enterprise, jobs are increasingly a patchwork of responsibility fitting into an overall mosaic, with overlaps and interfaces planned and executed by self-directed teams. Some of the more important job changes are as follows:

- An organizational design is used that is more flexible than the traditional structure based on specialization of work.
- There is increased reliance on alternative teams to deal with the change affecting the organization, particularly in the development of new and improved products and organizational processes.
- There is increasing acceptance of the belief that traditionally structured organizations are inherently designed to maintain the status quo rather than respond to the changing demands of the market and competition.
- There is less reliance on job descriptions or supervisor directions; rather, the team members take their direction from the changing demands of the team objectives.
- Workers develop the knowledge, skills, and attitudes to deal with individual effort and the collective responsibility of the team.
- Team members report to each other, look for facilitation and coaching from the team leader, and focus their effort on the resources needed to meet team objectives.
- A single job is important only insofar as it contributes to the bundle of capabilities needed to get the team's work done.

Since much of the team effort is temporary in the sense of delivering a capability to the organization on time and within a desired schedule, team members recognize that they will finish work on one team effort and be moving to another team for further work. As a result, peer acceptance, organizational cultures, and informal organizational and personal alliances change. A flexible organizational design becomes the norm rather than a rigid hierarchy of well-defined organizational units. A form of "disorderly" work and job assignments and performance standards emerges. Although they are disorderly in a sense, performance standards become more rigorous and better defined, with team members participating in the development of their individual and collective work and responsibility. The result is that people have a stronger commitment to their work and a sense of responsibility in bringing about continuous improvement.

Additional job changes are as follows:

- Policies on work hours, compensation, authority, and responsibility will be required along with new training programs, ranging from technical to social training, to develop people's ability to communicate, work on teams, and take on leadership responsibilities.

- Vacations will be taken between teamwork assignments, and retirement will become more an individual choice rather than the result of an organizational policy.
- Personal performance will not be constrained by organizational hierarchy and job performance, but it will be more independent and self-directed—people will be working in the spirit of a "bossless office."
- With all of the changes in the design and performance of jobs, middle managers will become rarer. Those that remain will be worker coaches, facilitators, organizational process guides, and counselors.
- Employees will act more like "owners" than people whose interests are restricted to doing only their job.
- The flow of information and the sharing of such information will be widespread throughout the enterprise. Such sharing will give employees considerable insight into the strengths and weaknesses of the enterprise, its problems and opportunities, and its future strategies. Participation in the development of both operational and long-term strategies will become more widespread throughout the enterprise, with exciting and broadened opportunities for contributions at all levels of the organization (in both follower and leader roles). One result of such participation will be enhanced work satisfaction, leading to both personal and organizational pride.
- Given the opportunity for enhanced leadership roles, employees will have much greater opportunities to make meaningful contributions to their work and organizational purposes, and they will contribute to developing a vision for the enterprise and the values required to make such a vision attainable.

The changes in the traditional definition and performance of work will require new and innovative training programs to prepare workers for greater responsibilities. Such training programs will provide employees with the ability to make decisions formerly reserved for managers. Employees will have to know how to obtain and use relevant information in making those decisions. In using information and making decisions, employees will need to know much more about the organization's purposes: its mission, objectives, goals, and strategies for the use of resources to meet the future. Finally, with the expanded role of employees in both the operational and strategic purposes of the enterprise, employees will expect to be rewarded beyond a simple wage or salary—to share the company's profits.

ORGANIZING AROUND PROJECTS

Project teams are valuable organizational mechanisms that focus the management of product and process development. Projects also provide a central point at which new knowledge, skills, and attitudes can be developed. As new technologies and resources are studied, evaluated, and developed for integration into the organizational products and processes, the need for changed and updated capabilities of team members becomes evident.

The development of new products and processes requires establishment of projects as an organizational mechanism to focus disciplines and resources. A project is any undertaking that has a defined objective, a cost parameter, and a time element for its development. Sometimes a project is defined as a cluster of activities that are pulled together to deliver something of value to a customer. A project is a miniature of the complete organization composed of team members from different disciplines of the enterprise, sometimes including customers, suppliers, and representatives from the unions, local community, and other interested and relevant stakeholders. Project teams provide for integration of the disciplines, technologies, and resources needed to take a project from concept through delivery of the results to the customer. Project teams provide an ongoing test of resource use, management systems, strategies, and values of the enterprise.

Projects enable an enterprise to come up with an enhanced capability, a product and a process that best fits the organization's overall strategy. Projects provide a rigorous test of the enterprise's ability to integrate its resources and position itself for the future. A project success in meeting competition depends on how well senior management has provided resources to the project team and reviewed its progress, and how well meaningful foresight and vision have been developed for the enterprise. Clear foresight and vision, strong enterprise, and project leadership enable a project to take off from the start and produce results throughout its life cycle, with success measured according to how well innovative organizational products and processes have been developed that give the enterprise timely competitive strengths.

ARE THERE ANY ALTERNATIVES?

What is the alternative to using projects to develop new products and processes? This question can be answered by reviewing some of the advantages that projects provide to the enterprise:

- An organizational and stakeholder focal point for integrating resources to create a product or process
- A strategic pathway for the commitment of people and resources to create value in future products and processes
- A learning opportunity for the development of knowledge, skills, and attitudes needed to support future enterprise purposes
- A model according to which progress can be measured in positioning the enterprise for its future

- A message to everyone that the enterprise's future can be developed through an integrating organizational design that is a key strategic management initiative for the enterprise

If the aforementioned elements are used, a project has been created. Considering our current understanding of managment discipline, there is no better means than projects to deal with ad hoc opportunities as building blocks of products and processes in organizational strategies.

The use of teams has reduced the number of management levels in organizations. As the organizational design provides for the use of teams as focal points for functional activity in the enterprise, fewer managers are needed—and those managers that remain take on different roles than they had under earlier, traditional means of organizing activities.

Management levels, according to Peter Drucker, manage nothing. Instead, they merely amplify faint signals coming from the top and the bottom of the infrastructure. Drucker reminds us öf the first law of information: Every relay doubles the noise and cuts the message in half. According to Drucker, most management levels neither manage nor make decisions—they serve only as relays. In the future, Drucker believes that few businesses will have more than two or three layers.[11]

INDIVIDUAL AND COLLECTIVE ROLES

Considering the number of teams that operate in the typical organization, the individual and collective roles that are carried out are important considerations. No longer can individuals perform their work without considering how they are expected to work with other people—many of whom can be outside their local organizational environment. The performance of organizational roles brings life to the enterprise. Organizations fail or are successful because members of the organization fail or succeed in their work. If people are unclear about what is expected of them in doing their work, the chances for difficulties or failure are greater. When employees have been empowered with more control over their jobs and are delegated authority and responsibility to do those jobs, role specificity is needed. If training, counseling, or team development strategies are needed, the more specific the expected roles that people will perform, the easier it will be to facilitate them in developing themselves professionally (to the point at which the empowerment that is given to them can be appropriately discharged). People will do a good job if they know what is expected of them and receive feedback on how well they are doing.

[11] Peter Drucker, "Infoliteracy," *Forbes ASAP,* August 29, 1994, pp. 105–109.

As one considers the breadth and depth of the strategic management of an enterprise, one asks why a strategic manager should be concerned with the specifics of individual and collective job performance. Regardless of how well the organizational mission, objectives, goals, strategies, and structure have been prescribed, if people do not perform their assigned and assumed jobs in an efficient and effective manner, the productivity of the organization will suffer and the quality of the products and/or services and organizational processes will likely suffer—leading to the potential for organizational failure or, at best, losses in efficiency and effectiveness.

LEADER AND FOLLOWER STYLE

The most important variable in the strategic management of an enterprise is the leadership that is provided in marshalling resources and providing direction for the organization. A leader's style is the distinctive manner or method of expression that is displayed. Style concerns the overall excellence, appearance, skill, and grace in performing the leadership role and preparing the enterprise for its future. A leader's (and a manager's) style can be autocratic, dictatorial, democratic, participative, empathetic, caustic, friendly, abusive, etc. The style exhibited by the leader tends to be emulated by the followers, sometimes unknown to them. If the leader possesses and professes a philosophy of strategic management for the enterprise, the chances are excellent that other managers will emulate that style. When the strategic manager approaches major decisions in a rigorous manner, takes time to develop the databases related to such decisions, and gets the people involved making that decision, such behavior will be copied by others in the enterprise. On the other hand, if the leader comes across as a quick, intuitive decision maker, others in the enterprise will act likewise. Examples of leadership style follow:

- "People at Goodyear headquarters say that CEO Stanley Gault's presence 'permeates' the corporate headquarters . . . [and] he is perceived as seldom giving orders, but everyone knows what he wants done . . . he runs the company based on trust."[12]
- At Siemens Company in Germany, "the management style is tailored to Germany's consensus-style corporate culture . . . [and] rigid hierarchy is out and an entrepreneurial drive is in."[13]

The collective style of the managers and professionals is reflected in the culture of the organization. An organizational culture is the complex of refined behaviors that people have and strive for in their organizational society. Cul-

[12] Peter Nulty, "The Bounce Is Back at Goodyear," *Fortune,* June 29, 1992, pp. 76–79.
[13] Gail E. Schares, et al., "The New Generation at Siemens," *Business Week,* March 9, 1992, pp. 34–39.

ture includes the totality of knowledge, beliefs, habits, attitudes, and the capabilities acquired and used in the organizational society. The term *culture* is most often used to describe the shared ideas and beliefs associated with a way of life in an organization.

The increasing use of teams is having extraordinary influences on organizational cultures. One impact is a growing recognition that the person doing the job knows the most about how that job should be done and can make valuable contributions regarding how the job should be done and how the management processes can be carried out. Thus, the strategic management of the enterprise must consider the cultural changes likely to come forth as more participative, team-driven cultures develop. Some examples illustrate the point:

- At the Levi Strauss Company, efforts are underway to have all employees feel as if they are an integral part of the making and selling of blue jeans. Strategies are underway to develop an "Aspiration Statement," which will help create a company culture that will make employee empowerment a reality and a competitive tool. Employees are evaluated by their superiors and by subordinates and peers—an evaluation whose process is not always pleasant. The use of teams to help solve production problems and to assume responsibility for the complete assembly of products has reduced cycle time from seven days to three. Under the team system, a worker's incentive pay is tied to team performance.[14]

When a new CEO takes over a company, a different management style is likely to set the tone for the culture of the enterprise. At IBM, a company facing enormous strategic challenges, CEO Louis V. Gerstner saw the changing of IBM's engrained culture as his toughest and most critical task: forcing changes in an entrenched, patriarchal culture. According to CEO Gerstner, "You can't graft a solution onto the old culture . . . it has to change from within. Unless IBM is prepared to accept a fundamental shift, one person can't change." The new CEO at IBM "rails" against the old IBM's "corporate arrogance." Instead of basic beliefs and employee policies, the company is focusing on the marketplace and profit and loss. Cultural factors that will come under close scrutiny and perhaps be changed include basic values and philosophies—decision making is one such process. A set of new IBM principles has been established and dictates the tone for management style and organizational culture:

- The marketplace is the driving force behind everything we do.
- At our core, we are a technology company with an overriding commitment to quality.

[14] Russell Mitchell and Michael O'Neal, "Managing by Values," *Business Week,* August 1, 1994, pp. 46–52.

- Our primary measures of success are customer satisfaction and share-holder value.
- We operate as an entrepreneurial organization with a minimum of bureaucracy and a never-ending focus on productivity.
- We never lose sight of our strategic vision.
- We think and act with a sense of urgency.
- Outstanding, dedicated people make it all happen, particularly when they work together as a team.
- We are sensitive to the needs of all employees and to the communities in which we operate.[15]

Considering the impact that an organizational culture can have on the abilities of an enterprise to succeed or fail, a philosophy of strategic management that gives due consideration to cultural ambience is important. Careful and deliberate planning must be carried out to develop the appropriate culture and then maintain oversight of the effectiveness with which that culture is carried out.

SYSTEMS AND RESOURCES

Two additional elements of the strategic management model are important. First, the systems that support the organization (such as software, hardware, accounting, information, marketing, production, design) are important. The technology offered by computer and information systems has changed the traditional role of the manager and the professional/worker and is changing the composition of the work force. A new worker elite is emerging that consists of technicians, the core employees of the digital information age. According to the Bureau of Labor Statistics forecasts, one of every four new jobs goes to a technical worker. Technicians are gaining new importance because of increasingly powerful, versatile, and user-friendly technologies. Organizations are depending more on front-line workers. These technicians are not just workers—they exert influence through empowerment and competence rather than a place in the hierarchy pecking order. As companies become more dependent on these technicians, cultural support is required to keep them productive and satisfied with their work environment. Cultural support is required along the following lines:

- Allow the technicians the opportunity to grow in their jobs, pay them well, and open promotion criteria for them.

[15] Laurie Hays, "Gerstner Is Struggling as He Tries to Change Ingrained IBM Culture," *Wall Street Journal,* May 13, 1994, p. 1.

- Since many technicians are working with customers and suppliers, they need to know a great deal about the business and the strategic direction of the enterprise.
- Provide the opportunity for technicians to compete for promotion into managerial ranks, and carefully nurture and train their technical and people skills.
- Make sure that technicians receive due recognition and rewards for their contributions to the enterprise.
- Finally, due to networked computing, information is becoming the common wealth of every employee. In earlier times, access to information was a jealously guarded privilege of management. No longer can a manager's style guard information availability—the management style must change accordingly.[16]

In the strategic management of teams, the core capabilities of people include technological skills at all levels of the enterprise, which are reflected in the knowledge, skills, and attitudes of the people. An important part of people's attitudes is their motivation and commitment to developing a capacity for action. Managerial systems are included as an important part of such core capabilities—managerial systems that provide for operational and strategic management of the enterprise that accommodates and provides for the widest participation of all employees in the enterprise's affairs. Physical systems, such as equipment, tools, and computers, are important. All of these capabilities must be tied together in a network of both vertical and horizontal organizational design, from the development and use of core capabilities in the disciplines supporting the enterprise, to the use of teams to focus the work, and finally to strategic management at senior levels of the enterprise to facilitate and develop the strategic direction.

As would be expected, the current fascination with a management style that encourages the use of teams is not shared by everyone. Elliott Jaques, a management-science professor at George Washington University in Washington, D.C., attacks executive development training that promotes such team concepts as quality circles, empowerment, participatory management, and cross-functional teamwork. According to Jaques, these teams are undercutting the importance of managerial accountability and leadership and having a dysfunctional effect by blurring lines of authority and responsibility and creating the perception that no one is in charge and the work gets done only after interminable delays.[17]

Attitudes are as important as abilities in strategically managing the enterprise. Attitudes are reflected in an individual's philosophy of strategic management.

---

[16] Louis S. Richman, "The New Worker Elite," *Fortune,* August 22, 1994, pp. 56–66.
[17] "Executive Education—When Things Go Wrong," *The Wall Street Journal,* September 10, 1993, p. R6.

PHILOSOPHICAL ATTITUDES

A philosophy is a way of thinking about how the strategic assessment should be carried out to prepare the enterprise for its future. In this way of thinking, attitudes held by the key leaders in the enterprise are important and include the following:

- A willingness to maximize the delegation of authority, responsibility, and accountability for operational matters in the organization to free time for developing future purposes
- An obsession with strategic thinking about the possibilities and probabilities of the future
- Deep belief that satisfaction with current organizational success means that the state has already been set for future failure
- The intellectual discipline to probe, experiment, and retry constantly in moving the enterprise to its future
- A predisposition toward leadership (doing the right thing) rather than management (doing things right)
- Use of alternative teams as integrative mechanisms to bring an organizational focus for both operational and strategic initiatives
- Recognition that teams should be used for the development of products and/or services, processes, and people for the support of future strategies

SUMMARY

A key question for those managers who want to manage the enterprise as if its future mattered is how to develop and implement organizational strategy. Development of such strategies requires a focus—an organizational point for the converging of resources directed to specific end purposes whose outcomes are building blocks in the design and execution of strategies. Market changes are usually reflected one way or another in changes in the way products and services are developed and offered to customers. The conceptualization, development, and manufacture (production) of such products and services require appropriate change in the organizational processes to create such changes. The enterprise's strategies ultimately must reflect such changes; how to manage such changes provides one of the more challenging tasks for the managers and professionals in the enterprise. It is work that is not, and should not, be the sole responsibility of leaders in the enterprise. It is work that can be done by employees as they go about their routine work and see the opportunity for improvement in the products and services they are creating, and the efficiency and effectiveness with which such output is achieved. Development projects managed by teams to improve or create new products and processes become the center of the organization.

Several key points have been discussed in this chapter:

- Change is inevitable.
- The key to development of timely strategies for an enterprise is to maintain a sustained flow of product and process innovations using teams as organizational focal points.
- Strategic management of the enterprise means keeping a balance of operational competency, strategic effectiveness, and functional excellence.
- A model of strategic management suggests that there are key checkpoints in following a roadmap to prepare the enterprise for the inevitable changes it faces in an unforgiving, competitive world.
- Alternative teams provide the linkages to bring the use of interfunctional and interorganizational resources together to prepare the enterprise for its future.
- The development and oversight of strategic performance standards provide valuable insight into how well the enterprise is meeting its intended purposes.
- Teams are the organizational design mechanisms in using projects as building blocks for the design and execution of strategies.
- Employees and managers must consider how they play leader and follower roles and how their personal style can affect the organizational members and culture.
- A philsophy of strategic management provides a framework for how one thinks and acts as both a leader and follower in the strategically competitive enterprise.

The next chapter will discuss how to get the organization ready to use teams.

PART II
DEVELOPING THE PLAYERS

____2
GETTING THE
ORGANIZATION READY

There is nothing permanent except change.
HERACLITUS OF GREECE, 513 B. C.

This chapter suggests a strategy for preparing an enterprise to use teams. The use of teams in the design and execution of organizational strategies is a major decision that will have serious impacts on all systems of the enterprise. People must be trained in the use of teams and learn how teams can modify existing cultures in the organization. Supporting systems in the enterprise, such as communication, computing, accounting, finance, marketing, and engineering, will need to change to support the teams as well as maintain the functional excellence of their disciplines. Attidudinal adjustment will be necessary: Employees will need to change the way they think about how the enterprise will operate under the emerging team strategies. Benchmarking of the "best in the industry" and competitors can catch the attention of managers, professionals, and workers. All personnel need to understand what teams can do to facilitate organizational success and, in contrast, how they are limited as instruments of corporate strategy.

The increasing use of teams has caused a change in managerial philosophies from the traditional concept of **bureaucracy** to an enlightened philosophy of **teamocracy.**

TEAMOCRACY[1]

We are entering the age of teamocracy—a time of changes in the leadership and management of organizations that will have a profound impact on how

[1] This is a term I coined on October 25, 1994, when I wrote this chapter.

things are done in the delivery of value to customers. The forces unleashed by teamocracy will affect product concepts, design, production, marketing, and after-sales logistic support. The move to teamocracy is an intellectual revolution for which there is no precedence in the history of management.

I have coined the term *teamocracy* to describe the use of teams in organizations as the basic design for bringing about cross-functional and cross-organizational work. In a teamocracy, the team is a social unit based on maximum empowerment and leads organization members' acceptance of responsibility and accountability. Teamocracy is the result of converting the traditional bureaucratic hierarchy. Instead of each organizational level rising in a pyramid (in which the greatest authority resides at the top), a network of authority and responsibility is widespread and permeates all levels of the enterprise. In teamocracy, new power foci emerge and reflect empowerment, dedication, trust, loyalty, and commitment. The team leads and manages itself within the larger strategic management context of the enterprise.

Teamocracy is the culmination of alternative teams working in operational and strategic harmony to deal with changes from within the enterprise and changes buffeting the organization from outside political, social, economic, competitive, and technological forces. Within teams decisions are shared, results are communal, and rewards may be equally divided. Workplace communities in the teamocracy accommodate self-directed teams as well as the more traditional configuration of the enterprise and include functional excellence, organizational autonomy, and performance standards. The hallmark of the teamocracy is that customer value is created principally through the efforts of teams and is sustained by organizational infrastructures that provide operational and strategic guidance, resources, empowerment, and performance standards. The teamocracy is dynamic and responds according to each situation to bring about continuous improvement (and sometimes dramatic changes) in products, services, and organizational processes. Characteristics of the teamocracy include the following:

- Everyone has the opportunity to be a leader and a manager. This results in a widely dispersed execution of leadership and managerial capabilities.
- Trust, respect, loyalty, conviction, and commitment permeate the culture.
- Everyone knows what is going on because there is a widespread sharing of information.
- All employees want to do quality work and be proud of that work.
- Team members subordinate their ego and needs to meet the needs of the team.
- Team leadership is shared; management of the team's resources is also shared.
- Interpersonal networks strengthen both individual and team behavior.
- The assumption is widespread that every product, service, or organizational process can be improved continuously.

- Setbacks in efficiency and effectiveness provide new challenges for doing better and moving ahead through improvement strategies.
- Individual status and pride are enhanced through the sense of belonging and freedom that people feel when working together as equals rather than as subordinates.

Since leadership and managerial activities are widely dispersed in the teamocracy, foresight and vision—two important responsibilities of leaders and managers—are shared throughout the enterprise. Leadership comes less from an appointed position and more from the summons that team members feel from within. Leadership is a fluid concept, and people exercise leadership when needed at appropriate moments. Senior leaders and managers do less trying to extend their authority from the top and more facilitating the cooperative effort of many people at many levels in the organization, who pursue their teamwork with a minimum of oversight from senior people in the enterprise. Leadership is more facilitative (or coaching, acting as a spokesperson) rather than a vertical power coming from a superior position proceeding down a chain of command.

In the teamocracy, self-managed work teams choose their leaders, who function as facilitators. Team members negotiate their individual and collective roles and assign duties and responsibilities. Everyone has the opportunity to be a facilitator. Customers and suppliers become contributing members of the teams, and the teams work at propogating a clear perspective of what it takes to create value for customers. Barriers between team members are reduced, a greater interpersonal compatibility exists, individual and team objectives and goals are better understood, and the team by its own functioning helps to develop the individual and the team in enhanced, productive performance.

Teamocracy is the flip side of bureaucracy in the sense that any bureaucracy has the potential to become a teamocracy if the leaders and managers are willing to change. In demonstrating that willingness to change, clear strategies need to be developed and executed throughout the enterprise, extending to key stakeholders such as customers and suppliers.

Teamocracy has affected the traditional roles of people in an organization who occupy positions of authority—who are in charge of other people. These people are becoming an endangered species.

THE ENDANGERED SPECIES

Traditional managers and supervisors, who believe and act as if they are in charge, are endangered if they do not change their ways of working and carrying out their previous in-charge duties. Team leaders and team members are performing many of the traditional duties of these in-charge people. When empowerment comes to the enterprise and is widely carried out by trained and competent people, both direct and indirect changes are seen that affect the role of the traditional managers. Some of the direct changes include

- Planning the work and assignment of the tasks by members of the team
- Evaluating individual and team performance in doing the work
- Moving toward both individual and team rewards
- Counseling poor team performers
- Participating in key decisions involving the work the team is doing
- Organizing the team members regarding their individual and collective roles
- Taking responsibility for the quality of the work, team productivity, and efficiency in the use of resources
- Developing initiatives to improve the quality and quantity of the output
- Seeking better ways of doing the work and, in so doing, discovering creative and innovative means of perparing for the team and the enterprise's future

The indirect changes are subtle but real. These include

- More interesting work
- A greater sense of control over individual, team, and enterprise destiny
- Greater esprit de corps and pride of both individual and team members
- Greater financial rewards due to improved delivery of products and services to customers
- A greater feeling of individual worth that stems from contributing to useful goals that are realizable and measurable
- Work that is more fun

The use of teams as instruments of corporate strategy has helped change the theory and practice of management. An enterprise that envisions the use of teams needs to consider the probable impact on the people and the culture that such use may have. The teams influence the culture and the culture influences the teams. Both the teams and the culture influence the thinking of other people in the organization, and in turn the organization influences all of the people. There is no beginning or end in how reciprocal influence is networked throughout the people and extending to internal and external stakeholders. That changes are likely to be encountered is clear, and senior management needs to recognize these changes, understand them, and decide how the knowledge, skills, and attitudes of the people must be adjusted, as well as how the culture of the enterprise needs to be fine-tuned.

ROLE CHANGES

The traditional manager is found less frequently in today's enterprises. Downsizing, restructuring, computer and information technology, and the use of teams have made many middle management positions superfluous.

The transition from the traditional manager/supervisor role to the facilitative, coaching, mentoring, and resource support role found in the team-driven organizations is difficult. For traditional managers and supervisors, the transition can be threatening because of

- A sense of loss of status or power—or even the job
- A lack of understanding of the reverberations set in motion by the use of self-directed teams (this lack of understanding causes a fear of the unknown)
- A poorly defined or misunderstood role of the team leader
- Fear of personal obsolescence and changes that require new knowledge, skills, and attitudes

The continued evolution of the roles played by managers and supervisors has paralleled the increase in the use of alternative teams in the strategic and operational management of enterprises. Peter Drucker has often written and spoken about the demise of the traditional supervisor. In one of his most forceful statements he said, "It can be argued that the traditional supervisor is an anachronism and an impediment to productivity."[2] Edward Deming, the father of the quality movement, has suggested that traditional management practices are obsolete and detrimental to the work force. In his usually candid way, he stated that "our prevailing system of management has destroyed our people."[3]

Although many managerial and supervisor jobs are being lost through downsizing and restructuring, does this mean that such jobs are not needed? Of course not, but the roles played by many managers and supervisors are changing—changes brought about to a large measure because of empowered teams, who are able to lead and manage themselves. Empowerment has always existed to some extent, and even organizations that do not use teams have some type and degree of empowerment. As organizations experiment with team strategies, the need for more formal and extensive empowerment becomes clear—usually when the value of empowerment begins to be seen in improved results.

The following suggestions can help supervisors change to nonmanagerial roles without slipping back into their traditional supervisory habit patterns:

[2] Peter Drucker, "Twilight of the First Line Supervisor?" *Wall Street Journal,* June 7, 1983, p. 1.
[3] Quoted at the Association of Quality and Participation's annual conference by Peter Senge, April 7, 1992, Seattle, Washington.

1. Be sure that the supervisor's role has been redefined, including responsibilities for mentoring, coaching, facilitating, and providing resources and support to the teams.
2. Have all supervisors undergo training and orientation into the expectations for the teams and supervisors in the new teamocracy.
3. Provide supervisors with feedback on how well they are doing.
4. Give assurance that supervisors will have job security if they are able to perform under the new order of teams.

Are teams simply a refinement of groups in the management of an enterprise? This question is examined in the next section.

TEAMS AND GROUPS

The decision to design and implement team management in the enterprise is a strategic decision of significant proportions. The outcome of such a decision will be a fundamental change in the way that both operational and strategic activities are organized and carried out in the enterprise. For many companies, a decision of this sort has been overtaken by events since there are teams—perhaps informal in nature—already working in the enterprise. A study of these teams, their origin, what is going on in these teams, and the results that are being produced can give valuable insight into the challenges likely to be encountered in broadening the use of teams in the enterprise. In examining existing teams, care should be taken to determine if teams or groups exist. There are subtle differences between the two. Groups usually emphasize individual efforts informally coordinated within an existing organizational structure. Teams, on the other hand, rely on individual efforts specifically integrated into collaborative output that contributes directly to the objectives and goals of the team. Table 2–1 summarizes ways of distinguishing groups and teams.

TABLE 2–1   Difference between Groups and Teams

Teams	Groups
Shared authority and responsibility	Limited sharing of authority and responsibility
All members share leadership	Leadership rests with one or few individuals
Individual and team accountability	Individual accountability
Shared results and rewards	Modest sharing of results and rewards
High degree of self-direction	Limited self-direction
Members work together to produce results	Results are produced by individual effort

Successful teams work out the details of how to accomplish their objectives and goals in response to a problem or opportunity put before them by higher management. Once a problem or opportunity is sensed, the team spends the time required to explore, understand, and agree on a strategy to deliver team-based results. Management spends the time required to facilitate the work of the team, provide resources, and maintain oversight over what the team is doing, using the team's objectives and goals and the enterprise's mission as performance standards against which to judge team efficiency. Union cooperation helps people identify more with the team than with the union.

Groups also have their objectives and goals—management of the people in the group toward successful accomplishment of the group's results is the responsibility of a single manager, usually in the organizational hierarchy of the enterprise. There is limited learning and rotation through all of the jobs of the group. Consensus decision making is limited; decisions are deferred to the authority of the person in charge. Objectives, goals, and priorities are set by the manager, with limited input from group members. If unionized, people may identify more with the union than with the enterprise.

Sometimes efforts are made to turn a group into a team, usually with little preparation of the people or alignment of the organization's management system to support the likely team. A hands-off approach of this sort turns teamwork into little more than an expenditure of everyone's time. Teams can work well, but they cannot do so by themselves. They need senior management involvement to ensure that objectives and goals are set, resources are provided, oversight of progress is maintained, and the people and management systems are aligned and effective.

Sooner or later after self-directed work teams are started, it becomes apparent that a traditional pay program based on fixed hourly rates, individual incentives, or merit will no longer suffice. Experience with self-directed teams has shown that several principal alternative reward programs are useful—profit sharing, gainsharing, employee stock option plans, skill-based pay, and team incentives.

As stated earlier, teams can work together and produce competitive improvement, but they cannot do this on their own. Setting the stage is important work in getting the organization ready.

SETTING THE STAGE

Shakespeare's wonderful words in *As You Like It,* Act II, scene 7, line 139—"All the world's a stage, And all the men and women merely players"—provide an excellent parallel for setting the organization's stage for the use of teams.

Senior managers are the stage managers in getting ready to use teams. As the strategic architects of the enterprise, these managers, by action and example, set the scene for how the organization prepares for and uses teams. As stage managers, these people are responsible for prescribing the strategic pathway for the enterprise, as outlined in Chapter 1. As leaders, these stage managers must do the right thing in preparing the organization.

This has been done in a remarkable fashion at one of the best-managed companies in the world. The transformation of the Motorola Corporation from a slowly declining American company to a worldwide, Baldridge award–winning legend can be attributed in part to the use of teams. The company's pioneering advances in self-managed work teams, reengineering teams, and product–process development teams, tempered with decentralized decision making, tearing down of organizational department boundaries, and promotion of cooperation between labor and management stand out as an example of distinctive competence in organizational renewal. Motorola has embarked on an ongoing journey to keep its workers energized, motivated, and dissatisfied with the status quo. A large part of the success of Motorola has been the philosophy of renewal: A willingness to renew product and process technologies and obsolete former technologies. Leaders in Motorola continue to sell quality, cycle-time reduction, and cooperative effort through a team organizational design that is envied in industry. Self-managed teams in the company hire and fire their own team members and schedule their own work. By empowering employees and using teams, Motorola's competitive advantage stands without equal in the world. In the strategic context, the company has launched a $4 billion project to interconnect wirelessly every square inch of earth through a constellation of 66 satellites orbiting 420 miles above the planet. When first announced, this development project struck many people as being wildly futuristic. This is indeed a vision of magnificent proportions, but it is likely to be achieved considering the company's remarkable track record. Without question, such accomplishments (which are being carried out through the team culture of Motorola) would not be possible without careful setting of the stage.

Setting the stage for the organizational players, and then keeping abreast of how well the players are planning and carrying out their roles, is the paramount responsibility of senior managers. Bringing forth and successfully using a philosophy of strategic management, as outlined in Chapter 1, is an important part of setting the parameters of the stage for using teams. Establishing and articulating a vision and code of values helps to develop a culture that encourages and rewards teamwork. Definitions of the types of teams and what is expected of them become important performance standards for the enterprise. Providing the resources and exercising oversight of how well the teams are developing and executing their strategies is a major senior leadership responsibility—an absolute necessity in determining how well the enterprise is doing regarding its uses of teams. Periodic evaluation of the results being produced by the teams, in whatever context, provides valuable insight into how well the enterprise is keeping on its strategic pathway. Ensuring that the right kind of documentation is developed to prescribe team roles, evaluating team performance, providing review and feedback on team activity, and providing teams with the resources to do the job (including whatever training is needed) are additional major responsibilities of senior managers. Indeed, the decision to move to a team-driven enterprise heightens and extends the responsibilities of senior managers. When senior managers launch the use of alternative teams in the operational and strategic arenas of the enterprise, they take on added responsibility not so clearly established under the traditional command-and-control enterprise.

STRATEGIC THINKING

When teams are used, more people are involved in doing strategic thinking about the enterprise—where it is going and how it is going to get there. By empowering the people and making available information on the problems, opportunities, and performance of the enterprise, people will start asking a lot of questions and will become more judgmental when they see something happening that they do not understand or with which they do not agree. The commitment of the people to participate more in an enhanced and empowered environment will make them more anxious to know what is going on and how their personal and organizational well-being will be influenced. As people participate more fully in the development of organizational mission, objectives, goals, and strategies at all levels, they will gain useful insight and thus suggest how these organizational performance standards can be improved (or thrown out if the standards do not make sense).

How well senior managers think through the probabilities and possibilities regarding what the enterprise can do and, in the process, engage many people from all levels and disciplines of the enterprise will largely determine how well the organization and its constituent parts play their respective roles.

There is important and inescapable work that senior managers must carry out in setting the stage:

- Develop, disseminate, and constantly propogate the strategic management paradigm in which the teams will operate and contribute to the future well-being of the enterprise.
- Ensure that adequate resources are made available to help the teams develop effective and efficient organizational mechanisms for meeting their objectives and goals improving operational and strategic improvements in product and process changes.
- Recognize that improvements in the knowledge, skills, and attitudes of all people who will be involved in using teams will be required and will best be served through substantial commitments to enterprise training programs.
- Keep close and ongoing oversight of how well the enterprise is doing in moving to its team-driven strategies, and provide members of the enterprise with feedback on how well things are going.

- Develop an organizational culture that facilitates the use of teams in enterprise strategy, and keep people motivated that the success of such a culture requires a continuous journey of self-improvement.

Few would doubt the need to deal with the issue of preparing the organization for the use of teams. Getting the attention of senior management to provide the leadership for a change to teams is an important challenge.

GETTING SENIOR MANAGEMENT'S ATTENTION

How can senior managers be convinced that a management philosophy that embraces a traditional organizational design and a command-and-control–managed enterprise is an anachronism—an out-of-date belief whose time has passed? A perusal of some of the leading business and management publications should catch the attention of managers—particularly if they see competitors using more current organizational designs and management philosophies. Once you have the attention of senior managers, benchmarking of the best in the industry and the most notable competitors can help to convince such traditional thinkers and managers of the need to change. But getting their initial attention to convince them that their enterprise is a problem—or an unexploited opportunity—is the secret. In this section, some of the experiences of the more successful enterprises that have used teams in both operational and strategic initiatives are presented.

General Electric (GE), a premier organization that is producing record earnings (making it one of the most profitable companies in the world) stands as a model of how teams can become key elements in the design and execution of organizational strategies. GE is using three basic strategies involving teams to empower employees:

- "Work-out" sessions, in which employees work together to take unnecessary work out of their jobs through working out problems and opportunities together.
- Best practices, which examine the secrets of a competitor's success. GE found that the successful companies focused less on the performance of individual departments and more on how they work together as products move from one to another department. These companies also outperformed their competitors in commercializing new products sooner and treated their suppliers as partners. GE also found that the best companies used a strategy of continuously improving processes—even in small ways—and that processes needed owners whose authority and responsibility reached through the walls between departments.
- Process mapping, through development of a flow chart that shows every step, no matter how small, that goes into making or doing something. Unnecessary steps become candidates for elimination.

What will this do to GE's hierarchy? Teams will move the organizational products and processes together, reaching into the core of the organization to get done what must be done to remain competitive. Managers will become those who facilitate, grease, and find ways to make the organization seamless and will not be controllers and directors.

GE operates almost entirely in traditional industries: electricity generation, appliances, lighting, medical systems, plastics, locomotives, and jet engines. CEO John F. Welch, Jr., has set the goal of increasing the company's productivity by 6 percent each year. He is a strong believer in human potential and is convinced that, if motivated, properly organized people can work near miracles. The team organizational design is a hallmark of GE. Getting people to talk, listen, and be open to new ideas, breaking down hierarchies, and ensuring that information flows up, down, and sideways in the company helps to facilitate the work of the teams. Old line supervisors are disappearing from the factories, and in many plants hourly workers manage their own jobs in teams. At the Erie plant in Pennsylvania, line supervisors are gone, and teams have been instrumental in cutting assembly times in half on new locomotives.

A more spectacular contribution of teams to the strategic management of GE was made in GE's Appliance Park in Louisville, Kentucky, where labor relations had regressed to the point at which the site was known as Strike City, USA. GE was about to launch a new washing machine, but because of high cost, poor quality, and poor labor relations, CEO Welch let it be known that GE might contract out production to another company. This got the attention of the manufacturing boss and the president of local union. After a trip to a GE silicone plant to study team problem solving, they decided to give teams a try at Louisville. A new team effort called Save the Park concentrated on cutting $60 million a year in costs and coming up with a better washing machine. The results of the team effort were that lucrative piece-rate pay scales were abandoned, job classes were reduced from 65 to 3, and no-supervisor work teams were adopted. The plant went from a $40 million loss in 1992 to a profit in 1994. The tone for the culture at GE is set in part by CEO Welch's belief that many of the problems that have come up at GE and elsewhere trace to similar causes: The people who know about the problem won't or can't or are afraid to get the message to the boss.[4]

TEAM BUILDING

Senior managers need to appreciate the importance of team building, both in the strategy of getting ready for the initial team organizational design and periodically when the teams are in operation, for the long term as long as teams are used as instruments of strategy. There are some team-building

---

[4] Paraphrased from James R. Norman, "A Very Nimble Elephant," *Forbes,* October 10, 1994, pp. 88–92.

fundamentals that senior managers need to recognize, and maintain oversight of, while preparing the organization to use teams:

- An ability of the different teams to work with each other and to respect each other's territory
- Recognition of the high degree of interdependence among the members of the team, and how that interdependence can be used as a strength for integrated team results
- A willingness of the team members to share their information and work with each other, leading to a high degree of collaboration among team members
- Recognition of the deliberate conflict usually found in team work—a conflict, often stemming from different backgrounds, which exists because of substantive issues and not interpersonal strife
- A more efficient way for team members to seek proactively ways to work out problems and opportunities through team members and reach a result in which each member sees part of his or her work in the solution
- A better understanding of the culture of the team, its thought and work processes, and greater willingness to give unselfish support to the team's objectives and goals
- Enhanced communication among the team members about their individual and collective work on the team
- Better understanding of the purpose of the team, its relationship with the work of other teams, and how everything comes together to support the mission, objectives, and goals of the enterprise
- Greater opportunity for a higher degree of esprit de corps, a sense of belonging on the part of the members, and pride in working together to accomplish desired ends

Part of the business of getting ready for the use of teams at Asea Brown Boveri's (ABB's) multinational organization (composed of more than 1000 companies) was training in cross-functional work and modern electronic data processing (EDP) software. After training was completed, center manufacturing teams were established that were responsible for the entire order process of a product, from the first customer contact to invoicing. The team reduced order cycle time by more than 90 percent, resulting in higher levels of customer satisfaction.

Ensuring that corporate strategy is developed, and then reviewing that strategy as it progresses, is a key responsibility of the senior organization members, including the board of directors. Development of strategy for moving the company to a team-driven organizational design is a key issue, the major elements of which the board of directors should review with care. A pending review by the board will send a clear message to the company: The use of teams in the company's organizational design is an important matter and should be dealt with accordingly. The development and adoption of courses of action and allocation of resources to carry out the transition to the use of teams in the management of the enterprise is a strategic initiative of the first order. The board of directors cannot be expected to work out a company's strategy for moving to the use of teams, but it is the duty of the board to make sure that the company has adequate strategies in place to use and get the best out of teams in both operational and strategic matters. Once the strategies have been launched to use teams, the board of directors should insist on periodically reviewing how effective those strategies are and how well the transition to teams is working out.

As such reviews are carried out and as the teams begin to be effective in their work, senior managers will develop an appreciation of what teams can do for the enterprise. As the teams continue to operate, they will influence the organization's culture. Senior managers need to know if that culture is supportive of the organization's mission, objectives, goals, and strategies.

Getting ready requires that people be invested with *de jure* authority. Such empowerment comes from a vision held by principal managers.

A VISION OF EMPOWERMENT

Getting ready requires that the senior managers coordinate and integrate their views concerning a vision for empowering the self-directed teams. Key elements of such empowerment should include a vision statement about empowerment and a set of basic truths or principles about empowerment that support the vision statement. A vision statement and set of principles are necessary to set the tone for how empowerment will function in the enterprise. The vision statement should address in specific terms how employees will be vested with both authority and responsibility to deliver value to both internal and external customers. A statement such as the following can be used as a template: "This company will be an organization in which all employees are vested with the authority and responsibility to participate in the self-direction of the efforts of the teams to which they belong." The supporting principles for the vision should include the following:

- Strategic management initiatives provide guidance for the utilization of resources by organizational units, functional entities, and self-managed teams in delivering customer value.
- All employees will be empowered through the specific decentralization of authority and responsibility to do their work and to self-manage that work in a team-driven organizational design.
- Sharing of information, an open organizational culture, a maximum communication of problems and opportunities, a minimum of bureaucracy, and deep personal dedication will be the hallmark of empowerment.

- The employees know the most about how to do their jobs, and given the opportunity through empowerment can make creative and innovative improvements in how jobs are carried out in the enterprise.
- Increased authority and responsibility reside at the organizational level where employees are doing their work through ongoing contact with managers and supervisors, peers, associates, and key stakeholders, such as customers and suppliers.
- Coaching, facilitating, mentoring, and collaborative skills are the principal means by which management and supervisory oversight is maintained.
- People will be expected to develop the multiple skills required for the team's work, and teams will, insofar as possible, choose their own leaders—with that leadership rotated throughout the team's membership.
- Performance standards for the enterprise, its subunits, and the teams will remain at the highest levels of quality and productivity expectations.

Another vision that senior managers should develop is that getting ready can be developed using a life-cycle approach.

THE LIFE CYCLE

It takes time to conceptualize and understand what self-directed teams are about, to prepare the teams and the organization for their use, to put teams into operation, and to transfer the technology involved in self-directed teams. The final result of this process is the recognition that teams have reached a level of adolescence and maturity and that they stand a good chance of becoming a way of life in the enterprise. Figure 2–1 portrays this life cycle.

The first phase, **conceptualization and understanding** involves building a probable paradigm of what self-managed teams can and should do, including

- Understanding of the need for the team organizational design
- Benchmarking of how and where teams have been used successfully

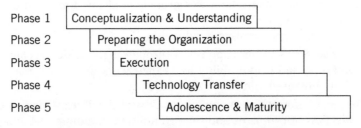

Phase 1	Conceptualization & Understanding
Phase 2	Preparing the Organization
Phase 3	Execution
Phase 4	Technology Transfer
Phase 5	Adolescence & Maturity

Figure 2–1. The life-cycle team design and execution.

- Likely problems and challenges involved in setting up and implementing the teams
- Appreciation of the reverberations that the installation of teams will create
- Insight into the training that will be required to move to team-driven initiatives
- An overall plan of how resources will be used to prepare the people and the organization to use teams

The second phase, **preparing the organization,** consists of developing the action plans required to transform the organization from its traditional mode of operation to one emphasizing the use of teams, including

- Development of supporting policy documentation, including team charters, delegation of authority and responsibility, work redesign initiatives, and new pay schemas
- Identification of training needs and supporting curricula
- Analysis of the organization's culture and the likely need for reinforcement of that culture to support team initiatives
- Benchmarking of other organizations that use teams to gain insight into what reverberations are likely and to develop remedial strategies to deal with such effects
- Identification and change of organizational supporting systems to help the teams do and manage their work
- Selection of areas in the enterprise best suited for demonstration projects in the use of the teams

The third phase, **execution,** provides for the on-line utilization of teams in the operating and strategic segments of the enterprise, including

- Assignment of people to teams charged with specific measurable objectives, goals, and tasks
- Implementation of new job design instructions, work rules, policies and procedures, pay and promotion policies, information requirements, and resource allocation schemas
- Measurement and evaluation of team results, including contribution to organizational performance standards
- Assessment of how well the teams are performing as integrated work units, team effectiveness, and the general need for further team development initiatives
- Effectiveness of feedback to provide insight into how well the teams are functioning, including insight into what fine-tuning is required to improve the teams' efficiency and effectiveness

The fourth phase, **technology transfer,** could be considered part of the execution phase. Yet the need to identify those technologies that support the teams is sufficiently important to distinguish technology transfer up as a separate phase including

- Identification of the computer and telecommunications needs to support the teams
- Assurance that the technology of the hardware being used in the enterprise is compatible with the capabilities of the people—such as on-line computers on the manufacturing floor
- Assurance that the technology being used in the products and processes is understood by the teams as they do their work
- The use of information to provide intelligence for the work of the teams as they work with customers, suppliers, and other stakeholders
- Assurance that the technology of team development is understood by the members of the organization and that mechanisms are in place to facilitate such development

The fifth and final phase, **adolescence and maturity,** is realized when the teams and the organizational supporting systems are working effectively and efficiently, delivering customer value. This stage is recognizable when the following conditions exist:

- Teams are acceptable in the organization, and people feel pride and status in being a member of a team.
- The cultural ambience of the enterprise sends out a clear message to those who want to listen: "Teamwork is simply the way we do things around here."
- Measurable benefits from the work of the teams can be traced to singular improvements in the global competitiveness of the enterprise.
- Team-based incentive pay and promotion schemas are ingrained in the values and traditions of the enterprise.
- Successful leadership of teams becomes a prerequisite for advancement to managerial levels in the enterprise.

Senior leadership responsibilities change as the successive stages of teamwork in the enterprise are carried out. Providing the vision and linking the proposed teams to the enterprise's performance standards are important elements of getting started. During the subsequent stages, senior managers need to facilitate the development process, keep the resources coming, garner feedback on how well things are going, and look for problems and opportunities that can be solved or exploited to strengthen the emerging team strategies. Accolades should be given to those teams and their members who have set new performance standards. Finally, as the teamwork in the enterprise moves into adolescence and maturity, senior managers should look for whatever fine-tuning can be done to make the successful teams even better. A final leadership challenge for all managers and leaders in the enterprise is to ponder the following question: What's beyond the use of teams and the reverberations that teams set in motion? Teams have brought important changes in the way contemporary organizations are managed. But teams are only a plateau for further changes in organizational design—changes that undoubtedly will spawn new ways of creating value for customers. As the use of teams becomes more commonplace they will become institutionalized, that is, they will reflect the attitudes that people have about the way the organization is designed and managed. The use of teams as instruments of organizational strategy will be more a state of mind than anything else. But teams are not the ultimate in the creation of innovative designs for the organization of the resources of an enterprise. Something else will come forth in the theory and practice of management. What that new paradigm will be no one knows, but if the evolution of the management discipline over the past one-hundred years is any guide, something different—and perhaps better—will likely come forth.

In the following example, two companies adopted a life-cycle strategy to introduce the use of teams. In a plastic-injection molding company and in a company that provides residential social services for people with disabilities, company managers believed in the value of teams for running a company. In setting up team organizational designs in these companies, several life-cycle phases were followed:

- *Feasibility:* Conduct a feasibility study to determine if teams will work and seek to determine such things as how long it will take to implement teams and what type of commitment on the part of everyone will be required.
- *Priorities:* Determine the most important needs for improvement, such as customer service, cost reduction, quality improvements, and productivity advances.
- *Mission and objectives:* Make sure that company performance standards have been set, including a common vision to condition the behavioral culture of the firm.
- *Discover and eliminate barriers:* Eliminate lack of expertise, narrow-minded processes, cultural barriers, territorial fiefdoms, or whatever else can stifle or kill the efforts to use teams.
- *Start small:* Begin team planning and execution in a small part of the company in which success is likely, and then expand from this base.
- *Training:* Upgrade the capabilities of all the people—senior managers, functional managers, team leaders, and team members.
- *Let go:* Managers must give up control, allow teams to manage themselves, and allow them to make mistakes.

- *Provide feedback and support:* It is necessary to offer modest feedback to guide the team development effort and support the personal development of the individuals on the teams.
- *Expect results:* Insist on specific, measurable improvement in a specified time period.[5]

Improvement of existing products and processes and development of break-through new products and processes spring from an idea—a visible representation or conception—that someone associated with the organization had. Through a design and development process, the idea is transformed into something real that can be sold to and will create value for customers. When people serve on teams and are provided with resources and a culture that encourages creative thinking and innovation, a wealth of ideas develops. Not all of the ideas are good ones. Most of the good ideas that are further explored and developed will not survive to reach a product or process contribution. A high mortality rate is to be expected, the best way to get a good idea is to have plenty of ideas. Emerging ideas should be tested in the mainstream of the enterprise so their merits can be evaluated.

If there is a viable alternative to using teams to meet the challenges of an unforgiving global marketplace, such alternatives are not apparent. Should such alternatives come forth, it is highly probable that teams will be used in some context to focus the use of organizational efforts.

The emergence of teams changes the way organizations are managed. These changes have taken on the characteristics of systems changes. The introduction of self-directed teams into the strategic management of the enterprise triggers widespread and deep changes in the enterprise's operational and strategic posture. Every innovation carried out within the context of teams acts as a trigger of change, precipitating a series of events that, in turn, touch off other events and additional reverberations. Teams cause trigger effects in the enterprise's community, leading to further changes in what becomes a continuing sequence of interconnected events.[6]

TRIGGER EFFECTS

Reverberations from the use of teams are extensive and profound, affecting individual and collective roles, reward systems, organizational design, and the manner in which the management functions (planning, organizing, motivation, direction, and control) are carried out. Traditional management and first-level supervisory duties shift from the direct superior–subordinate relationships to

---

[5] Bradford McKee, "Turn Your Workers Into a Team," *Nation's Business,* Vol. 80, No. 10, July 1992, pp. 36–38.
[6] I have picked up on James Burke's phrase "The Trigger Effect" in Chapter 2 of his book *Connections,* Little, Brown and Company, Boston, 1978, pp. 1–14.

reciprocal relationships among superiors, subordinates, peers, associates, and stakeholders such as customers and suppliers. Managers and supervisors become facilitators, coaches, mentors, advisors, teachers, trainers, counselors, consultants, guides—roles in which they exercise less command-and-control direction and take on added responsibilities of leadership to expedite and ease the useful employment of resources in the enterprise. The former role of being in charge of the people in the organization is now more one of providing an environment for the people to work together with economic, social, and psychological satisfaction during the process of creating value for internal and external customers. Considering such changes in roles, managers and supervisors need to rethink what they do and develop attitude changes that enable them to demonstrate expertise as leaders in getting diverse constituents to work together. The sharing context of the project-driven organization becomes critical—there is a greater sharing of resources, authority, responsibility, accountability, problems, opportunities, results, and rewards.

As senior managers plan to move the enterprise to take on the characteristics of the team-driven organization, they must recognize that a substantial and critical part of getting ready rests with them as leaders and facilitators of the forthcoming change. Recognition of the probable trigger effects likely to affect the enterprise includes

- Redefinition of the individual and collective roles in the enterprise
- Reduction of the number of management and supervisory personnel
- Broadened empowerment of all people—particularly those people who hold membership on the alternative teams being used in the organization
- Extensive training of all people, leading to improvement in their knowledge, skills, and attitudes and greater expectations on their part to participate more fully in operational and strategic matters, including access to relevant information about all aspects of the enterprise
- Likely greater expression of creativity and innovation by all people, which, if properly facilitated and nurtured, can lead to improved quality products, services, and organizational processes
- Enhanced contact with enterprise stakeholders, particularly customers and suppliers, whose expertise and resources can be better marshalled for improvement of the enterprise's abilities to deliver value to customers.

Customers that have redesigned themselves to strengthen the use of teams as inherent units of strategy and have enjoyed trigger effects as a result include the Hewlett-Packard Company. In 1989, the company had flat sales in electronic instruments, and its flagship minicomputers were battling a slowing market. More significant was that the company was lagging in fast-growing new markets, such as workstations. A traditional organizational design, buttressed by management by committee, had taken on an extraordinary level of inefficiency. Three dozen committees maintained oversight over most decisions. One major result was a delay in developing new products and processes.

A broad corporate move to improve performance and get products out the door sooner using product and process development teams was undertaken. Employees accepted the challenges to serve on teams to rethink every process, from product development to distribution to customers. As the team-driven culture developed at the company, two layers of management were eliminated, product groups were given their own sales staffs, and more up-front time was spent to define product opportunities and to form small teams that would develop products faster than the company's former traditional development organization.[7]

In one company, senior management was concerned about some of the trigger effects that would affect the enterprise when teams were formed and used as key elements in organizational strategy. To test the water, senior management set up several demonstration teams to help in transforming the company's approach to manufacturing from a single integrated factory to one that had several focused factory cells, dedicated to a narrow, newly developed product line. The teams studied the concept of the focused factory configuration and recommended a $40 million investment in equipment, reliability testing, automatic tool adjustment, and programmable control of manufacturing equipment. By advancing the state of the art of the equipment and manufacturing processes, the company realized a continuing source of cost and quality advantages. The success of these demonstration projects in manufacturing encouraged the formation of other team initiatives in product and process development and quality improvement and paved the way for the use of self-directed production teams. People in the enterprise were kept appraised regularly on the progress and the problems being encountered by the teams. Not only did the demonstration projects make improvements in manufacturing, but their success and the candid disclosures of what the teams were doing convinced people that teams, properly formed and used, could improve both the operational and strategic posture of the company.

THE LARGER WHOLE

For teams to do well, they must fit into the larger context of the enterprise in terms of the major characteristics of the enterprise: (1) strategic and operational direction, (2) culture and values, (3) management systems, (4) reward systems, and (5) strategic and operational performance standards. Compatibility of the teams with the larger whole should be one of the key reasons for developing and presenting training and orientation programs. Setting up a senior-level team design and implementation initiative to study where the

---

[7] Robert D. Hof, "From Dinosaur to Gazelle," *Business Week/Reinventing America,* October 23, 1992, p. 65.

enterprise stands regarding these characteristics and then suggest a strategy for taking the enterprise to a team-driven culture is an important endeavor. Once the vision for the team has been accepted by senior management as presented by the design and implementation team, resources can be allocated to bring about the changes needed. The implementation team should monitor vigilantly how the team development efforts are going and should provide corrections as needed and feedback to key people in the enterprise. Benchmarking of competitors and the best in the industry and evaluating strengths and weaknesses can contribute to an understanding of the changes that will be needed to launch an initial and subsequent successful transition to teams in the enterprise's strategies. It is necessary to assess the likelihood of the culture to assimilate teams, the degree of empowerment felt by employees, the present level of productivity, product or service and process development, and whatever other performance indicators can be reviewed to judge the likelihood of the teams being successful. A study of the organization's past, its current successes and failures, how well it has done in being competitive, and the probability of continued success can be done by sampling the judgment of people in the enterprise, all who contribute to such questions as the following:

- What cultural and value issues will influence the introduction of teams in the enterprise?
- What resources will be required to bring about the changes needed to introduce and use teams?
- What is the likelihood of success in this endeavor?
- How do we get started, and how will it be known how we are doing as we set out to design and implement teams for the enterprise?

HOW LONG WILL IT TAKE?

The time that it will take to get the teams up and working effectively in the enterprise varies, depending on what experience the enterprise has had with teams. If an organization is introducing teams for the first time, it will probably take three to four years to ensure that the teams are operating effectively and to implement the supporting systems and cultural fine-tuning that are needed. Some of the changes that will come from the use of teams will be that fewer traditional managers are needed and the number of employees can be reduced since the work that is being carried out in the enterprise will be done more efficiently.

Managers who hope to install teams must think about how such teams will fare in prosperity and adversity. An effective way of getting ready is to practice what you preach—use a design and implementation team to plan for and maintain oversight over the process of getting ready for teams.

Major responsibilities for the design and implementation team include the following:

- Provide for the transfer of the enterprise's vision and values to the teams.
- Develop documentation for the teams, including a supporting charter, authority-accountability-responsibility relations, work redesign, and general cultural support.
- Provide both conceptual and work linkages between the teams and the other organizational elements.
- Evaluate existing reward systems for compatibility with the team organizational design.
- Become the champion for the transformation of the enterprise from its traditional configuration to one characterized by team modes, values, and processes.
- Provide general support, including allocation of resources.
- Evaluate how the teams will interface with the functional expertise, strategic management, and cultural characteristics of the enterprise.
- Recommend training initiatives to support the transition to a team-driven enterprise.
- Assess the existing supporting technologies, such as computer and information systems, to support the team architecture.

Finally, the design and implementation team should present strategies, as they are developed, to senior management regarding how the enterprise can best bring about the changes needed to support the new team organizational design. A key point to remember is that although a champion is needed at the senior levels of the enterprise to help in the transition to teams, champions are needed at every level—advocates who can provide the inspiration and model for moving to the team-driven enterprise.

SUMMARY

Teams working in cross-functional and cross-organizational environments are becoming the only real and effective way to develop viable operational and strategic initiatives to meet global competition. The building of effective and useful teams in the organizational design of the enterprise is becoming a major challenge for contemporary managers. Three major benefits occurring to the enterprise from the use of teams are (1) better problem solving and opportunity realization, (2) higher productivity, and (3) more effective use of resources. Success in the timely accomplishment of the organization's mission, objectives, and goals and the successful execution of its strategies comes from the use of teams.

Getting ready means that specific strategies need to be designed and implemented by way of

- Understanding why the concept of teamocracy is replacing the traditional paradigm of managing organizations
- Appreciating the changing roles of managers and supervisors, and how such changes need to be considered in preparing to use teams as instruments of strategy, including the acceptance that many traditional roles are endangered and will be replaced by members of the team, who manage themselves
- Developing insight into why teams are different from the traditional groups in the management of the enterprise
- Developing strategies in setting the stage for change to teams
- Understanding that senior managers play a pivotal role in preparing the enterprise for the use of teams, including development of a vision of how teams will be empowered in the organization
- Using a life-cycle process that includes the key elements of work to be done in each life-cycle phase toward the use of teams
- Understanding that the use of teams has changed the traditional activities carried out by managers and supervisors
- Acknowledging that the trigger effects coming about from the use of teams are real and should be considered when strategies are developed for the use of teams

Changes stemming from the use of teams are so important that every means must be used by senior managers to anticipate such changes and plan for and commit the organizational resources necessary to facilitate and understand these changes. In the next chapter the concept and process of project management will be described as a philosophy to use in getting the teams ready to perform their duties.

_____3
GETTING THE
TEAMS READY

You may fire when you are ready, Gridley.
ADDRESSED TO THE CAPTAIN OF
GEORGE DEWEY'S FLAGSHIP AT THE
BATTLE OF MANILA BAY, MAY 1, 1898.

This chapter describes the basics of project management. These basics are important—the theory and practice of project management affect the way in which other teams are organized and managed. The reader should consider how the techniques discussed in this chapter can be applied to the other types of teams described in this book. This chapter will provide insight into the key elements of planning, organizing, and maintaining oversight of project team activities.

The strategic pathway to the use of alternative teams in organizations was preceded by the concept and practice of project management, an idea whose time has come. Project management emerged in an unobtrusive manner in the late 1950s and began to take on the characteristics of a discipline in its own right. No one can claim to have invented project management. Its beginnings are found in the construction industry, and in later years project management was used in the development and procurement of military systems. Since its origins, project management has spawned a rich abundance of literature describing its conceptual framework, the processes used in managing projects, and the prescription of ways and means for managing diverse stakeholders, who participate in the design, development, and delivery of project results. Project management is a performance capability, delivered on schedule and within a planned budget and consistent with the strategic direction of the enterprise.

For example, the use of projects as building blocks in the design and execution of organizational strategies is found in the management plan for the city of Tucson, Arizona. The city has several strategic priorities: environment and development, capacity of the city organization, the future city, Tucson and the global economy, and youth and crime. Management values have been developed to support the city's strategic management system. These values include diversity, leadership, integrity, loyalty to an ideal public service, teamwork, organizational pride, and excellence in performance. The organizational design philosophy of the city is meant to facilitate having employees and managers "crash through department walls, coalescing and collaborating in order to efficiently utilize limited resources to meet the challenges of our strategic priorities as well as day-to-day operation." A project management system (PMS) defines the priority work to be undertaken in the city. Projects are designed to meet specific performance requirements, on time and within budgets. The PMS provides for a careful, calculated use of the city's limited resources.[1]

One of the trigger effects set in action by the emergence of project management has been the development of specialized approaches and techniques to manage projects, which are ad hoc activities carried out to create something that does not currently exist but is needed to enhance the capability of a user. New highways, buildings, bridges, computer systems, and manufacturing facilities are a few examples of the many new capabilities that can be created using project teams. The use of teams in organizations has fostered new concepts and processes in the field of management that are dedicated to manage an ad hoc activity, such as a project as a building block in the design and execution of organizational strategies. These concepts and processes include specialized network scheduling techniques, and project management information systems to report on the progress of the project as it goes through its life cycle have been developed and refined. Distinct project planning strategies have come forth to use in developing a plan of action for project development. Project evaluation and control methodologies have been created to monitor, evaluate, and maintain control over the effectiveness and efficiency with which projects are managed.

PLANNING PROCESSES

Planning for the use of project teams and alternative types of teams in the enterprise deals with the development and dissemination of foresight regarding the possibilities and probabilities of using resources to attain end purposes. Depending on the extent to which the teams are self-managed, this planning can be carried out by the team members with support by managers acting in the capacity of coaches, facilitators, mentors, and resource providers. Two

---

[1] *Blueprint for Organizational Renewal,* Brochure, City of Tucson, undated.

key modules are involved in the development of plans for a team: (1) the elements of team planning, and (2) development of a work breakdown structure (WBS) of tasks to be performed. These modules are briefly discussed next.

The Elements of Team Planning

In supporting organizational strategies, team planning is carried out through the development of key supporting elements. These elements include

- A delineation of the **team objectives**—the desired future position of the team in terms of costs, schedules, and performance capabilities.
- A determination of the **goals or milestones** that, when completed successfully, will lead to adequate completion of the team's work. Goals are defined in the context of the work breakdown structures leading to work packages, whose completion is essential to completing the team's goals. Strategies are the plan of action required for the team along with accompanying policies, procedures, and schemas, which provide general direction for how resources will be used to accomplish the team goals and objectives.
- The **organizational design** of the team and how that team interfaces with the parent organization and other organizations that provide products and services to support the effort. Such as organizational design usually includes some variation of the matrix-driven organizational structure. The organizational design includes identification, negotiation, and resolution of individual and collective roles to support the team's deliberations. The common denominator of this organizational design is reflected in the authority and responsibility patterns within the overlay of the team on the existing functional elements of the organization.
- The **leadership style** of the team leaders, and how that style is reflected in the knowledge, skills, and attitudes of the team in its organizational environment.
- The **information** required to develop and support the team in planning for, organizing, and controlling the resources.
- The **cultural ambience** of the organization in which the team is being designed and executed. This ambience is a reflection of the beliefs, customs, knowledge, practices, and conventional behavior of the social groups in the project and its environment. The cultural ambience will influence the character of the team and the efficiency and effectiveness with which the work is managed.
- The **techniques and methodologies** used to gain insight into how the project resources should be allocated. These techniques and methodologies include action plans, policies, procedures, resource allocation schemas, and programs. Since teams are building blocks in the design and execution of organizational strategies, they play an important role in preparing the organization for its future. Conceptualizing a team's work

and bringing it to a successful conclusion involves creating something that can be used to support a customer's future operational needs. Senior managers of an enterprise need to consider the strategic fit of the team's work in supporting the strategies of an intended user or customer. Organizational planning provides the context in which team planning can be carried out.

The Work Breakdown Structure (WBS)

The WBS is the basic cornerstone of the team's work. A WBS is a product-oriented family tree division of hardware, software, services, and other work elements that organizes, defines, and graphically displays the product or service to be created as well as the work to be accomplished to achieve the specified purpose of the work. The logical subdivisions in a WBS are the specific **work packages.** A work package (WP) is a unit of work required to complete a specific job, such as a piece of hardware, a report, or an element of software; it is the responsibility of one operating unit within the organization. Identification of a work package provides for assignment of the work package to a unit of the organization, to which responsibility and accountability can be charged. In the development of the WBS, a scheme is contrived for dividing the work into subelements: Major groups are divided into tasks, tasks are subdivided into subtasks, and so on. The organization of the WBS should follow an orderly identification scheme: Each WBS element is given a distinct identifier. For an aircraft, for example, the WBS might look like this:

1.0 Aircraft

1.1 Fuselage

1.2 Engines

1.3 Wings

1.4 Communication equipment

1.5 Ground support equipment

1.6 Etc.

A graphic representation of the WBS can facilitate its understanding. By using succeeding indented numerical listings, an understanding of the total team's work and its integral subsystems can be facilitated. For example,

```
1.0
     1.1
          1.11
               1.1.1.1
                    1.1.1.1.1
                         Etc.
```

Figure 3–1 is an example of a WBS for an antenna rotating system for an aircraft fire control system.

Use of the WBS. When properly developed, the WBS can serve many key purposes in the planning and control of the work. These purposes provide the means for

- A model of all the products and services involved, including support and other team's tasks.
- A way to show the interrelationships of the work packages to each other, to the overall team's work, and to other activities in the organization.
- A way to pinpoint authority, responsibility, and accountability in the structure of the organization matrix created by the overlay of the team on the existing organizational functions. Each work package can be assigned to a specific individual on the team.
- A focus for estimating cost, schedules, and risk assessment on the work. Each work package can be assessed by an expert drawn from somewhere within the supporting organizational units (i.e., that individual can assess the work package's cost, schedule, and risk considerations). By breaking down the total work into the work packages, a unit of work is sufficiently defined that the required organizational expertise can be brought to bear on the evaluation and planning of the work.

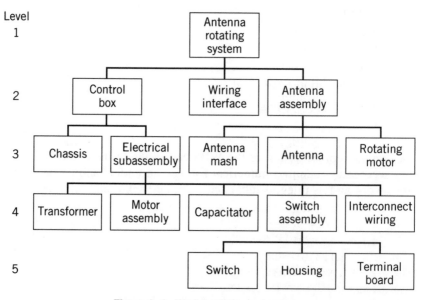

Figure 3–1. Work breakdown structure.

- A basis for controlling the application of resources.
- A reference point for getting committed to the team. Each member of the team, as well as other participating people, can identify with a development of that work package.

The WBS provides a common identifier and management thread by which the project can be developed, produced, and put in its operational environment.

ORGANIZATIONAL DESIGN

In its simplest terms, the organizational design prescribes the manner in which authority, responsibility, and accountability are allocated to the teams, to the supporting functional resources, and to those managers who provide for the strategic management of the enterprise. The modules that are important for organizational design include

- Identification of the individual and collective roles to be played out on the teams and in the supporting functional elements.
- Identification of the major responsibilities of the team leader and the team members. The team leader is responsible for (1) working with the team members in the selection of the objectives, goals, and strategies for the team; (2) sharing leadership with team members so they are motivated to seek opportunities for leadership in their areas of expertise; (3) setting the example for the management style used in the team; (4) being willing to seek team member ideas, input, and opinions in the management of the team; (5) facilitating, coaching, training, and supporting the needs of the team members in doing their work; (6) executing the management functions of leading, planning, organizing, motivating, directing, and controlling, including appropriate instruction and guidance so team members participate in the self-direction of the team; and (7) keeping out of the team's way as it goes about its work.

    The responsibilities of the team members are complementary to the team leader's and include (1) being willing to participate wholeheartedly in the technical and management affairs of the team; (2) attending the team meetings; (3) accepting leadership of the work packages for which they are responsible and seeking other opportunities for leadership in the deliberations of the team's work; (4) being willing to be adversial and "blow the whistle" when they sense that something is not right in the workings of the team; (5) executing the management functions in their area of responsibility; (6) being proactive in identifying opportunities for improving the working of the team and its output; and (7) working at effective communication with the team members and other stakeholders.

The Initial Meeting

An important part of the organization design for teams is a carefully planned and orchestrated initial meeting of the teams. Setting an initial supportive climate for the first meeting will strengthen the individual and collective roles of the team members and make an important first step in developing a cultural ambience that strengthens the bonds of professionalism among the team members. In the initial meeting, questions like the following can be presented and discussed to help set the stage for a team that will work together with social and psychological satisfaction:

- What understanding do we have of the specifics of the individual and collective roles to be carried out in the team?
- What needs to be done to provide added clarification of these roles if required?
- Do we have any concerns about the expectations for the team's work or for the manner in which the team members work together?
- What expectations do we have of each other?
- What needs to be done to sharpen our understanding of these expectations?
- Are there any issues concerning the team's work, the resources available, or other matters that, if not properly understood, could slow down an effective start in the team's work?
- Can we accept the idea that the team members are expected to be adversial when they see something amiss or inconsistent with the team's operation or its purposes?
- How will disagreements and controversies be handled?
- What will be done about a member of the team that might not be satisfying his or her responsibilities on the team?
- How can we ensure that an effective consensus process is carried out in making and implementing decisions in the team's work?
- Do all members of the team fully understand how the team's work, results, and rewards are to be shared?
- How can we develop and continually strengthen the bonds of trust, faith, loyalty, and commitment among the members of the team?

Continued Feedback

After the teams are in operation and provisions have been made to review the teams' progress regularly, there should be continued examination of how well the teams are doing. The teams can perform a self-examination of how well they are functioning as an effective team. By examining themselves and developing feedback due to such self-examination, improvement can be instituted. By seeking answers to questions like the following, valuable and critical feedback can be obtained:

- How well are we doing in working toward attaining our objectives and goals?
- What is going right in the team's work—conversely, what might be going wrong?
- What do we see as the team's strengths? Weaknesses?
- If there are weaknesses, what should be done to correct these weaknesses?
- Are the strategies used by the team in the use of resources effective? If not, why?
- How would we describe the culture that is emerging in the team?
- Is there anything that needs to be done to improve that culture?
- Are we an effective team? If not, why?
- What image does the team have among its stakeholders?
- Do the team members help each other improve their knowledge, skills, and attitudes in the working of the teams?
- Are we proud of our team and the results that it is producing?
- Do the members of the team feel empowered in their roles on the team?

As the team members meet and deliberate on these questions, valuable feedback can be obtained regarding how well the team is doing; strategies for improving the operation of the team can be developed.

Planning for the organization design of teams requires that the issue of authority and responsibility be dealt with in a forthright manner as soon as possible. One of the biggest challenges in getting a team organized is to understand the characteristics of the matrix organizational design.

Usually, organizations that use teams have the teams take an active role in the redesign of the teams' work and the organization of the teams, including redefining the roles of team members and expanding the depth and breadth of their work. Teams that engage in getting themselves organized enjoy that they do not have a lot of specialists and bosses—from industrial engineers to quality control experts—telling them how to do their detailed work.

In traditional practices, work was organized around disciplines. In the design of teamwork, work is organized around meaningful organizational processes. For example, at Asea Brown Boveri's (ABB's) plant in Vaestreras, Sweden, a cross-functional team, the center manufacturing team, was responsible for the entire order process of a product, from the first customer contact to invoicing. With the aid of cross-functional training and modern EDP software, the team reduced its order cycle time by more than 90 percent, resulting in higher levels of customer satisfaction.[2]

[2] "World Class Quality: The Challenge of the 1990s," *Fortune,* July 1991, advertisement, pp. 36–45.

UNDERSTANDING THE MATRIX

In the matrix configuration, personnel are drawn from the organizational functional units to perform a specific task; the organization is temporary in nature, built around the purpose to be accomplished rather than on the basis of functional similarity, process, product, or other traditional bases. When such a team is assembled and superimposed on the existing organizational structure, a matrix organization is formed. Figure 3–2 is a model of the matrix organization.

The matrix model is a network of interfaces between a team and the functional elements of an organization. As additional teams are laid across an organization's functional structure, more interfaces come into existence. These interfaces, depicted in the lower right-hand corner of Figure 3–2, are where the focus of authority and responsibility come into play, largely determining who works with whom in the project affairs. A cursory review of Figure 3–2 would raise the suspicion that the individuals at the interface between the project and functional organizations would be working for two bosses, an apparent violation of the principle of unity of command, which

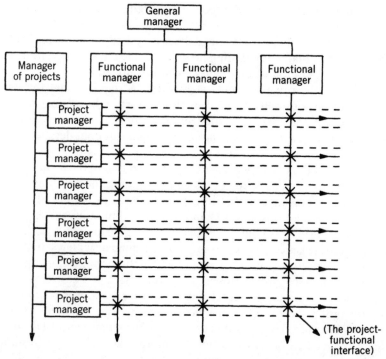

Figure 3–2. A basic team management matrix. (From D. I. Cleland, *Project Management: Strategic Design and Implementation,* 2d ed., McGraw-Hill, New York, 1994, p. 187. Reproduced with permission.)

TABLE 3–1   The Team–Functional Interface

Team Manager	Functional Manager
• What is to be done?	• How will the task be done?
• When will the task be done?	• Where will the task be done?
• Why will the task be done?	• Who will do the task?
• How much money is available to do the task?	• How well has the functional input been integrated into the project?
• How well has the total project been done?	

Source: David I. Cleland, *Project Management: Strategic Design and Implementation,* Tab Professional and Reference Books, Blue Ridge Summit, Pa., 1990, p. 142.

states that one should receive orders from only one individual in the chain of command. This apparent violation can be avoided by describing the basic dichotomy found in the matrix design around the syntax of the statements shown in Table 3–1. This basic dichotomy used to describe the organizational forces in the matrix organization should be used as a polícty statement—a guide to the way people should think about their role in the matrix organization. The management of the organizational relationships in the matrix setting is multidimensional. The team manager relates upward to the boss, horizontally to members of the team, and diagonally to the functional managers and to other representatives of organizations that have a vested interest in the project, including customers, vendors, government agencies, local communities, and other stakeholders.

The literature in project management has given considerable attention to describing the matrix model of organization. All too many projects have been inefficiently and ineffectively managed because of a failure to understand and properly apply the matrix model of organization. In others, the nuances of the perceived violation of unit of command and the resulting confusion have caused difficulty. Today, thirty years after the first experiments with the matrix configuration, there are still problems with its application and in its understanding.

An important part of team organizational design planning is to plan for the organizational arrangements that will be used in the management of the team. The team is like a football team. The individual and collective roles on the team must be planned in advance so all the players know their own authority and responsibility and that of the other players. Project team organization charting can serve a useful purpose.

PROJECT ORGANIZATIONAL CHARTING

A **linear responsibility chart** (LRC) is a model of an organization that goes beyond the simple display of formal lines of communication, gradations of organizational level, departmentalization, and organizational territory portrayed in the traditional organizational chart found in most offices. The LRC reveals the work package–organizational position couplings in the organization. It shows who participates and to what degree when a task on the project is to be carried out. It also helps clarify the authority expectations when two or more organizational positions have overlapping involvement; it clarifies the authority relationships that arise when people share common work. Figure 3–3 shows the basic structure of an LRC in terms of organizational position and a work package, in this case conduct design review. The symbol P indicates that the director of systems engineering has the primary responsibility for conducting the system design review. Figure 3–4 shows an LRC for team management relationships within a matrix organization. A different symbol is used in this sample. The development of such a chart as part of the organizational planning activities of the team, combined with the inevitable discussions that usually accompany such a development, can help facilitate an understanding of how the team is organized and how the day-to-day team roles will be carried out.

ORGANIZATIONAL DESIGN REALITIES[3]

Designs that are coming forth to support the team-driven enterprise take on the characteristics of the horizontal enterprise, a term used to describe the matrix organizational design that emerged in the 1960s literature describing project management. As we gain further understanding of how the alternative use of teams changes the culture of the enterprise, we can identify some of the key characteristics of the horizontal enterprise. These characteristics include

- A reduction in the number of organizational levels, resulting in a flatter hierarchy with an increased number of people reporting to a manager. At the Sun Life Assurance Society, a Bristol-based insurer managing $24 million in assets, most middle management positions have been eliminated and the once isolated customer service representatives, each in charge of a tiny part of processing a customer's file, now work in teams that handle jobs from start to finish. Turnaround time to settle claims has been reduced by 50 percent while new business grew by 45 percent.[4]
- An elimination of unnecessary work that fails to add value to the enterprise. Activities within organizational processes are reduced, and teams are used to manage the processes of creating value for a customer.
- An organizational design based on processes, such as product development, order entry, or quality improvement initiatives, rather than func-

---

[3] The article by John A. Byrne, "The Horizontal Corporation," *Business Week*, December 20, 1993, pp. 76–81, has influenced the ideas expressed in this section.
[4] Jane A. Sasseen et al., "Rethinking Work," *Business Week*, October 17, 1994, p. 92.

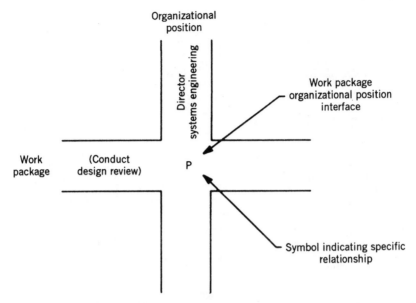

Figure 3–3. Essential structure of a linear responsibility chart. (From David I. Cleland, *Project Management: Strategic Design and Implementation,* 2d ed., McGraw-Hill, New York, 1994, p. 210. Reproduced with permission.)

tions or departments. Each process has an individual who acts as a focal point for the development of strategies for that process.

- The use of empowered teams as the building blocks in bringing a focus to the management of change within the enterprise. Teams have specific objectives and goals—a common purpose—and share resources, results, and rewards and are held responsible and accountable for results.

- The use of suppliers and customers in important working positions on the empowered teams. Team members are brought into direct and ongoing contact with suppliers and internal and external customers. Quality and performance in the creation of value for customers drive the teams and the enterprise. Organizational results and rewards follow from providing value to customers.

- The use of training as a way of life in the enterprise to improve individual and collective knowledge, skills, and attitudes in technical, social, and managerial expertise. Through empowerment, people develop extraordinary technical, managerial, and leadership skills as they serve on teams that, for all practical purposes, manage themselves.

- The use of management across and diagonally in the enterprise, which is more critical than managing up and down in a traditional organizational structure. Organizational boundaries are eliminated or reduced as empowered interdisciplinary teams work together to perform core processes, such as product development or sales generation.

Activity	General manager	Manager of projects	Project manager	Functional manager
Establish department policies & objectives	1	3	3	3
Integration of projects	2	1	3	3
Project direction	4	2	1	3
Project charter	6	2	1	5
Project planning	4	2	1	3
Project–functional conflict resolution	1	3	3	3
Functional planning	2	4	3	1
Functional direction	2	4	5	1
Project budget	4	6	1	3
Project WBS	4	6	1	3
Project control	4	2	1	3
Functional control	2	4	3	1
Overhead management	2	4	3	1
Strategic programs	6	3	4	1

Code

1: Actual responsibility   4: May be consulted
2: General supervision   5: Must be notified
3: Must be consulted   6: Approval authority

Figure 3–4. Linear responsibility chart of project management relationships.

Some companies now prepare budgets based not on functions or departments but on organizational processes, such as after-sales support to customers. Other companies are moving toward having business units organized as teams rather than traditional profit centers. Xerox Corporation uses "microenterprise units" of empowered teams with total life-cycle—beginning to end—responsibility for products and services.

The Change Factor

An organizational design that moves from the neatly arranged boxes on the traditional organizational chart to a team-driven design is an enormous and, at times, painful change. Getting people to quit thinking as marketing, finance, or manufacturing experts alone and to think more synergistically, which is required if teamwork is to manage processes, can be threatening and disquieting for people. Traditional organizational boundaries—the boxes on the traditional chart—cause territorial imperatives to arise and interruptions in the flow of the processes needed to deliver value to customers. At the General Electric Company, CEO John F. Welch speaks of building a "boundaryless" company in responding to customers. At GE, teams of people manage over

100 processes or programs worldwide, from product development to manufacturing, to create customer value. The use of teams at GE has brought about major changes in training, performance appraisal, and compensation systems—for example, "360-degree appraisals," in which peers and those above and below an individual evaluate performance. Employees are paid on the basis of the skills they attain rather than just the work they perform.[5]

At the senior managerial levels, people are appearing who have multiple competencies, rather than narrow specialities, and work more toward providing a culture and the resources for the teams to work rather than the management of the day-to-day activities that are done by the teams. Senior managers have more time—and rightly so—to work at the strategic management of the enterprise.

The development of strategies for the use of team-driven initiatives has been done more at the middle and lower levels of the enterprise. However, organizations are looking at how teams can be used as focal points at higher levels in the hierarchy (e.g., Plural executive teams, such as management committees, or the president's office). For example, a large chemical company replaced several executives in charge of key functions with self-managed work teams. Instead of an individual in charge of manufacturing, a self-directed team was appointed that consisted of all plant managers. Decision making was decentralized to the teams—a major change from the previous organizational design.

A word of caution: Experience has shown that functional departments can become powerful fiefdoms. But so can teams. Teams should always be considered as an organizational design that brings a focus to organizational processes to support enterprise goals, objectives, and mission. Teams are complementary to the functional expertise in the enterprise and are integrated with the functional entities in bringing a cooperative, interdependent focus to the creation of customer value. However, a functional entity should not have an independent mission, but rather a mission that recognizes the interdependence that supports organizational processes. Strong functional leaders can grow powerful along with their departments; this harms the overall enterprise as the leaders fight to build and protect their territory. Functional expertise, focused in a center of excellence within the organization, is a necessity to maintain specialized performance standards, provide a pool of resources for teams to draw on, and ensure that the state of the art in the discipline is maintained and improved.

Titles will be altered as more team-driven strategies emerge. Organizational core processes will likely not have managers in the traditional sense but will have someone called "champion" or "owner." This is done at the AT&T Network Systems Division, in which thirteen core processes are used to track and allocate day-to-day operations or processes. The owners focus on the

---

[5] Reported in the *1993 Annual Report, General Electric Company*, pp. 1–5.

operational matters, whereas the champions ensure that the process keeps close linkage with overall business strategies and objectives.

Providing an environment that facilitates motivation of people is important in the use of teams, as it is in other organizational settings. A few of the basic ideas about motivation as related to teams are discussed next.

MOTIVATION

Motivation provides the opportunity for people to realize social, psychological, and economic satisfaction in their work. Since the early 1930s, increasing attention has been focused on providing an organizational environment in which people will feel motivated and will work toward continual improvement of their interpersonal skills and enhancement of the cultural ambience. To motivate is to provide incentives, inducements, or conditions that stimulate people to dedicate themselves to attaining the organizational mission, objectives, and goals in such a manner that enhanced competitiveness will result.

Sociologists, psychologists, psychiatrists, and behavioral scientists are a few of the professionals who have studied the theory and practice of motivation. Anyone who has had responsibility for other people has had to deal with this question: What brings out the best in the performance of people? In the team-driven organization, motivation becomes a concern of everyone: managers, supervisors, team leaders, team members, suppliers, customers, and other stakeholders. An in-depth description of the theory of motivation is beyond the scope of this book, yet everything that is described in this book, in one way or another, contributes to the conditions whereby people are motivated—or demotivated. We will discuss a few of the fundamentals in motivating people to do their best.

An early and enduring concept of motivation was put forth by Abraham Maslow in his hierarchy of needs. This hierarchy was developed to describe certain levels of human needs that motivate individuals (Figure 3–5).

In 1960, Douglas McGregor, in his *The Human Side of Enterprise*,[6] described a set of attitudes held by managers about the nature and behavior of people that will be reflected in how successful that manager is in leading people toward the organizational purposes. For theory X, these assumptions are as follows:

1. The average human being has an inherent dislike of work and will avoid it if he or she can.
2. Because of this human characteristic of dislike of work, most people must be coerced, controlled, directed, and threatened with punishment

---

[6] Douglas McGregor, *The Human Side of Enterprise,* McGraw-Hill, New York, 1960.

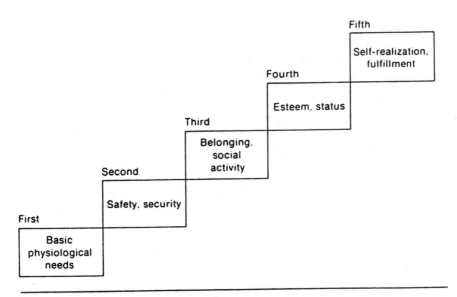

Figure 3–5. Order of priority of human needs. (Adapted with permission from Keith Davis, *Human Relations at Work,* 3d ed., McGraw-Hill, New York, 1967.)

to get them to put forth adequate effort toward the achievement of organizational objectives.

3. The average human being prefers to be directed, wishes to avoid responsibility, has relatively little ambition, and wants security above all.[7]

Theory Y assumptions about human behavior are in dramatic contrast to these:

1. The expenditure of physical and mental effort in work is as natural as play or rest. The average human being does not inherently dislike work. Depending on controllable conditions, work may be a source of satisfaction (and will be voluntarily performed) or a source of punishment (and will be avoided, if possible).

2. External control and the threat of punishment are not the only means for bringing about effort toward organizational objectives. People will exercise self-discretion and self-control in the service objectives to which they are committed.

3. Commitment to objectives is a function of the rewards associated with their achievement. The most significant of such rewards (e.g., the satisfaction of ego and self-actualization needs) can be direct products of effort directed toward organizational objectives.

[7] Ibid., pp. 33–34.

4. The average human being learns, under proper conditions, not only to accept but to seek responsibility. Avoidance of responsibility, lack of ambition, and emphasis on security are generally consequences of experiences, not inherent human characteristics.

5. The capacity to exercise a relatively high degree of imagination, ingenuity, and creativity in the solution of organizational problems is widely, not narrowly, distributed in the population.

6. Under the conditions of modern industrial life, the intellectual potentialities of the average human being are only partially utilized.[8]

Taken together, the concepts of Maslow and McGregor provide the basics for enhancing an environment in which people feel motivated to do their best work. There are other conditions that need to be created and also affect how motivated people feel in doing their best. These conditions are as follows:

• There must be careful prescription of the individual and collective roles that people are expected to carry out in their work on the team and in other capacities in the enterprise. "What is expected of me?" is an important question that people have about how they are expected to work with others in attaining organizational purposes. On pages 67–68, the use of an LRC was described as a means of having people participate in the development and understanding of these roles. If people do not understand these roles, or if the roles are ambiguous, the opportunity for enhanced activation is reduced.

• By having members of the team fully participate in the design of team strategies, a greater understanding of those strategies and their rationale is gained. People will support strategies that they have had a role in developing, particularly as they sense that their input into the team strategies has been recognized. The productivity increases found through the use of self-directed teams have been caused, in part, by involvement of the team members in leading and managing the team.

• There should be maximum sharing of information with team members regarding the performance of the team and the enterprise in terms of the realization of mission, objectives, and goals. When the team members are kept informed regarding how well their efforts are contributing to team and enterprise success, they will feel a greater sense of motivation. By sharing such information, an important message is sent concerning trust and faith in the organizational culture.

• There should be ongoing, continuous improvement of the interpersonal skills of everyone—from senior managers to the employees who are members of the teams. Training in social skills, knowledge about the theory and practice of motivation, and practice in the common courtesies

[8] Ibid., pp. 47–48.

of professional life are important. Working at creating an environment characterized by trust, loyalty, faith, conviction, and commitment on the part of everyone will help improve the interpersonal skills of everyone. Perhaps the Golden Rule says it best: Treat everyone as you would like to be treated.

- It should be recognized that some of the more important characteristics of a fully integrated, motivated team include satisfaction of individual needs within the shared interest of the team members. A strong sense of belonging to the team and pride and enjoyment due to the team's work are important. A commitment to team members and to the team's objectives yields important advantages. Minimum conflict, comfort in the interdependence ambience of the team, and a high degree of intrateam interaction increase motivation. A strong commitment to attaining the performance standards that have been set for the team and the enterprise is important.

- Conditions to enhance an environment in which people are motivated include a training program to improve their knowledge, skills, and attitudes. A training program to enhance everyone's perception of motivation should include insight into the basics of leadership and management as well as how team building can help people understand what they can do individually and collectively to improve motivation. It is important to discuss the strategies needed to facilitate cooperative effort, keep people informed about what is going on, and communicate to them the inevitability of change and how that change will affect the enterprise and everyone in it.

- There should be candid discussions with team members about the important change that the use of teams brings to the enterprise and about the fact that such teams will not be successful without careful preparation on the part of everyone. Teams are not a panacea, and their use has been criticized by some management theorists and practitioners. According to one psychoanalyst, teams undercut the importance of managerial accountability and leadership. The use of teams devalues management at the first and middle levels, undercutting the influence of the first-line manager. Lines of authority and responsibility are blurred, nobody is in charge, and work gets done only after interminable delays. Some executives feel that team training has ruined relationships with subordinates.[9]

Teams are like any other organizational unit in that care must be exercised in prescribing objectives, goals, and strategies. Organization of the team and delineation of individual and collective roles must be done so people know how they are expected to relate in terms of their formal capacity in the

[9] "Executive Education—When Things Go Wrong," *Wall Street Journal,* September 10, 1993, p. R6.

enterprise. Given that people accept their formal roles in the enterprise, they will be more likely to assume informal roles that will help to improve the performance of the enterprise. These are important roles that they can and will assume if given the opportunity to participate in a leadership capacity in the team and in the enterprise.

Executives that envision using teams as key elements in their strategies need to recognize that teams provide a focus for encouraging more employee participation. Without an organizational design dedicated to focusing participation, people will be reluctant to seek involvement in the affairs of the organization. Some of the obstacles to participation include size, hierarchy, passive motivation, and lack of understanding about what degree of participation is appropriate. In large organizations, people can feel insignificant, without names, and fearful of exerting influence on the work being done. If managers are jealous of their power and prerogatives, employees can feel helpless and unable to influence decisions. If managers refuse to let employees make any decisions for themselves, participation will be a charade. By having people work on teams, an organizational unit of appropriate size exists in which people have a sense of belonging, control over their work affairs, and a comfortable feeling of participating in making and executing decisions.

Other impediments to participation include the defined roles of managers, their status and pay, and the perceived position of power that they occupy. Some companies have decided to hire managers only after they have been interviewed and accepted by all their future subordinates. Manager effectiveness is increasingly being evaluated by subordinates through the company's merit evaluation plan. When employees sense that they are being treated as adults, are provided the necessary resources, and are assigned to an organizational unit such as a team, their willingness to participate is increased markedly; they begin to sense that someone is listening.

Teams must be managed like any other organizational unit. Maintaining an overview of what the team is doing is an important executive responsibility. Getting the teams ready should include instructions in the role of monitoring and evaluating performance.

TEAM MONITORING, EVALUATION, AND CONTROL

Team control follows planning. Control is the process of monitoring, evaluating, and comparing planned results with actual results to determine the status of the team's cost, schedule, and technical performance parameters. Control also involves the constraining of resources through corrective action to conform to the plan. The managerial function of control may be visualized as having distinctive steps in a cycle, as depicted in Figure 3–6. Effective control requires suitable information that provides insight into how well the team is accomplishing its purposes. By gleaning suitable information from all of the activities that are underway, explicit comparison can be made of the plan and

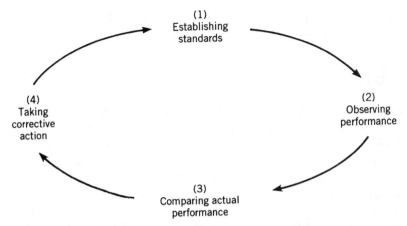

Figure 3-6. The control system. (From David I. Cleland, *Project Management: Strategic Design and Implementation,* 2d ed., McGraw-Hill, New York, 1994, p. 285. Reproduced with permission.)

the results to date. Control is done not so much to determine what has happened (although this is important) but rather to become the basis for predicting what may happen if the team's current thrust and trajectory are continued without any changes in the application of resources. There are several distinct steps involved in the control process, as reflected in Figure 3-6. Control can be carried out only if appropriate performance standards have been developed.

PERFORMANCE STANDARDS

A standard is a touchstone—an acknowledged measure of comparison for determining value, such as the value of the progress that has been made in the team's work. The expected value to be gained on that work is the degree to which the organizational resources have been used. Standards to use in determining the efficiency and effectiveness with which the work is being managed are derivatives of the plan. Some key standards commonly found in team plans and used in the control process include scope of work, work breakdown structure (work packages), work specification, cost estimates and budgets, master and ancillary schedules, financial forecasts and spending plans, quality, customer satisfaction, team satisfaction, senior management satisfaction, reliability, physical quantities of work, vendor plans, productivity, and strategic fit in the strategy of the owner's organization. It is often forgotten that effective control is preceded by effective planning. In the development of plans, careful foresight should be exercised to determine if the plans that are being developed contain the needed standards of performance against which monitoring, evaluation, and control can be carried out. Once the standards of performance have been developed and accepted by the team, over-sight of the work activities must be carried out.

PERFORMANCE OVERSIGHT

Oversight of the team's performance is watchful surveillance of what is hap-pening in the use of resources that is affecting the cost, schedule, and technical performance parameters of the team's work. To maintain oversight means that sufficient information is available on the work to make an intelligent comparison of planned and actual performance. Such information can come from formal reports and team meetings and from letters, memoranda, and other documentation. Informal sources include casual conversation, observa-tions, "management by walking around," and listening to everything that is being said about the team's work. Sometimes rumors and gossip can give insight into problems that are arising in the work.

Review meetings are a useful place in which to garner information on how well things are going. Review meetings should be held at the following levels to determine the indicated status of the project:

- The work package level (cost, schedule, and technical performance)
- The functional manager's level (quality and quantity of the technical resources brought to bear on the project)
- The team level (total synergy of all the project's parameters)
- The general manager's level (adequacy of project and functional support)
- The customer's level (strategic fit)

Review of all of these levels is important. All of the effort underway on the project should be focused at the project team level so the cost, schedule, and technical performance considerations can be evaluated.

The basic purpose of carrying out a review of the team's work is to determine how well the project is doing and, if there are deviations from the performance standards, what caused these deviations.

COMPARISON OF PLANNING AND ACTUAL PERFORMANCE

To compare is to examine and thus to note the similarities or differences among planned and actual results. Two key questions need to be asked on a continuing basis: (1) How is the team doing? and (2) If there are deviations in the planned allocation of resources, what caused these deviations?

Both the managers and the team should maintain oversight of activities. By analyzing the planned results vis-à-vis the actual results, the proper corrective action can be determined. For example, the original cost estimates may have been faulty. Perhaps there has been an unproductive use of team resources.

Teamwork, which requires a notable advancement of the technology in which unknown forces operate, always runs the risk of overruns. A deviation such as a cost or schedule overrun is not the problem. In all likelihood, such an overrun is a symptom of something else and should be investigated accordingly.

Corrective action is required when the oversight of the team's work indicates that reallocation of the resources is needed.

CORRECTIVE ACTION

Corrective action can consist of replanning, reprogramming, reallocating, or realigning the resources. Perhaps the way in which the team is managed and organized requires correction. Since the corrective action on the project usually centers around cost, schedule, or technical performance parameters, care should be taken to ensure that the ripple effect of the action is considered. If the team's work is behind schedule and resources, such as personnel, are added, the cost of parameters will change. If the objectives are in jeopardy, putting more resources on the team will change the cost and schedule parameters. The additional resources may affect other development efforts underway in the enterprise. Under such conditions, the senior managers need to evaluate carefully the strategic fit of the team's work—for if the work is behind schedule, it may be that an important goal of the enterprise is in trouble. In highly competitive product development efforts, such delays can put the enterprise out of the competitive game.

Corrective action is a people-based activity. Sometimes team and senior leaders forget this and only provide for the development of sophisticated information systems buttressed by computer technology, which provides impressive output documents on the status of the project. These can be valuable if the managers recognize that the information in such documents is time dependent and may not reflect the true status of the team's work.

SUMMARY

In this chapter, the basics of the management functions of planning, organizational design, motivation, directing/leadership, monitoring, evaluation, and control have been presented. These functions are basic to the management of any organizational unit, including teams. Each of these management functions was presented in the team context to serve as guides for those individuals who lead teams, serve on teams, or maintain oversight of team activities. The major points to remember include the following:

- Project management, an idea whose time has come, set the stage for the knowledge and skills needed today to manage alternative teams in the strategic and operational management of an enterprise.

- The use of teams sets forth trigger effects in all facets of the enterprise and creates changes that are a significant departure from the traditional management paradigm.
- There are growing numbers of organizations that use teams effectively in improving their operations.
- The fundamentals of identifying the key elements of team planning, including development of a work breakdown structure and its associated work packages, set the stage for further planning schemas on how the team can and should use resources.
- An organizational design for teams defines how authority, responsibility, and accountability are to be assigned to the individual members of the teams, including a designation of how the team members are to work together with other team stakeholders.
- The matrix organization paradigm is basic to the use of teams and should be defined adequately so people understand how they are to work within the matrix and the larger context in which the teams operate.
- There are many important evolving elements in today's organizational design realities.
- Providing an environment in which team members are motivated is as important in the management of teams as it is in the management of any organizational unit.
- Leadership is a role to be carried out by all members of the team, the team leader, and others in the enterprise that play some role in developing and implementing organizational strategies.
- Monitoring, evaluating, and initiating corrective action is an important management function to be carried out in the use of teams.

In the next chapter the development of a team will be presented.

___4
TEAM DEVELOPMENT

The by-product is sometimes more valuable than the product.
LITTLE ESSAYS OF LOVE AND VIRTUE, HAVELOCK ELLIS,
1859–1939

Team building and development are the act and process of forming, growing, and improving the knowledge, skills, and attitudes of individuals with different needs, backgrounds, and abilities into an integrated, high-performing team. Basic assumptions about the behavior of people that facilitate their willingness to become contributing team members include the following:

- Individuals closest to the work being done in an organization know the most about how that work should be planned and executed.
- Participating as a contributing member of a team increases an individual's commitment and loyalty, resulting in high morale, work satisfaction, and quality work performance.
- Meaningful work can be a source of personal satisfaction and, given the right conditions, people will seek responsibility and accountability.
- An individual's fullest potential is best realized in work that encourages freedom of thought and action, initiative, and creativity.
- People are inherently creative and can be developed to improve continuously their technical and leadership capabilities.
- The more people are kept informed about their work and the performance of the organization to which they belong, the more dedicated and capable they will be to make and implement decisions in their work responsibilities.

79

Investigation into motivation research indicates that people are motivated more when the work environment offers them a cultural ambience in which they feel that they belong, in which they can make a difference, in which there are growth opportunities, and in which the work has meaning. In the participative culture of work teams, people can be empowered. However, there will never be an empowered employee team unless the managers are willing to share control of the resources and express that sharing in terms of delegated authority, responsibility, and accountability.

Team members must be allowed to have a key influence on their work environment. Given the chance, they will accept work as being as natural as play. They will exercise self-management and self-direction when they become committed to objectives and goals in which they have played a role in developing. A person's commitment to the objectives and goals of the work unit will be related to the rewards associated with achieving them. People have the capacity for a high degree of imagination, creativity, ingenuity, and dedication in their work. Given the opportunity for personal development, people will be contributing members in continuously improving the quality and productivity of their work, leading to sustained high team and organizational performance.

The preceding conditions do not come about automatically in an organization or in a team. A proactive team-forming and team-building strategy must be developed and be improved continuously.

AN EFFECTIVE TEAM

The following are characteristics of an effective, fully integrated team:

- Members of the team feel that their needs for participating in meaningful activities in the enterprise have been satisfied through active membership on a team.
- Team members contribute to the team's culture of shared work, interests, results, and rewards.
- People on the team feel a strong sense of belonging to a worthwhile activity, take pride in the team activity, and enjoy it.
- Team members are committed to the team, its activities, and achievement of its objectives and goals.
- People trust each other, are loyal to the team's purposes, enjoy the controversy and disagreements that come out of the team's operation, and are comfortable with the interdependence of working on the team.
- There is a high degree of interaction and synergy in the team's work.
- The team's culture is results oriented and expects high individual and team performance.

Some cultural changes due to the use of teams strike at the heart of bureaucracy. Chrysler's concurrent engineering initiative in developing the Viper racing car brought the vehicle to a reality in slightly over two years at a budget much lower than the historical cost for a major vehicle. The concurrent engineering team was led by an executive engineer who became a champion, coach, referee, house mother, and even a chaplain. The team at Chrysler pulled down bureaucratic walls. There was no middle management level—on the Viper team there were team members, team leaders, and a team executive leader. Under normal development at the company, five or six hierarchial levels would have been involved.[1]

A winning team is likely to be the one that has affirmed the greatest loyalty and commitment to and trust in its team members. A team that has this demonstrated commitment will have created the greatest sense of belonging for its members. It will have carried out its own team development, through the internal workings and empathy of team members. In such a team, people are able to speak openly, without fear of criticism or ridicule or hestiation because what they are saying might be counter to what the manager wants to hear. The team leader has a strong working knowledge of the team's work and can function as an objective and knowledgeable leader, irrespective of the emergencies or trauma that the team might be going through. As Rudyard Kipling wrote, "If you can keep your head when all about you/Are losing theirs and blaming it on you," you will succeed. A winning team is like an open forum, in which team members participate in the decision-making and decision-execution process as experts in their particular area of capability.

Team development, as a continuous process of self-development, requires that the team engages in an ongoing audit of its effectiveness.

CONTINUOUS TEAM DEVELOPMENT

An important part of team development can be carried out when the team meets to review its progress. Questions like the following can be used as prompters for a discussion concerning how well the team is working. At the same time, they provide feedback to team members on how well they and the team are performing:

- Are we effective in achieving our purposes? If not, why?
- What is going right on our team? What might be going astray in our team's work and in the way the team is being led and managed?
- What are the strengths of our team? What are its weaknesses?

[1] Eugene E. Sprow, "Chrysler's Concurrent Engineering Challenge," *Manufacturing Engineering,* April 1992, pp. 35–42.

- How well are we doing in settling controversies and disagreements?
- Are we developing a distinct and supportive culture for the team? If not, why?
- What is our image with our stakeholders?
- Do we help each other in making our team an effective entity?
- Are there any nonparticipants on the team? If so, what are we going to do about these individuals?
- Are the team leader and the team facilitator fulfilling their roles?
- Is working on this team enjoyable, and do the team members feel that membership on this team is beneficial to their personal and career objectives?
- Is there anything that we would do differently on this team if we were given the opportunity?

The key components in team development include several elements: (1) Team members believe that a cultural ambience of trust, respect, loyalty, commitment, and dedication is characteristic of the team; (2) people understand their individual and collective roles and are dedicated to carrying out those roles as they work on the team; (3) team members clearly understand the objectives and goals of the team and the strategies that are needed to attain them, and they are actively involved in developing the team's reason for existing; (4) people on the team work hard at communicating with other team members, with the team leader, facilitator, and key stakeholders; (5) team members understand the processes, techniques, and tools that will be used in the work of the team; and (6) the team is willing to assess periodically its work and the leadership of the team with purpose of constantly improving the team's credentials, its work, and its management.

Team development is not a one-time activity consisting of training seminars or exhortations from management about what the capabilities of the team should be. From the time a team is organized and throughout its life cycle, there are abundant opportunities to improve the knowledge, skills, and attitudes of team members. Although formal training seminars or classes are useful, the best team development comes from being part of the action and facing and resolving the challenges facing the team. The team leader must work constantly at developing a team culture in which personal and team development is a way of life as the team meets its challenges and strives to achieve its objectives and goals.

EARLY OPPORTUNITIES

When a team is first formed, the following situations usually emerge:

- There is confusion concerning individual and collective roles on the team. Unfortunately, some teams never get beyond this point if specific means are not used (such as linear responsibility charting) to establish these roles. Unclear authority, responsibility, and accountability relationships result. These relationships must be documented appropriately early in the formation of the team.

- There is uncertainty regarding the distribution of work among team members. By getting the team members actively involved in determining the distribution of the work, this uncertainty can be removed early in the team's life cycle. Otherwise, task assignments are unclear. Team members should know their own abilities and what tasks they are best suited to perform.

- Objectives, goals, and strategies for the team's performance are unclear. Again, full participation of team members in establishing the team's basic performance standards—its objectives and goals—will reinforce the development of the team.

- There is distrust and a lack of respect among team members because they do not know each other well enough. Trust and respect take time to develop. A frank discussion of these forces and their importance will start building the foundation for trust and respect and will lead team members to develop and reinforce these essential forces.

- Team members are unable to relate their personal objectives to the objectives of other people and the team itself. This takes time: By working as an integral unit in developing the team's objectives and goals, team members will begin to see how their personal motives are related to the team's purposes as well as to the personal objectives of other team members.

- Performance standards and the means to measure individual and team performance are unclear. Each team member wants to do a good job but needs guidance on the expected performance standards for his or her personal work and for the team itself. The team leader must take an initial and ongoing proactive role in working with team members in developing these performance standards.

- Team members have a limited understanding of how the team will make its contribution to both the technical and managerial work of the team. Team members will know how to perform their technical work since they have probably established their credentials in doing such work in previous assignments. For those who have not participated in the overall leadership and management of a team, there will be many questions (and even fears) about what is expected. Providing all team members with an intensive training course in the fundamentals of management and leadership will help alleviate fear and uncertainty.

- There is little or no team spirit. Among team members, devotion to and enthusiasm for each other, the team, and its purposes is a vital and motivating force that will enhance the team's performance. A spirit of fellowship, companionship, and comradeship can be developed among team members and should start with the recognition that each team member is an expert in some technical work that the team needs. The team leader's challenge is to take this technical expertise and add to it the team member's attitudes about the fundamentals of a team esprit de corps, what it is, how it can be developed, and how important it is in reinforcing the culture of the team.

- Team direction and leadership is unclear and untested. Although preliminary objectives and goals were established when the original charter was given to the team, that is just a start. By taking these preliminary objectives and goals and building realism into them, team members will better understand them, accept them, and relate their personal objectives to the team's purposes.

- There are opportunities for power struggles and conflict. When team members do not understand what is expected of them, when their roles are unclear, and when they do not understand their limits of authority and responsibility, the stage is set for conflict and political power struggles. The way to defuse such power struggles is to talk about them during the early team meetings: how such conflict and power struggles will be handled and how these struggles will be reduced as the team moves toward organization and technical work.

EARLY QUESTIONS

Team development can and should start when the team is initially organized and meets for the first time to discuss team initiatives. Team development, what it means, and how it is best carried out can be one of the first topics for discussion. A frank discussion of the following questions should be undertaken:

- What questions do the team members have about the team, its purpose, and how it will operate? What questions do the team members have about their individual and collective roles on the team?
- What are the likely objectives and goals of the team and the expectations of team members for their role in meeting those objectives?
- What do team members expect of each other?
- How will a team member's shortcomings or nonparticipation be handled? What do team members expect of the team leader? The team facilitator?
- How will decisions be made on the team? How will checks for consent and consensus be carried out?
- What can the team, its leader, and its facilitator do to build and maintain a cultural ambience of trust, loyalty, respect, candor, and commitment?[2]
- How will conflict be handled on the team?

[2] I have paraphrased and added to the material presented by Judith Mower and David Wilemon, "A Framework for Developing High Performing Technical Teams," in Harold Kerzner and David I. Cleland, *Engineering Team Management,* Van Nostrand Reinhold, New York, 1986, p. 104. Questions similar to these were suggested on pp. 62–63.

Conflict is normal on any team. The real question is whether it is destructive or constructive conflict.

CONFLICT

Managers increasingly understand that organization members devote a lot of psychological and social energy to suppressing conflict. Conflicts that are not confronted and resolved may be played out in subtle and destructive ways in organizations, and interpersonal friction usually arises when conflicts over substantive issues in the enterprise are not resolved. When team members can acknowledge and have agreed on means of working toward conflict resolution, the team will have made important strides in its development and in creating and propagating a culture that has a greater capacity to innovate and adapt.

Controversy and opposition are expected behavioral actions within a team. Conflict can arise because of member behavior, substantive disagreements about the work of the team, disagreements due to differing professional viewpoints, concern about how the team's work is progressing, and so forth. A cardinal rule in dealing with conflict is to confront the issues and not the person. Focusing on issues demands considerable objectivity. A team leader who constantly works at developing a team culture in which disagreement is expected and welcomed will find that meaningful conflict is a way of life on the team that facilitates better solutions and recommendations.

Disagreement about the behavior of team members is usually more difficult to accept than disagreement about ideas, technical approaches, or processes. Team members should be aware of the differences in conflict about ideas and conflict about team member behavior. A good discussion of personal behavior that is likely to affect the decision making and decision execution of the team should help individual members recognize those differences. Here are a few guidelines:

- Behavioral controversy is normal when people of different experiences, credentials, and values work together.
- Behavior that is personal or petty has no place on any team. If the team leader or the teamwork facilitator is unable to resolve such behavior, a specialist in counseling should be brought in from human resources.
- Disagreement about substantive matters pertaining to data, perception or interpretation of facts, or relevance of data should be clearly distinguished from personal behavioral issues. Open and honest discussion of the former can contribute to effective conflict resolution.

Sometimes controversy arises when someone jumps in with a quick-fix solution without going through the processes that the team went through to arrive at this point of conflict. In such cases, a professional facilitator can help the team work through a systematic process that requires patience in resolving the disagreement. However, the team can usually resolve its own conflict because a process exists for such resolution, and team members accept and respect that process.

CONFLICT RESOLUTION

There are ways to resolve conflicts on a team. A simple and workable model for conflict resolution is discussed in this section. The steps in this model are (1) understanding the facts; (2) determining the relevant issue(s); (3) understanding the potential organizational impact; (4) considering the alternatives; and (5) making separate and/or collective recommendations.

The team leader should try to resolve the conflict by open and frank discussions with team members of the issues that are involved. If doing so does not lead to resolution, then the issue should be referred to the management level that appointed the team and that expects to use the team's output in operating the organizational unit. However, before the conflict is "kicked upstairs" for resolution, several steps should be taken (i.e., the aforementioned model should be used) toward a satisfactory resolution:

1. The team should reach a full understanding of the facts behind the conflict. The facts of the conflict are known with certainty and objectivity—they have been verified as certain and usually have been established by full analysis buttressed by expert opinion. There may be disagreement over the facts, how they were determined, who identified them, and how relevant they are. If the team insists on developing a database to establish the indisputable nature of the facts, even the most recalcitrant team members are likely to assume that the facts are correct. If not, then further discussions will be needed to get those doubters to assume that the facts are correct.

2. The team should reach agreement on the issue(s) that are involved. Achieving a resolution here will test the mettle and patience of the team leader. An issue is a point of discussion, debate, or dispute over a substantive matter in the team's work. For example, a concurrent engineering team will find that the manufacturing and marketing representatives on the team disagree over the configuration of a new product. A self-managed production team will find that there will be disagreements over a proposed new manufacturing process. Whatever the disagreement, the team leader must take time to give everyone on the team their "day in court" to express their opinion and listen to what everyone else on the team has to say. Bring in expert opinion from outside the team can help the discussion reach a consensus point. If there are still honest differences of opinion, the basis for those differences should be

documented and made available to all of the team members so they can appreciate the impact the alternative views of the issue might have on the next step in the conflict resolution process—the team's and enterprise's output.

3. The team should consider the organizational impact, which is the effect that the outcome of the conflict, and how it is resolved, will have on the team and on the organizational unit to which the team is assigned. Conflict over the design of a new product or service, and how that conflict is resolved, will affect the product's or service's introduction on the market. The potential impact could have financial implications for the organization. A conflict that is not resolved in a timely manner could delay the commercialization of the product, with the possibility that market share may be lost if competitors get to the marketplace sooner. Guidelines for assessing the organizational impact include the following: (1) What will be both the short-term and long-term meaning of the outcome of the conflict? (2) What specific, measurable effects might be involved on the team, in the organizational unit, and in the competitive posture of the company involved in the conflict? (3) When negative effects are involved, are the senior managers of the enterprise willing to assume the risk and uncertainties of the likely impact? (4) Has enough analysis been done to determine the probable and possible impact on the enterprise's business? The impact will likely be affected by the choice of alternatives in resolving the conflict.

4. The team should consider the alternatives. Substitute solutions are likely to be available and should be examined in terms of their likely costs and benefits relative to the conflict in question. Insight into which alternatives would be available in a conflict over product configuration could be gained by benchmarking a competitor's product. A conflict over which manufacturing process to use could involve benchmarking the best in the industry in manufacturing capabilities. Each of the probable alternatives should be evaluated rigorously by the team, and this evaluation should provide insight into which alternative is likely to have the best fit in the enterprise's operational or strategic direction. Examining the alternatives is part of doing the homework; a perceptive senior manager will ask what alternatives have been considered.

5. The team should document the recommendations based on the conflict resolution process. If there are majority and minority opinions, these should be put forth for resolution by senior management. Recommendations should be backed up by the consensus decision process of the team. However, if there are members of the team who feel strongly about the issue and do not agree with the consensus, their views should be made available to senior managers. After considering all of the circumstances and the issue resolution process that the team has gone through, senior managers decide which alternative best fits the purposes of the enter-

prise. If senior managers believe that there is additional information that the team has not considered, they should send the issue back to the team for further study and efforts at resolution.

In reality, as the team goes through the several steps outlined here, the chances increase that the final course of action will become apparent to the team, and they will make the appropriate decision. If senior managers have to make the final decision and if they are familiar with the processes that the team has gone through in trying to resolve the conflict, they will be confident that the risks, uncertainties, and facts about the issue have been considered. It will be easier for them to make the best decision.

During the conflict resolution process, it is essential that the team members and other stakeholders in the conflict continue to communicate. Open discussions of the issue, with open minds and full disclosure of the facts, assumptions, and unsubstantiated opinions, will contribute to meaningful conflict resolution.

ONGOING DISCUSSIONS

The team leader and the team facilitator should not forget that the success or failure of the team depends more on the knowledge, skills, and attitudes of the individual team members than on anything else. As part of the team development strategies undertaken to improve the synergy and dedication of the team, there should be ongoing discussions with team members about what it takes to achieve participatory involvement:

- Are team members truly comfortable serving on a team in which the members are expert in diverse fields and will show independence of thought and action?
- Do team members truly value the ideas and opinions of other members?
- Can individual team members accept disagreement and controversy?
- Do team members really want to know what is going on with the rest of the team members, or do they think that what they do is the most important and that things, if let alone, will fall naturally into place?
- Do team members really enjoy working on a team?
- Would some of the team members rather be working alone? If so, they can still make contributions to the organization's purpose and would be better off working by themselves. There are some people who are not team players unless they are in charge of the team.
- Do team members enjoy and value contributing to the growth of fellow team members? Are team members pleased to see a member of the team receiving special recognition for doing something well, or is there likely to be jealousy when a team member is singled out for recognition?

- Do team members show true and dedicated interest in making and implementing the best possible decisions to support the team's work?

Asking questions such as these during team development meetings is better than making statements about such considerations in developing the team. By encouraging free expression of ideas, concerns, and beliefs, the preceding questions will help team members understand each other and increase their individual and collective willingness to contribute to the team's objectives and goals.

Team development includes building understanding about the team's authority, its responsibility, and its accountability for producing useful results.

RESIDUAL RESPONSIBILITY AND ACCOUNTABILITY

To what degree should a team be held collectively accountable for producing the results expected of the team? When things go wrong and the team fails to attain its objectives and goals, where should the blame and subsequent consequences be placed? Traditional management theory holds that the person having the residual authority and responsibility for doing a job should be held accountable. That idea works pretty well for an individual, who can suffer a poor performance evaluation, reduction in pay, or reassignment or be sent for further training to improve job performance. But what happens when the team is held accountable? When a team fails, should all members of the team suffer the same fate? Should the entire team be given a poor performance evaluation, suffer a pay cut, or be reassigned to other work? There is little evidence to suggest that an entire team has been fired for doing a poor job; conversely, how often has an entire team been promoted for doing an outstanding job? When a team fails, the team leader is blamed—often demoted or reassigned. That leader may have done everything right, but for often complex reasons, the team has not been able to achieve its objectives and goals.

There are a few things that can be done to enhance the team leader's ability to build and maintain an efficient, effective, and accountable team. The team leader should be responsible for the following:

- The final decision regarding who will perform which work assignments on the team, including deadlines and performance standards.
- The final decision regarding who serves on the team, and the right to request reassignment of a team member who is not performing adequately in spite of continuing counseling.
- The right to comment in writing to the team members' immediate supervisors about performance evaluations of team members. This right should include recommending people for special recognition, bonuses, or exceptional merit increases.

- The right to set the tone for reviewing individuals' and the team's ability to produce results. Schedules, deadlines, reporting protocol, finances, and daily oversight of the team's operation are key responsibilities of the team leader.

Team members should play a key role in selecting their leader, but the final decision should rest with the responsible manager based on knowledge of all of the candidates for the job, their knowledge, skills, attitudes, and judgment, as well as their image in the organization. In some cases, the position of team leader is rotated (such as on self-managed production teams). Team facilitators from the Human Resources staff can help the team leader get the team organized and functioning.

Traditional management theory holds that only one person should be held accountable for the performance of any organizational unit. Yet it is possible that two or three people can serve effectively as leaders of a team. However, under the best of co-leadership, an accountability challenge emerges. Co-leadership can be used as a way to obscure or evade the anxiety of a single, responsible, and accountable leader. Nonetheless, co-leadership is possible and workable *if* care has been taken to identify the individual and collective work packages for which the co-leaders are responsible. For example, the author of this book is co-director of the University of Pittsburgh Manufacturing Assistance Center (MAC), a working factory whose mission is to provide manufacturing systems technology (MST) assistance to small and mid-sized manufacturers in western Pennsylvania. The MAC is run by a team of dedicated professionals who are expert in some technology of MST, such as metrology, computer-aided design, computer-aided manufacturing, and automated materials handling. The two co-directors have identified the principal work packages that are necessary to manage both the operational and strategic context of the MAC. Each co-director has principal authority, responsibility, and accountability obligations for assigned work packages. Certain work packages require that both co-leaders be involved in decisions concerning those work packages. On others, the responsible co-director can make the decision without counseling with the other co-director. The co-directors, as a matter of policy and practice, keep in touch on a daily basis, informing the other about their activities, the decisions they are considering, and how well their particular work packages are being carried out. This co-directed team has worked out well in its collective role of managing the MAC because of the reciprocal respect and trust between the two co-directors.

Whatever the team's objectives and goals, its culture should establish clear and understandable performance standards that make leaders and team members accountable for their work. Ambiguities in authority, responsibility, and accountability damage morale, allow things to fall between the cracks and allow political solutions to replace reasoned business solutions. Final accountability is a fundamental principle of sound enterprise management and must be designed into the team management philosophy.

Teamwork is the hallmark of the successful team. Leadership is what makes teamwork happen.

TEAM LEADERSHIP

As the use of alternative teams grows in an enterprise and as leadership of certain teams, such as self-managed production teams, is rotated among team members, training and education in the art of leadership needs to be extended to more people.

The team leader's role is to facilitate and help the team work together to achieve common purposes. Rather than trying to control the team, the team leader's role is to help people become involved in the team's activities and to encourage their participation in both the technical and managerial aspects of the team's work. Effective team leadership is a matter of what the leader does to promote the team's productive functioning. Helping team members feel relaxed and comfortable while working toward common objectives and goals is the core task of the team leader. This section presents a few important guidelines that will help team leaders make the team an effective organizational unit. Being able to listen well and be sensitive to the feelings of team members is important. Criticism and ridicule should be avoided at all costs; rather, the team leader should work carefully to make each team member feel needed and important. Being receptive to all ideas is important. When disagreement happens—as it will—the disagreeing individuals must be allowed to express their opinions, and then the team leader should make the decision on behalf of the team. A team leader who is a role model in cooperative behavior and is truly interested in everyone on the team will solidify the culture and work of the team.

Providing feedback to the team on a regular basis about how well the team is performing is important. Sharing all information with the team is important as well—both the good and the bad news. As the leader works with the team, the individual motives of team members should become apparent. Once these motives are identified, the skillful leader will find a way for these motives to serve the best interests of the team. Having each member of the team report regularly on the work packages for which they are responsible will help team members identify their role in the team's work. Allowing all members to ask questions about the overall team's effort—and the effort of individual team members—will bring issues into the open and build individuals' perception that they are part of the action. Constantly encouraging team members to uncover conflict and volunteer all information—both good and bad—will reduce the probability of hidden, festering conflicts. Hidden conflicts can hurt the team's work and, without a timely resolution, compromise the work of the team and damage the team's culture.

Working on a team is an intensive activity. How well the team meetings are managed can contribute to or detract from the effectiveness of the team's work. The team leader should insist that team members do not interrupt one another in meetings. Helping the team distinguish between fact, inference, and opinion is important. Constantly insisting that an adequate database be reviewed when decisions are being made is important as well. If the building of a database is not possible, then team members should recognize that a decision is being made without an adequate database and the role that assumptions and probabilities will play in that decision should be understood. It is useful to keep an ongoing, summary set of minutes concerning the major work packages of the team. As future meetings are held, these minutes become the agenda for the team's deliberations. In addition, keeping a summary set of minutes reduces the probability that issues will fall between the cracks in the team's work.

The basis of successful team leadership is to work continually at developing the team and to create a culture in the team that unleashes team members' abilities to contribute to the technical and managerial work of the team. When the team knows where it is going and how it proposes to get there, the outcomes of team action will benefit the team, the parent organization, and every member of the team, including the team leader.

Skillfully led team members work well and produce meaningful results. In addition to their technical and managerial responsibility to the team, team members have other key responsibilities:

- They must regularly attend team meetings and participate fully in team meetings.
- They must assume responsibility for assigned work packages on the team and for reporting on the progress of those work packages to the rest of the team. If no progress is being made on the assigned work package, this lack should be reported and discussed at the regular team meetings. It is possible that during the discussion, someone will have insight into a strategy that will lead to progress.
- They should listen to and respect the views expressed by other team members. From time to time, the team should engage in brainstorming activities. In doing so, a lot of ideas will be put forth that have little merit, but a few good ideas can emerge. However, even those ideas that look ridiculous should be encouraged and respected.
- They should accept responsibility for bringing their unique and diverse abilities to the team's work, and they should work to improve their input to the team's deliberations.

THE TEAMWORK FACILITATOR

A teamwork facilitator designated to work with a particular team can be a valuable member of that team. A facilitator can monitor the process of team interaction to keep members on track. A person in this role is usually not concerned with the substantive work of the team, but rather how the team is able to work together in a process of effective and efficient interaction. A professional facilitator should be knowledgeable and experienced in team interaction, in cultural considerations, and in the management of change. Other important attributes include a demonstrated track record in team leadership, sensitivity, discipline, and the ability to influence and motivate people to work together in satisfying their individual needs and the team needs. The facilitator must be comfortable in dealing with change, ambiguities, and conflict—particularly in resolving conflict so there is a win-win solution for everyone. In addition, the facilitator should keep the team focused on its purposes, train and coach the team leader, provide feedback to team members on how well they are doing as a team, and constantly encourage open expression of ideas on the team.

SUMMARY

As the act and process of forming, building, and improving the knowledge, skills, and attitudes of team members, effective team building is a continuous activity for team leaders and members. The team leader and team members should understand some of the basic assumptions that condition team members' behavior. This chapter discussed some of the commonly accepted assumptions about people based on research and on the empirical experience of teams. In addition, it discussed team building. Specifically, no opportunity should be missed to carry out team-building initiatives when leading or functioning as a contributing member of a team. The daily operations of any team provide ample opportunity for team-building initiatives. Formal team-building seminars or training exercises can build on the capabilities of the team. However, these formal training initiatives cannot explore many of the informal, daily opportunities to make the team and its work better. The characteristics of a fully integrated team were presented to give the reader a benchmark against which to judge to the effectiveness of team-building strategies. Several key strategies, and the key components of team building, were presented in light of a continuous improvement philosophy of team building.

The typical problems and questions that a new-formed team encounters were presented, along with guidelines for dealing with these initial problems. Conflict was offered as a normal and expected force on any team. Conflict over substantive issues on teams, suitably resolved, can reduce the likelihood that the disagreements will deteriorate into interpersonal stress. The basic idea is to confront the issue and not the people. A model policy was suggested for resolving conflict in a way that maximizes the probability that the team will resolve its conflict without appeal to a higher authority.

Ongoing discussions by members of the team, when properly led and executed, are a subtle and effective way of developing the credentials of every member of the team. Demarcation of the expected authority, responsibility, and accountability relationships of the team is vital to the team's subsequent success or failure and to its meaningful development. The bottom line in the design and execution of any team development initiatives rests with the team leader and how well that individual provides enlightened leadership of the team.

Finally, team development will happen even if it is informal. A team that is being poorly led, that has not properly organized itself, that neglects the resolution of conflict, that is nonproductive, and that turns out poor-quality work does in fact carry out a team development effort that affects the team's culture—unfortunately in a debilitating and wasteful manner. A form of negative team development will impair the team's efficiency and effectiveness. Thus a carefully designed and executed program of both formal and informal team development promises enormous benefits for the team, its members, and the quality of the team's work.

In the next chapter the concept of a team culture will be presented.

____5
TEAM CULTURE[1]

A culture is in its finest flower before it begins to analyze itself.
ALFRED NORTH WHITEHEAD, 1861–1947

In this chapter, the concept of organizational culture is presented along with a brief description of how the use of alternative teams affects that culture.

Culture is a set of refined behaviors that people have and strive toward in their society. Culture, according to anthropologist E. B. Taylor, includes the totality of knowledge, belief, art, morals, law, custom, and the other capabilities and habits acquired by individuals as members of a society.[2]

Anthropologists have long used the concept of culture in describing primitive societies. Modern sociologists have borrowed this anthropological concept of culture and used it to describe a way of life of people. In this chapter, the term is used to describe the synergistic set of shared ideas and beliefs that is associated with a way of life in an organization.

More attention is being paid to the culture of an enterprise because the use of alternative organizational designs is affecting the way things are done in today's organizations.

---

[1] This chapter contains substantial material that has been paraphrased from the author's article, "The Cultural Ambience of Project Management—Another Look," *Project Management Journal,* June 1988, pp. 49–56. In addition, portions of the paper "Professional Development in the Team-Driven Enterprise," presented at the Project Management Institute '95 Seminar/Symposium, New Orleans, Louisiana, October 1995, have been integrated into this chapter.

[2] Paraphrased from E. B. Taylor, *The Origins of Culture,* Harper & Row, New York, 1958 (1871).

EXAMPLES OF ORGANIZATIONAL CULTURES

The Nucor Steel Company has created a culture that has reduced the number of corporate staff members and doubled its sales in the last seven years while its marketing, administrative, and other expenses have remained virtually flat. The ratio of managers to production workers stands at a rock-bottom 1 to 300 in an industry that is notorious for bureaucratic bloat. Operating units have become self-sufficient businesses, with delegated authority for all decisions except buying health insurance and raising capital. Planning and forecasting monthly production schedules are done by one person—the sales manager at each operating level. Bonuses tied to return on assets keep the operating units from building up their own management layers.[3]

The management style of CEO Andrew Grove of Intel has propogated a "constructive confrontation" culture at the company. CEO Grove sits in a cubicle precisely to eliminate barriers between chief executive and staff. Anyone can stop by and talk with him; he believes that there is no time for anything as inefficient as bureaucratic protocol. The current crisis at Intel over the replacements of the Pentium chips was in part because of the notion that Intel's engineers simply could not grasp consumers' demands that the Pentiums be replaced. By focusing on the technical objective of being able to double the number of transistors on its chips every eighteen months, management has difficulty seeing the big picture. The centralized power of Grove, the tremendous profitability, and the confrontational culture have become a blinding light. Many "students" of Intel believe that Grove is going to have to reexamine his stubbornly analytical style, his signature combativeness, and the culture that has grown up around it.[4]

Motorola, Inc., a giant organization, is much more nimble than other large corporations. In part, Motorola's nimbleness comes from its ability to change, to foster a participative culture, and to use teams as a way to organize workers and professionals to do productive, quality-driven work. Motorola has an elaborate corporate culture that kindles rather than stifles conflict and dissent, finds promising but neglected projects, and generates a constant flow of information and innovation from thousands of small teams, which are held to quantifiable goals.

Intelligence gathering in Motorola is done through a department that has as its mission the reporting of the latest technological developments gleaned from conferences, journals, rumors, and such. Intelligence gained from many sources helps build "technology roadmaps," which assess where breakthroughs are likely to occur and how these breakthroughs can be integrated into new products and processes. The culture of conflict helps identify and fix mistakes quickly, unmasks and eliminates weak or illogical efforts, and keeps senior managers abreast of problems and opportunities in the market-

---

[3] "Lean Management—Nucor," *Financial World,* September 29, 1992, pp. 50–51.
[4] Robert D. Hof, "The Education of Andrew Grove," *Business Week,* January 16, 1995, pp. 60–62.

place. Sometimes, however, the conflict leads to missed opportunities. As described in the *Wall Street Journal,*

> In 1986, a chip team in Austin, Texas, designed a new high-speed workstation microprocessor called the 88000, many times more powerful than Motorola's by now successful 68000 line. But the 68000 project group lobbied against the new chip and tried to persuade customers to ignore it. The conflict led to delays and to a critical decision by a potential customer, Sun Microsystems, Inc., to design its own chip after initially leaning toward the 88000. Sun's design is now the brains for its market-leading workstations. Motorola officials have conceded that 88000 was late to market and that "jealousy" was a factor.[5]

Traditional managers—bureaucrats—may fight more for their turf than for what is right for the enterprise. This fighting slows decision making and prevents people from trying anything new. These turf battles contributed to IBM missing the early markets for laptop computers, notebook computers, and workstations. IBM also sat back and procrastinated while competitors exploited mail-order distribution of personal computers. Even in more mature product lines, IBM came months late to the market—a failure to capitalize on what concurrent engineering can do for commercializing products sooner. Part of IBM's current problems came out of their early success in the 1980s, when the company had so many successes that the managers began to lose touch with competitive realities. With the success of the 1980s, IBM's culture became complacent, and the "measure of success became how high someone could rise in the company. The highest compliment someone could pay a rising star was: 'He's good with foils'—the transparencies used on overhead projects in all IBM meetings." Foils became such a part of the culture that senior executives started having projectors built into their beautiful rose-wood desks.[6]

The chairman of Kao believes that his objective is to create a culture for his organization that exhibits "biological self-control"—an enterprise that responds to crises just as the body does. When things go wrong in one area of the company, those people in other areas of the organization sense the problem and respond to provide help without being asked. The CEO of Intel, Andrew Grove, tells his people to display the teamwork and dedication that an emergency team must have to respond to disasters, forgetting self-interest and territoriality for cooperation and mutual support. Under the circumstances just described for Kao and Intel, cooperation and individual action for the common mission must be a deeply held cultural force.[7]

---

[5] G. Christian Hill and Ken Yamada, "Staying Power," *Wall Street Journal,* December 12, 1992, p. 1.

[6] Paul B. Carroll, "The Failures of Central Planning at IBM," *Wall Street Journal,* January 28, 1993, p. 1.

[7] Sumantra Goishal and Christopher A. Bartlett, "Changing the Role of Top Management Beyond Structure to Process," *Harvard Business Review,* January–February 1995, pp. 86–96.

According to the *Wall Street Journal,* Louis Gerstner, the new CEO of IBM, is struggling in his toughest and most critical task: forcing changes in an entrenched, patriarchal culture. Some of the artifacts of the old IBM culture include a "corporate arrogance," a feeling of entitlement to jobs, and a sense of lethargy pervasive in the company. CEO Gerstner makes much ado over his distaste for the white shirts IBMers always wore and for the overhead projection devices that IBM executives always used in their presentations. Protective employee policies and generous benefits, a no-layoff policy, a shunning of unions, and a turnover rate of less than 3 percent a year were other hallmarks of the IBM culture, with the result that people became conditioned into dependence at the company.

A new training program at IBM focuses on the marketplace and profit and loss rather than on the former basic beliefs and employee policies. A set of new IBM principles heralds the development of a new culture at IBM:

- The marketplace drives everything IBM does.
- IBM is a technology company with an overriding commitment to quality.
- Customer satisfaction and shareholder value are the primary measures of success.
- The company operates as an entrepreneurial organization with a minimum of bureaucracy and a constant focus on productivity.
- Sight of the corporate strategic vision is never lost.
- Urgency paces IBM's thinking and acting.
- Outstanding dedicated people working as a team make things happen.
- IBM shows sensitivity to employee and local community' needs.[8]

VALUES AND CULTURES

Values are principles, standards, or qualities considered worthwhile or desirable in influencing people to think and act in a supportive manner for an organization. For example, values play an important role in the culture of Levi Strauss & Company. The company has embarked on a "grand social experiment" to live up to a lofty vision of how to run a modern corporation. The vision combines traditional liberal idealism with a modern set of management precepts, including an emphasis on empowerment. To guide employees and set the tone for the corporate culture, an "Aspiration Statement" was crafted by senior management at Levi's.

CEO Robert D. Haas has launched a strategy to make all workers an integral part of the making and selling of blue jeans. Employees are evaluated by superiors, subordinates, and peers—a process that is not always pleasant.

[8] Paraphrased from Laurie Hays, "Gerstner Is Struggling as He Tries to Change Ingrained IBM Culture," *Wall Street Journal,* May 13, 1994, p. 1.

Over 6000 employees have been asked for advice on what Levi's should be doing differently. Since the company sells 200 styles of blue jeans, CEO Haas believes that there is no way that senior management can keep up with the fashion trends without help from deep within the organization.

Workers at Levi's are grouped not by function but in multitask teams of twenty to thirty workers that are responsible for completing individual orders by assembling full pairs of pants from waist to hem. Teams are given weeks of training.[9]

CULTURAL FEATURES

An organization's culture consists of shared explicit and implicit agreements among organizational members regarding what is important in behavior as well as attitudes expressed in values, beliefs, standards, and social and management practices. The culture that is developed and becomes characteristic of an organization affects strategic planning and implementation, team management, and everything else.

At the Chase Manhattan Corporation, strategies to improve the corporate culture included definition and development of key values—highly esteemed principles, standards, or qualities considered worthwhile as cultural characteristics of the enterprise. Five key values were defined: customer focus, respect for each other, teamwork, quality, and professionalism.[10]

Corporate culture may be reflected in the key slogans put forth by an organization, such as General Electric's "Progress is our most important product," Dupont's "Better things for better living through chemistry," IBM's "IBM means service," and 3M's "Never kill a new product idea." These slogans can set the tone for the entire corporation. Or a corporate culture may be altered by a structural change in the organization. In some organizations, such as Hewlett-Packard, General Electric, and 3M, the crucial parts of the organization are kept small to encourage the personal touch in an environment of spirited teamwork.

Corporate culture usually is explained in terms of organizational values and beliefs and the behavior of members of the corporation. In the corporate setting, the value orientation and leadership example set by senior managers greatly influence employee behavior.

A cultural unit has many subcultures: the company, the work group, and the teams. Together these also determine individual behavior. Managerial behavior is affected by the culture in which the manager operates. This culture, in turn, is reflected in the subordinate elements of the organization. Culture influences managerial philosophy, which in turn affects the organizational

---

[9] Russell Mitchel and Michael Oneal, "Managing by Values," *Business Week,* August 1, 1994, pp. 46–52.
[10] Kelly Holland, "A Chastened Chase," *Business Week,* September 26, 1994, pp. 106–109.

philosophy. Organizational culture can be affected by a lack of management philosophy on which plans, policies, procedures, guidelines, rules, and basic values important to the growth and survival of the organization are based, which in turn affects the organizational philosophy.

A culture can be analyzed by examining the organization's technology, manner, visible or audible behavior patterns, and documents, such as charters, plans, policies, and procedures, as well as its organizational structure and leadership style and the individual and collective roles played in the organization.

An organization's culture is its social and intellectual formation, the totality of socially transmitted behavior patterns, beliefs, institutions, and all the products and services of human work and thought characteristic of the community or population. Culture can also be described as the style of social and artistic expression peculiar to a society or class. Culture includes the basic way things are done in the enterprise.

An enterprise's culture can be its major strength when it is consistent with its strategies. There is a shift in the culture of the organization when teams are used. This shift usually follows a shift in the management philosophy and style of the key principals in the enterprise. The change that is created comes about through the push of senior managers to use alternative teams in the operational and strategic management of the enterprise.

It is possible to identify common cultural features that positively and negatively influence the practice of management and the conduct of technical affairs in an organization. Such cultural features develop out of and are influenced by

- The management leadership-and-follower style practiced by key managers and professionals
- The example set by leaders of the organization
- The attitudes displayed and communicated by key managers in their management of the organization
- The managerial and professional competencies
- The assumptions held by key managers and professionals
- The organizational plans, policies, procedures, rules, and strategies
- The political, legal, social, technological, and economic systems with which the members of an organization interface
- The perceived and/or actual characteristics of the organization
- The quality and quantity of the resources (human and nonhuman) consumed in the pursuit of the organization's mission, objectives, goals, and strategies
- The knowledge, skills, and experiences of members of the organization
- Communication patterns
- Formal and informal roles

The role of an enterprise's culture in an enterprise remaining competitive is keynoted by an article in *Fortune* magazine, which suggests seven steps toward being the best company in the world. One of these steps is directly related to the company's culture: "Communicate with employees as if your life depended on it." Keep the employees focused on the realities of the marketplace—customers and competitors. Define a clear vision that creates a sense of urgency, and help people understand the impact of their own behavior.[11]

CULTURAL STRENGTH

A strong working culture is like magic. The team is of one philosophy in approach, in creativity and innovation, and in style. An informal and unspoken mutual approval process exists. Every decision made by the team is deliberate; every policy and procedure has a defined and understood purpose. The team members stick together in their daily work. There is a common purpose that transcends the objectives and goals of the team, reaching out to bring forth creativity and innovation in the team processes and output.

There are subtle yet powerful cultural changes found in the team-driven enterprise. As employees serve on teams, they expect further in-depth participation in the development and execution of both team and organizational strategies. Employees find that their opinions are valued and that they are being treated as key organizational members. Employees feel as if they are being treated as thinking adults rather than just appreciated for the "brawn" that they bring to their place of work. The special perks—such as reserved parking places and executive dining rooms—formerly provided to senior managers begin to disappear, which heightens the cultural ambience of personal equality. The cross-functional and cross-organizational work that is carried out creates strong interdependent relationships among people from different disciplines and different organizational levels. There is a high degree of interdependence among everyone—workers, staffers, supervisors, managers, and senior management. Crossing functional, discipline, and organizational boundaries is common. This high degree of interdependency causes people to assume a greater responsibility for the quality of the processes that they are performing. Total customer satisfaction becomes the minimum expected of all people in the enterprise.

Each team has a distinct culture that partly reflects a universal culture in all teams. The team is an organizational entity devoted to the integration of specialized knowledge for a common purpose: delivery of team results on time and within budget to support organizational strategies. The team must be organized for creativity and innovation and be organized as a force for

---

[11] Stratford Sherman, "Are You as Good as the Best in the World?" *Fortune,* December 13, 1993, pp. 95–96.

continuous improvement and constant change in positioning the enterprise for dealing with a changing global marketplace. Appointment and empowerment of a team are an explicit recognition that creativity and innovation in products, services, and organizational processes are both possible and essential to organizational survival.

Every organization must maintain surveillance over the real and potential changes in its environment and then design ways for the organization to manage the change and thus remain competitive. This means that the organization must have the discipline to abandon those products, services, and processes that are currently successful and provide the means for an orderly, disciplined, and systems strategy to develop new organizational initiatives. Several strategies are needed to bring a team focus to the management of change in the enterprise:

1. Enhance the organizational culture so that people at all levels and in all specialities are encouraged to bring forth ideas for improvement in their areas of responsibilities.
2. Develop an organizational culture that seeks to abandon that which has been successful through the continuous improvement of existing products, services, and processes.
3. Become a learning organization through explicit recognition that all organizational members will have to retrain and relearn new technologies to escape obsolescence.
4. Organize the enterprise's resources so that explicit opportunity is available to bring an organizational focus (a team focus) to the development and implementation of new organizational initiatives that will bring forth new products, services, and processes.
5. Provide a strategic management capability by which organizational leadership is proactive in providing the resources, vision, and disciplines to manage the future through the use of product and process projects.

The team—a body of companions—dedicated to the creation of something that does not currently exist in the enterprise provides a way of decentralizing the organization of resources to deal with change. The team members represent those different specialities needed to create value and thus satisfy the needed change in products, services, and processes. The nature of the task needed to bring about the change determines the organizational membership in the "body of companions." The organizational membership, in turn, influences the culture of the team—and, to a certain extent, that of the participating stakeholders as well. Since each member of the team comes from specialized areas of the enterprise and represents parochial areas of expertise, the objectives, goals, and strategies of the team must be unequivocal—crystal clear to all the stakeholders. Only focused team objectives, goals, and strategies will hold the team together and enable it to create something that does not currently exist in the enterprise, in an efficient and effective manner.

The team is comprised of knowledgeable people who must be led, not supervised or managed in the traditional sense. Team loyalty is obtained by providing members with the opportunity to put their knowledge to use; the team is an organization of peers, colleagues, and associates who are bonded together by the focus of the team to create and innovate continuous improvement in organizational products and processes. Teams are clearly not an organization of supervisors and bosses or any form of the traditional supervisor–subordinate relationship that has been characteristic of traditional organizations. How do you "boss" knowledgeable workers? It cannot be done—if attempted, the team members will find ways of leaving the team to seek more motivational environments. Yet there remains the need for someone to make decisions on behalf of the team after a consensus process that actively seeks the expertise of the team members is carried out. The leader who makes decisions on behalf of the team must be willing to be held accountable for those key decisions that arise from the team's deliberation. The leader must inspire the team, provide the means for a vision to be developed for the team, provide the teams with the resources needed to do the job, seek participation and consensus on key problems and opportunities, and provide the means for the team's performances to be evaluated on an ongoing basis.

One author has called the most executive level of leaders **culture team leaders** because they have the residual responsibility for creating the conditions for team empowerment and cultural change throughout the enterprise.[12]

Organizational cultures are affected by many forces. Consider how the forces in the following systems changed the culture of the enterprise.

CULTURAL MOVERS

Technological System

At the modern IBM digital factory in Charlotte, North Carolina, each worker has a computer screen hooked into the factory network and self-managed production teams build many different products at once, such as hand-held bar-code scanners, portable medical computers, fiber-optic connectors for mainframes, and satellite communication devices for truck drivers.

Social System

At Levi Straus & Company, a Diversity Council (which is a direct link to senior management for groups representing blacks, Asians, Hispanics, gays, and women) plays a role in the decisions made within the company.

---

[12] Kimball Fisher, *Leading Self-Directed Work Teams,* McGraw-Hill, 1993, p. 8.

Political System

The Republican victory in the 1994 elections created changes during 1995 in the staffing of U.S. congressional offices. There are new people in office who bring to the job their unique view of the political world and who hire staff who desire to work in Washington to please their new leaders as well as their constituents.

Economic System

Changes are occurring in contemporary organizations as a result of reengineering, downsizing, restructuring, and other measures to reduce costs and become more competitive in the global marketplace.

Legal System

Each new law or regulation that is passed affects in some way the manner in which business is conducted. OSHA, The Fair Labor Standards Act, Affirmative Action legislation, and even changes in the tax law have trigger effects on the way businesses conduct their affairs.

Teams as Cultural Systems Changers

The introduction of teams to the strategy of enterprises has introduced a radical cultural change as well. The supporting systems of the organization are affected—in particular, the personnel selection, performance assessment, compensation, and recognition systems. Personnel evaluation before hiring includes interpersonal skills and aptitude for serving as a contributing member of a team. Performance assessment policies and procedures need to be evaluated to determine the balance between individual and team performance. Compensation policies for people serving on teams need to be reviewed to determine pay for former supervisors who become facilitators and how pay will be rewarded based on individual and/or team performance. Under traditional organizational designs, recognition systems usually go to individuals. Members of a team may want to have the freedom to recommend their peers on the team for special rewards. Although team performance rewards may be appropriate, some people have a strong need for individual recognition and should be so acknowledged in addition to team recognition policies.

TEAM CULTURES

The key elements of a team-driven organizational culture include the following:

- Teams are used as the principal strategy for managing change in the enterprise. As teams design and develop building blocks in the planning and execution of organizational strategies, managerial and supervisory roles are modified because the teams do most of the work of managing themselves. Teams have a common purpose, have the authority and responsibility for the substantive technical and managerial work of their members, and are held accountable for measurable performance objectives and goals.

- The organizational hierarchy has been flattened as managerial and supervisory roles are modified, some are eliminated, and teams manage themselves. Cross-functional processes are handled through the teams. As the teams examine their operation, there is a tendency to eliminate work that fails to add value, and the work involved in all organizational purposes is reduced or eliminated. Yet at the same time, core values in the enterprise are created through the use of teams that are driven by cross-functional and cross-organizational activities.

- The traditional organizational structure was organized around functions, disciplines, or departments, and the enterprise is organized around several core processes, which are assigned specific performance objectives. Teams are used as the basic organizational element to manage these cross-functional/discipline and cross-organizational activities. Customers and suppliers play key roles in the team-driven enterprise. Customer satisfaction becomes the principal driver of organizational initiatives and ultimately the measure of the enterprise's performance. Teams provide the medium through which supplier and customer contact is kept up. Supplier and customer people work on the key teams of the enterprise.

- Education, training, and a willingness to share all information with employees become a way of life in the enterprise. Key decisions in the enterprise are made by team members once they have developed the knowledge, skills, and attitudes needed to meet the high performance standards set by the teams.

When an enterprise elects to use alternative teams in its operational and strategic strategy, significant cultural changes will ultimately come about. Although there is little rigorous research that has established the nature and extent of these changes, there is empirical, practical, experience-based evidence that shows that subtle yet powerful changes have come into the culture of the enterprise using teams as the principal focus for managing change in the organization. Table 5–1 shows these cultural characteristics prior to the use of teams. Table 5–2 shows the characteristics of the culture after teams have been used successfully in the enterprise. There are more cultural characteristics described in Table 5–2 than in Table 5–1. The current fascination in the literature with using teams in contemporary organizations probably accounts for this.

TABLE 5–1 Cultural Characteristics before Teams

There are formal rules and procedures to govern individual behavior.
There is hierarchical managerial authority.
There are narrow definitions of work responsibility.
There is a Bureaucratic culture.
Change comes about through top-level–directed programs.
There are more organizational levels.
Leadership comes out of the organizational hierarchy.
Reorganizations come from the top.
Individual efficiency and effectiveness are paramount.
Authority and responsibility flow within the hierarchy.
There is a command-and-control mentality.
There is considerable risk of overmanaging.
Organizational and system boundaries are preserved.
There is individual responsibility for decisions.
The organization is non-team oriented.
There is individual thinking.
There is blurred organizational identification.
Individuals are reluctant to assume additional responsibility.
Individuals identify primarily with individual goals.
People follow their leader.
People feel a limited degree of involvement.
People are given responsibility.
People are managed.
Managers assume responsibility for execution of the management functions
(planning, organizing, motivation, leadership, and control).
Managers assume responsibility for quality.
Managers are responsible for the performance of their subordinates.
Managers make the decisions.
People are reluctant to seek additional responsibility.
Managers supervise.
There is limited participation by people in the affairs of the organization that affect
them.
The culture reflects the titles of superiors and subordinates.
There is limited sharing of organizational results.
Rewards are based on individual performance.
Problems are owned primarily by the managers.
People tend to withhold their opinions until the manager gives his or her opinion.
Responsibility for strategic decision rests primarily with the managers.
Project management is viewed as a special case of management.
People are reluctant to change since they usually have little participation in the
development of the rationale for the change, the selection of the strategies to
bring about the change, or in the execution of change strategies.

TABLE 5–2 Cultural Characteristics after Teams

There is systems thinking.

There are blurred organizational boundaries.

There are formal and explicit interdependencies.

There are closer relationships between customers and suppliers.

There are changes in the implicit contract about what employers and employees owe to each other.

External environmental considerations (home, family, school) are put on the organization's agenda.

Problems and opportunities are seen as systems related to larger systems.

Project management is seen as an element of strategy to deal with and to facilitate change in the organization.

Organizational people are working at thinking together.

Organizational hierarchies are being shortened.

Ad hoc and other forms of teams are becoming commonplace in the strategic and operational management of the organization.

The gap between organizational potential and performance is being reduced.

People accept, even insist, on greater responsibility for their own work, for their management, for the organizational products and processes, and for the organization as a whole.

People fly like geese rather than plod like cattle.

People are truly involved in the business of the organization.

People participate in the management of the organization: the design and execution of the planning, motivation, leadership, and control of the organization.

Managers become facilitators and coaches.

People manage themselves.

Organizational managers manage the context; they provide and allocate resources; they design (with the help of the teams) and implement the systems.

Managers (with the help of the teams) provide the required organizational design.

People assume responsibility for quality.

People are responsible for their own performance.

Teams work with the customers and suppliers.

It is recognized that the people doing the job know the most about how the job should be carried out.

Teams evaluate the performance of the team as a whole and of the team members.

Team members counsel team members on individual performance; the team may recommend the release of those individuals who do not perform at the standards expected of their teams.

Organizational decisions, results, and rewards are shared.

Teams take over the functions performed by individual managers in the hierarchy.

The number of organizational layers is reduced.

Teams assume the supervisor functions, and those jobs change considerably or disappear.

People perform a wide range of work in their jobs.

There is a greater sharing of information about the organization, its problems, opportunities, successes, and failures.

Senior managers recognize their limited power in mandating organizational change and renewal from the top. They encourage a nondirective change process.

(*continues*)

TABLE 5–2 Cultural Characteristics after Teams (*Continued*)

Managers work at creating a culture for change in the organization and a culture that supports the operation of different kinds of teams.

The main thrust in change gains momentum at the periphery of the organization and spreads to the core of the organization.

Change is viewed as a learning process for all of the organizational members.

Coordination, information sharing, and teamwork become critical to making the organization function efficiently and effectively.

Commitment, loyalty, trust, and confidence become clear characteristics of the culture.

Willingness to seek new knowledge, develop new skills, and change attitudes becomes socially acceptable in the organization.

A shared vision for the organization and its purposes and an appreciation of the importance of competitiveness become apparent to organizational members.

Words like *supervisor, employee,* and *subordinate* fall into disuse; everyone is called associates, members, coordinators, or coaches.

Promotions are based on results as well as the learning, teaching, coaching, and facilitating role of people.

People are committed to the organization, to individual and organizational goals, to members of the peer group, and to the continual improvement of the organization.

A permanent change in the way the organization is run has been undertaken.

People like being able to influence the affairs of the organization to which they belong.

People's expectations are driven by their own motivations and by how they see themselves fitting into the vision shared by organizational members.

Learning (by everyone in the organization) takes on new importance.

Management's job is to promote the vision, provide the conditions for people to share in that vision, facilitate the use of resources in the organization, and build a culture in which the individuals' and the organization's best interests are served.

Change is seen not as a goal but as an endless journey from the present to the future.

Status in the organization becomes less dependent on the organizational role held and more on the results one is able to accomplish, both individually and as a member of the organizational teams.

Senior managers are concerned with the strategic management of the organization in the sense of managing and orchestrating change so that values are created for the organization and its stakeholders that did not previously exist. The oversight role of the senior managers during the change process (which is continuous) becomes a critical responsibility.

Change and organizational renewal come about without imposing them.

Members of the organization become more aware of the competitive pressures facing the enterprise. Knowledge of the competition dictates high standards for individual and organizational performance.

Managers alter fundamentally the way of doing things—there is less chance that they will overmanage the organization.

TABLE 5–2 (Continued)

Authority through the use of knowledge, interpersonal skills, leadership capabilities, building and maintaining alliances, and expertise—totaled in the ability to influence people—becomes more important than the authority of the formal role that an individual holds in the organization.

Leadership becomes a criterion for promotion at all levels in the organization. People's careers are directed to encourage further development of their potential leadership skills.

The organizational culture tends to facilitate creativity, innovation, productivity, and quality. Consequently, there is an enhanced chance for continuous improvement in the way in which the organization does business.

Participative management and consensus decision making become key characteristics of the organizational culture.

Distinctions between managers and workers become blurred.

People have more fun at work.

Policies, procedures, and rules still exist, but people have a greater understanding and respect for such guidelines to influence behavior.

There is a reduced number of organizational levels.

There is a dicuss-and-decide mentality.

People feel involved.

Everyone participates, at some level, in the organizational decision processes.

People do not wait for problems and opportunities to be assigned to them; they look for problems and opportunities that can be undertaken either individually or through an organizational team.

Leadership for change rests with everyone in the organization.

There is less resistance to change in the organization. Since people play vital roles in discovering and bringing about the needed change, they find that the change is less threatening.

People become more outspoken, questioning the existing order of things, questioning decisions and the right of people to make decisions.

More people understand the management processes, develop improved interpersonal skills, and see the larger systems context of problems and opportunities; individuals develop empathy for the people who have responsibility for improving organizational performance.

Closer working relationships with suppliers are realized.

Introducing and using any of the alternative teams described in this book can affect the culture of the enterprise. For example, the decision by the Boeing Company to bring its suppliers into the concurrent engineering process at the company aggravated the unionized machinists at Boeing. When the Seattle-based aircraft manufacturer announced that Rockwell International Corporation would produce large wing sections for its newly upgraded 737 airliners, the unionized machinists, already decimated by more than 24,000 job cuts, angrily protested the contract with Rockwell International. Boeing's union engineers generally favor efficiency gains that are good for the company, but they are wary of potential job losses.[13]

At one company that launched a concurrent engineering effort, a team of 50 people started out in one large, open room, literally tearing down walls between design and manufacturing to maximize communications and working interrelationships. Subtle cultural changes resulted. The team represented all aspects of product design: development, manufacturing, marketing, finance, and after-sales support. With everyone closely situated, communication got better; conversations were no longer private, and everyone was encouraged to develop an awareness of what was going on in the conversations and get involved if they desired. This up-front conversation enabled the team to resolve many problems as they were identified and reduced the office rumors and politics that typically arise from distorted or inadequate information.

A subtle cultural change was created by the open-room geography of the concurrent engineering team. One difficulty in the cultural change was to get the design engineers to cut their approval ties with their departments. Under the process of concurrency, there was no need to slow down for the decision approval process because all decisions were made by the team in the open room. The company worked hard to break down the barriers between departments. A new cultural philosophy emerged: Put the people together, give them their assignments, provide the resources, focus on the importance of the work they are doing and the value of their output to the future of the enterprise—and then get out of their way and let them go to work. Senior managers had the teams come by every two weeks for a briefing on how well the development effort was going—its particular problems and the timely opportunities that were emerging.

SMASHING BARRIERS

Developing a strategy to change the culture of an enterprise to facilitate team-driven strategies includes breaking down the likely barriers that exist in the organization:

- Organizational barriers between functions
- Barriers existing between the company, its suppliers, customers, and other key stakeholders
- Physical barriers, such as walls between departments or departments being located in different buildings or in different parts of the country
- Psychological barriers, such as attitudes, values, and prejudices that make it difficult for people to work for someone other than their normal supervisor, such as a team leader

---

[13] Neal Templin and Jeff Cole, "Manufacturers Use Suppliers to Help Them Develop New Products," *Wall Street Journal,* December 19, 1994.

- Barriers due to the differences that people have in their background, education, previous work experience, or perception of how decisions are to be made in the enterprise

Viewing an enterprise in cultural terms means being less concrete and more concerned with less easily measurable aspects. The cultural view means to examine processes, methods, attitudes, and the values held by organization members. One company emphasized three key aspects of the cultural side of the enterprise:

1. Creation of a shared vision
2. Use of cross-functional teams
3. Reflection on and revisiting of the results.[14]

At Honda, workers are called production associates and are supported by a culture that can be characterized as follows:

- Any idea should be able to find its way to people who are willing to listen.
- Workers and managers eat together in the same cafeteria.
- The person on the production line knows the most about how the work is to be done.
- Significant decisions are left to the workers—such as a new layout of the production line to accommodate a new product.
- The people working on the teams are actually doing managerial work.
- Extensive training is given to prepare the workers for the new culture in which they will have to work.[15]

THE TRUST FACTOR

A key challenge to the team leader is to manage the team members and the other team stakeholders, so one of the key characteristics in the team's culture is trust—a security concerning the integrity, ability, and character of people associated with the team. To trust is to have confidence in the abilities and personalities of the team. To trust the team is to feel that team members will be responsive and responsible in making and implementing decisions affecting the team, the organization, and the other stakeholders. Trust must exist between the team and higher management, and these managers must have a

[14] T. M. Haalien and M. Sense, "Managing the Cultural Environment for Better Results," *Proceedings, Vol. 1, 12th INTERNET Congress on Project Management,* Internet, Oslo, Norway, June 1994, pp. 90–102.
[15] Paraphrased from Myron Magnet, "The Truth about the American Worker," *Fortune,* May 4, 1992, pp. 48–64.

vision of how the team's purposes fit into the larger goals and objectives of the enterprise.

Trust in a relationship takes years to develop and can be damaged or destroyed by a single act of imprudence. Trust is easy to violate; it requires that members of the team open up to each other and let each other know where they stand. Trust is particularly challenging to develop and maintain on a team because people from different disciplines have to pull together for the common team goals and projects. Jack Welch, CEO of General Electric, said in GE's 1991 annual report that the corporation would be built on mutual trust and respect and that "trust and respect take years to build and no time at all to destroy." The bottom line of trust is that a person's word is his or her bond.

By becoming sensible to these factors, the team leader can enhance the positive aspects of the culture. Team leaders must be change managers and, at the same time, participate with other organizational leaders in designing and facilitating a culture that brings out the best in people.

OPERATIONAL STRATEGIES

The person who is able to function as a team leader along with the other managers (leaders) of the parent organization is responsible for arranging the conditions conducive to a creative and disciplined culture supportive of teamwork. Certain actions can help develop and maintain such a culture:

1. Team leaders must design and implement an ongoing, disciplined approach in planning, organizing, and controlling the **team management system.** This is a fundamental first because team members must have a model to use in managing the work of the team. This is one of the first task-related actions to let people know where they stand and what is expected of them on the team. Team leaders must provide as much leeway as possible for team members to try new ways of getting their jobs done. This includes encouraging experimentation without fear of reprisals if mistakes are made.

2. Team leaders must give team members a reasonable amount of attention through team reviews, strategy meetings, and checking in on a regular basis to see how things are going. Too much attention can be counterproductive and might be interpreted as meddling. Too little attention might be construed as disinterest on the part of the team manager.

3. Team leaders must make sure team members understand in specific terms their authority, responsibility, and accountability so that they know what's expected of them on their work package. If team members know their assigned work packages, there is less likelihood that they will become overburdened with the minute details of their jobs. Creativity

requires the opportunity to reflect on the totality of the job being done. If members are too busy with details, it's easy for them to miss the big picture.

4. Team leaders must give team members part ownership in the decisions affecting the team. When the team members know that their opinions are valued, their self-confidence is bolstered and the chances for creative thinking are enhanced. By encouraging participation in decision making on the team, the general culture of the team will be improved. When team members see their work on the work packages as challenging and the goals as realistic, they are more likely to exhibit creative behavior and be happier in their work.

5. Team leaders must maintain proper oversight of the team's objectives and goals. A team leader is not a supervisor in the usual sense of the word, although such a person should have supervision of the team, should know where the total teamwork stands, and should know where the team stands on cost, schedule, and technical performance at all times. The team leader maintains oversight of the work by watching and directing the major activities and course of action of the team. Most team members who have maximized their creative potential would prefer a low level of oversight by the leader. The oversight effort should be focused on those activities most directed to achieving project results.

6. Team leaders must encourage the use of creative brainstorming approaches to solve the many unstructured problems that arise during the team's work. Many different types of unstructured solutions will be needed to solve these problems. The use of a single routine problem-solving approach would be inappropriate since such an approach assumes too often that there is one best and correct solution. Teams create something new. Innovation and creativity are required to deal with something so new.

7. Team leaders must provide timely feedback to the team. In this way, the team's leader will encourage open communication in the team's culture. If the team members sense that key information is being withheld or that the leader is less than candid with them, dissatisfaction and disenchantment could result, thus adversely affecting the team's culture. If feedback is provided too late for the team members to make adjustments, their work could suffer and team members could become discouraged.

8. Team leaders must provide the resources and support to get the job done. This is another fundamental and positive contribution that the leader can and must make to the culture. Adequate resources are required to do the job and to facilitate a creative and innovative culture. A shortage of resources may allow people to use their innovative and creative skills, but in the long run adequate resources are needed to ensure a supportive culture.

9. Finally, team leaders must recognize the key people-related cultural factors and utilize them. These factors include the following:
   • Rewarding useful ideas
   • Encouraging candid expression of ideas
   • Promptly following up on team and member concerns
   • Assisting in idea development
   • Accepting different ideas—listening to that team member who is marching to a different drummer
   • Encouraging risk taking
   • Providing opportunities for professional growth and broadening experiences on the project
   • Encouraging interaction with the project stakeholders so that there is an appreciation by the team members of the project's breadth and depth

At Dupont's Fibers Division, the company's largest chemical business, a unique approach to people development, called the Empowered Learning Team Process, is being used. A concentrated team leader development process for 2500 employees combined with an eighteen-month development process for 19,000 team members starts with "Playing to Win" and "Leading Empowered Teams" seminars held at Dupont's five regional training centers. Training includes outdoor team adventure experiences and indoor sessions that challenge employees to improve products, services, and processes continually. Basic values of trust, respect, truth, and accountability provide professional standards for the team leaders and members to attain. Team-building learning is combined with total quality management concepts and processes, leading the team members and leaders to recognize that continuous improvement of products, services, and processes is a way of life at Dupont.

Changing a culture means that people have to change. For some, change is difficult if not impossible.

WHY CHANGE?

Individual and group behavior in an organization is controlled as much by the basic relationship that people have in the organizational culture as by anything else. This behavior includes organizational policies and procedures and how perceptions, rules, and expected behaviors are carried out.

Enterprises are organized to exploit the user acceptance of their products and services. The process of innovation can help improve that profitability. But there is a larger dimension of innovation—the abandonment of old ways and the creation of new products, services, and organizational processes needed to bring something new to customers. To innovate means to challenge the existing order or the prevailing viewpoint and to assume risk, uncertainties, and the enmity of those who wish to preserve the status quo—those who encourage the traditional viewpoint, who postpone evaluating existing strategies, and who tolerate mediocrity and even failure because of a fear of what change might bring. We all have a litany of old saws that serve to protect us and rationalize the status quo:

Don't rock the boat.
The way to get along is to go along.
Why change?
I'm only a couple of years from retirement.
What we are doing now is good enough.
I like things the way they are.
The good old days were the best days.

Responses of managers in their attempts to remain competitive include the following:

- Respond with defensive strategies of cutting costs, reducing the number of products and even product lines, and emphasizing the most profitable products and services.
- Make innovation a way of life in the organization, and energize and empower every member of the enterprise to look for new and better ways of doing things—both in doing things for the internal customers and in providing products and services to outside customers.
- Work at building a culture that encourages and rewards creativity and innovation, and tune the organizational management and cultural systems to make innovation a way of life—to be accepted by everyone at every level in the enterprise. Everyone in the organization is protected from criticism of any sort for brainstorming and is on a constant quest for new ways of working and serving the organization.

SUMMARY

In this chapter, the general nature of an organizational culture was described along with some of the likely changes that will come about as an enterprise that uses alternative types of teams pursues its mission.

Organizational cultures are dynamic and likely to be affected whenever political, legal, social, economic, technological, or competitive forces affect the enterprise. Yet despite all of these forces, a basic core of values within the enterprise can preserve the fundamentals of the enterprise's culture or change the culture to the organization's benefit.

Whenever managers are considering the introduction and use of teams in the enterprise, the likely cultural impact of such teams should be considered. Once the enterprise's culture is understood, strategies need to be developed to change that culture to be supportive of teams in the design and execution of strategies.

The key messages of this chapter include the following:

- Culture is a set of refined behavioral patterns found in an organization. It includes attitudes, beliefs, ethics, morals, prejudices, predispositions, policies, procedures, and leader and follower styles. It is included in the fundamental belief among the members of the enterprise that "this is simply the way we do things around here."
- The introduction of teams to the operational and strategic purposes of an enterprise changes the culture.
- Values held by the members of an organization influence the culture. Values are principles, standards, or qualities considered worthwhile or desirable to influence people to think and act in a certain manner and to support organizational purposes.
- A strong team culture supports the team's purposes and provides a common base for expected behavior of team members.
- Organizational cultures are affected by many forces. The systems context in which the organization operates will affect, and be affected by, the cultural forces at work in the enterprise.
- Although an organization's culture is real, its appearance and influence on the members of the organization are subtle. Viewing an enterprise in cultural terms means being less specific and being concerned with less easily measurable aspects.
- The development and propagation of a new organizational culture means that people have to change. For some, the change is difficult if not impossible.

The following chapter will review teams and the competitive edge.

PART III
USING TEAMS

____6
TEAMS AND THE COMPETITIVE EDGE

We trained hard . . . but it seemed that every time we were beginning to form up into teams we would be reorganized, [and] I was to learn later in life that we tend to meet any new situation by reorganizing: and what a wonderful method it can be for creating the illusion of progress while producing confusion, inefficiency and demoralization.

PETRONIUS, ARBITER, GREEK NAVY, 210 B.C.

If reorganization into teams has produced only the "illusion of progress" and left us with only "confusion, inefficiency and demoralization," then we have not learned much since 210 B.C. about psychology, efficiency, or the building of high morale in any organization. Survival is based on the ability to organize and reorganize to meet problems as they arise. The project teams that are described in the current literature have given rise to a wide variety of teams that are organized to meet specific needs of organizations. The reorganization into project teams and their subsequent reorganization into other kinds of teams has brought about a basic, fundamental, and salutary change in organizations. At the same time, as with any change, there may be temporary dislocations, but there are ways of forestalling them or dealing with them.

In this chapter, teams are described as competitive tools—the medium through which organizational strategies are conceptualized, designed, and implemented. Examples show how teams have improved an enterprise's ability to compete in the markets that contemporary organizations face. Team results are described as the building blocks in competitive strategies, and the benefits of teams are presented. In addition, values created by teams, the changing role of traditional managers, and cultural support are discussed, as well as how recalcitrant individuals can resist the use of teams. Finally, this chapter presents a way of classifying teams.

ORGANIZATIONAL EFFECTIVENESS

The survival and growth of an enterprise depend on the ability to sustain a flow of products and services that meet customer needs faster and more efficiently than those of competitors. The use of product and process development project teams within the context of concurrent or simultaneous engineering can deliver results sooner than using more traditional development methods. The ability to survive and grow in long-term competitive markets can be tested by a constant overview of how well the enterprise is doing in bringing new and innovative products and organizational processes into the mainstream of the enterprise's business. Such innovative products can be those that represent a minor improvement of previous products, or they can be breakthrough products that set a new competitive standard in the marketplace. Development products and processes provide the basis for a thorough and rigorous testing of the enterprise's ability to innovate. In the process of innovation, they test the organization's ability to integrate the many disciplines needed to prepare for its future.

Integration within an enterprise takes many forms. First is the integration required to maintain functional excellence in the disciplines needed to support the organization's mission. Second is the integration needed to provide coherency in organizational units, such as departments, divisions, and profit centers. Third is integration of the entire enterprise's efforts to support the overall mission, objectives, and goals. Fourth is the need to integrate the core capabilities of the enterprise so that development projects can be carried out—this is the best way to prepare for survival and growth.

Integration of the disciplines in the enterprise always raises territorial issues—managers and professionals want to protect their turf. If the enterprise is committed to the use of teams as instruments of strategy, the chances are improved that serious territorial issues will not arise, and the wisdom of using teams as focal points to integrate disciplines and resources will be recognized.

Ideas for improved and new products and processes often originate at the worker or professional level in the enterprise. In companies such as 3M and Texas Instruments, policies exist whereby a person with a new idea is authorized to form a small ad hoc team off-line and experiment with the idea to see if it has sufficient merit for further study. Such policies result in many ongoing product and process ideas, some of which survive and become projects for new product and process development. Corporate strategy is affected by these ideas, and the employee empowerment engenders a feeling of ownership among team members. Development efforts and strategic initiatives move ahead faster, often with little management stimulation, because of the culture, which facilitates empowerment and creativity. Teams that are able to develop new products and processes successfully experience a great sense of accomplishment, particularly as they see their results reflected in an emerging enterprise strategy with a likely impact on the future pathway of the company.

RESULTS THROUGH TEAMS

It has been estimated that about one in five U.S. employers operate self-managed teams today. By the end of the twentieth century, 40 to 50 percent of the companies in the United States could be using such teams. When these teams are used, labor costs drop, morale rises, and signs of alienation between workers and managers are eased. In general, in recent years the team work ethic has improved in U.S. industry.

For example, in the mid-1980s, an automobile manufacturer was ready to shut its oldest plant, a dingy and rundown components facility in the midwest. The plant was beset by heavy absenteeism and worker alienation. In 1986, management decided to try self-managed teams; workers were renamed technicians, and line supervisors, some of whom left over the power loss, became team advisors. Time clocks were removed.

The new organizational design teams worked well. The plant's seventy-seven teams now assign tasks, confront sluggish performers, order repairs, talk to customers, and even alter work hours after consulting a labor–management steering committee. Extra training earns technicians extra pay. Employees have, in a sense, taken over ownership of the plant. Absenteeism has plummeted, grievances have tumbled, and there has been a dramatic improvement in the quality.

The use of teams for improving manufacturing operations is gaining favor. For example, at the Packard Electric Division of the General Motors Corporation located in Warren, Ohio, self-directed teams have been instituted in Plant 16's modular cutting area. Teams are staffed with six hourly employees to operate four modular cutters on a continuous-run basis. The teams do their own scheduling, servicing, auditing, and packaging. One of the first jobs that the team members undertook was to design their job classification and decide on the layout of the module where they spend eight hours a day. The team members also share such tasks as set-ups, service, binding, and packaging of the wiring for motor vehicles. They also serve as technicians to help evaluate machine improvements and problems. Team assignments rotate on a daily basis. Training to serve on the teams is extensive, including both technical and social training.[1]

Sometimes teams take over a company's operation. This happened at Amgen, a biotechnology firm located in Thousand Oaks, California, where teams are used to maintain a small-company atmosphere and to facilitate the growth

[1] "Plant 16 Installs Third Self-Directed Team," *Direct Connection,* Packard Electric Division, General Motors Corporation, P.O. Box 431, Warren, OH 44486. Used by permission.

of the company. Starting off with the use of teams in the research and development side of the company, the effort was so successful that now teams are used for everything. Two general types of teams have emerged: product development teams, which are concerned with everything related to bringing a product to market, and task forces, which do everything else. Members of these teams come from the different disciplines of the company. The teams range in size from six to eighty people, and they report directly to senior management. Department heads, called facilitators, work for the teams, making sure they have the resources that are needed. Teams meet weekly, monthly, or whenever the team members see fit. The vice-president for human resources at Amgen calls the team system "our family jewel."[2]

An important reason for using teams is the expected cost savings that are likely to result. The H. J. Heinz Company figured that it would generate $200 million in annual savings within four years by listening to teams of employees enlisted to boost productivity and team waste. In one such effort, teams at the Starkist factory in Puerto Rico found that tuna was being wasted because workers were not able to keep up with a faster processing line. By spending $4 million for additional equipment and $5 million a year for extra workers, the company realized a savings of $100 million annually.[3]

The use of teams gained acceptance in the auto industry because of the success at the Saturn plant. The Saturn automobile has become the highest-quality American-made brand, competing with the Japanese Hondas and Nissans. Worker pay at the Spring Hill, Tennessee, plant is tied to quality goals. These workers have demonstrated that they do not compromise quality. Everyone is on salary, including the line workers. Workers are given a voice in all management decisions, with 20 percent of pay linked to quality, productivity, and profitability. Workers are chosen carefully from within GM ranks; only those that GM considers adaptable and able to work on teams, and only those who have good communication skills, are chosen to work at Spring Hill. Teams hire workers, approve parts from suppliers, choose their equipment, and handle administrative matters, such as team budgets.

At the Saturn plant, a revolutionary labor agreement makes partners of Saturn's blue- and white-collar workers and gives everyone the authority to solve quality problems. Workers who find defective parts often phone the vendor to recommend a fix. A fourteen-member door team at the plant made specific recommendations to rearrange machinery to improve quality productivity.[4]

Suppliers to automobile manufacturers have found success through their use of teams. At the Freudenberg-NOK auto parts factory in Ligonier, Indiana, three shifts a day produce 123,000 engine mounts a month for the Ford Motor

---

[2] Andrew Erdman, "How to Keep That Family Feeling," *Fortune,* April 6, 1992, pp. 95–96.
[3] *Wall Street Journal,* September 7, 1992.
[4] Woodruff, David, and Kathleen Kerwin, "Saturn," *Business Week* (Industrial Technology Edition), August 17, 1992, pp. 86–91.

Company's Aerostar van and Ranger pickup trucks. On a fall day in 1993, a twelve-member self-managed team was given ambitious goals: Boost capacity by 20 percent, raise productivity by 15 percent, and reduce work-in-process by 50 percent. Team assignments of this sort are typical for the forty such teams that work in this factory. The teams dubbed GROWTH teams (for Get Rid of Waste through Team Harmony) are helping the company move toward attaining the goal of doubling sales by the year 2000 to $1 billion, without adding more people or factory space. Over a dozen other plants in the company are undergoing similar teamwork, with the hope that by the end of 1995 over $1 million will have been invested in teams, with their results providing an impressive payback of $12 to $20 million.[5]

Teams can help the transition from an old plant to a new one—a major strategic initiative for a company. This occurred at the H. J. Heinz plant in Pittsburgh, Pennsylvania. Teams were used to design and implement plans for the shutdown of a traditional factory that had served the company for decades and to get a new factory with over 553,000 square feet of space up and running. Behind the teams' work were massive investments in training directed to enhancing the knowledge and skills of the work force. An array of training tools, such as evaluation of basic skills, educational counseling, literacy education, classroom instruction, and training on the factory floor, was provided.

Remarkably, during the transition from the old to the new factory, not one day of production was lost. According to the general manager of the Heinz plant, for "the people who make this project happen—the trainers, the computer programmers, the process engineers, the people on the line—it was more than a job, it was a commitment. And they lived it passionately." The teamwork on this new factory brought an unprecedented degree of employee involvement and flexibility in solving problems and taking responsibility.[6]

Heinz used teams for other purposes as well, including quality and safety efforts that slashed workers' compensation costs by 60 percent and helped make the company the quality leader of the pet food industry. In England, at Heinz's Harlesden and Kitt Green factories, worker-led process evaluation teams are helping to streamline factory operations, improve quality, and, in some cases, reduce overhead by as much as 40 percent. These are self-managed teams that developed their own plans, got co-worker approval on the plans, and successfully implemented the changes with little or no intervention by management. One of the hardest things to do at Heinz was to allow the teams make their own mistakes and to meld those mistakes into the learning process of the organization so that everyone had useful learning experiences.[7]

The use of teams has become a global phenomenon. In the new Mercedes-Benz plant at Rastatt in Germany, there are no traditional foremen and few

[5] James R. Treece, "Improving the Soul of an Old Machine," *Business Week*, October 25, 1993, pp. 134–136.
[6] "Working Smarter," *The H. J. Heinz Company 1993 Annual Report*, p. 16.
[7] Ibid., p. 17.

conventional production lines. Instead, self-directed teams work in bays and assemble and produce the Mercedes midrange 200 series cars. Even with realizing the productivity gains of self-directed work teams, the company has the highest labor costs in the world, far ahead of similar costs in the United States. Part of the blame for these high labor costs has been an unparalleled generosity with entitlement programs and unemployment benefits and the lack of manufacturing leanness to meet global competition. Another part of the problem is the failure of Mercedes to design its cars for new and lean manufacturing techniques. Any remedial strategy to get labor costs down will have to be accepted by the work directors that sit on the board of supervisors of the company—ten out of twenty slots at the company. Although the company is reducing jobs slowly through a mix of early retirement and attrition, it may not be enough to get Mercedes costs down. Mercedes, once hugely profitable in the car business, now sees sales being snatched away by Lexus, BMW, and Infiniti. Even more humbling for Mercedes, for the first time ever, BMW has overtaken Mercedes sales in Germany.[8]

Japanese countries who pioneered an early use of teams have found that teams can produce unusual results. For example, a team at Honda Motor Company developed a new diesel car engine that promises to meet California's strict emissions standards and is expected to attain 48 miles per gallon (mpg) in town and 55 mpg on the highway. The technology used is described as "lean-burn"—an incremental improvement by the Japanese—and Detroit's Big Three had always insisted that only a major breakthrough would make a lead-burn engine a success. The Honda team developed the incremental improvement that led to the new engine by pulling "together everything that we know." Brainstorming by the team helped provide the insight needed to develop the technology, particularly in the alteration of an intake part on the cylinder head. The Honda engine project was developed in its early phases through "cajoling" colleagues into asking for prototypes from the designer's drawings. The head of research, Nobuhiko Kawahiko Kawamoto, now Honda's president, gave tacit approval to the "bootleg' project.[9]

When teams are used, employees become empowered, which leads to enhanced personal satisfaction and added responsibilities. Organizational cultures are changed as new work relationships come forth—as well as new challenges for everyone.

At Goodyear, employee teams are empowered to make key process and product decisions. The company executives turned Goodyear's corporate culture on its head when they decided to implement a team approach to process and product development and problem solving. Goodyear began extensive training for all employees—from executives on down—to introduce and im-

---

[8] Templeman, John, "Downshift at Daimler," *Business Week* (Industrial Technology Edition), November 16, 1992, pp. 88–90.

[9] Karen Lowry Miller and Larry Armstrong, "55 Miles per Gallon: How Honda Did It," *Business Week,* September 23, 1993, pp. 82–83.

plement the team concept. At Goodyear, internal teams exist in functional and cross-functional areas. In addition, the company also has cross-corporate teams that partner suppliers, customers, and employees together. By integrating people into teams, Goodyear has "unleashed the power of the people" and moved away from the idea that managers are doing all the management. Gaining a flatter hierarchy is part of the justification for forming many teams in the company. Position descriptions have been rewritten to put challenge and risk into each one. Performance appraisals now focus on the ability of an individual to work as a team player. Employees have greater opportunity to brief senior officials of the company on projects underway. Top officials have gained a better awareness of who the employees are in the company and what their abilities are. That awareness has facilitated the continued building of a participatory style of management and decision making at Goodyear. It has also helped to push decision making down to the level at which information can be developed.[10]

Union Involvement

When teams are used, unions are often involved. The support of a major stakeholder like a union is absolutely necessary. As union and company leaders have seen the advantages of teams, formal agreements for joint teams have come forth. By joint agreement, unions, workers, and management are forming problem-solving teams to evaluate and report back to leadership committees on specific problems or projects likely to affect the work force, the use of technology, or other situations that can influence current production productivity. Adequate resources are provided to these teams, as well as problem-solving training and information so members can participate fully on such teams.

The mission statement of the USS Gary Works, shown in an employment involvement charter, makes a commitment to increase the degree to which workers have a say in how they will accomplish the responsibilities of their job. An employee involvement process is expected to build a climate of respect and trust by success in joint efforts. The areas of joint effort include safety, product quality, on-time delivery to customers, product cost, secure employment, improved job satisfaction, and the full utilization of human resources to ensure continuous improvements. USS Gary Workers commits to training, education, and information sharing to help employees make better decisions. Employment protection is provided through a commitment that "no employee shall have his/her employment involuntarily terminated or his/her earnings reduced as a result of any employee involvement project." Other provisions cover such matters as discussion of alternatives to layoffs, voluntary participa-

[10] Frederick J. Kovac, "Goodyear Agility Focuses on Collaboration, Technology and Employee Empowerment," *Focus,* National Center for Manufacturing Sciences, June 1993, pp. 2–3.

tion on problem-solving teams, open communication, and the protection of existing union or management rights.[11]

For self-directed production teams to succeed, union cooperation is essential. Many unions today recognize the use of teams. Sharing of information and decision-making authority and responsibility at all levels of the enterprise is becoming policy in the strategic partnerships of successful labor–management–union relationships. A commitment to work together that extends from the board room and the executive office to the shop floor and the union office is driven by a shared vision of the need for continuous improvement in joint decision-making processes; employee participation; relationships among labor, management, and union; and all aspects of business. Memoranda of agreement are being signed by all parties to bring about closer strategic partnerships in enterprises. Working together to respond quickly to changes in the marketplace, having process technology serve both the business and the workers, and understanding the realities of worldwide competition are becoming the accepted way of thinking and doing in unionized companies. The need to design and implement training programs for workers, management, and union officials is recognized. Joint leadership committees are being established to work toward achieving improved productivity levels throughout plants as well as union involvement in company decisions to make technological changes and to provide guidance to problem-solving teams. When unions, workers, and management do not agree, traditional grievance and arbitration are used.

The use of teams to bring about progress in the cooperation of unions, workers, and management toward enhanced competition in the marketplace changes the culture within organizations and enhances a cross-organizational culture that can markedly improve productivity and quality. The use of teams also reduces the *we* versus *them* syndrome that was characteristic of traditional labor–management relationships of the parties.

Recovery Teams

Sometimes the impetus for the formation and use of teams is due to an urgent desire to retrieve a failing product. On the Mustang sports car, a projected $1 billion development cost seemed to be too expensive to undertake. The Ford Motor Company organized Teams Mustang of about 400 people and used a frugal budget to develop a modified sports car. The team broke many of the policies and rules that governed product development in a rigidly disciplined company. A special team spent six months visiting and benchmarking competitive cars in Germany and Italy, seeking clues about how rivals were able to develop new cars for hundreds of millions of dollars less than Ford had been spending. All team members were put under one roof, and the project's manufacturing chief held veto power over car design changes

---

[11] USS Gary Works, Employee Involvement Charter, undated.

that would have required new factory tools. Team members were grouped into "chunk teams" with responsibility for a particular piece or chunk of the car. Vendor bidding processes were thrown out, and the team leaders awarded contracts to suppliers on a best-qualified basis without competitive bidding— and on the basis of supplier willingness to enter a strategic partnership with the Mustang team. At one time the project nearly died, but the cost and schedule advantage gained by negotiating directly with the suppliers on a strategic partnership basis saved the project.[12]

Other Uses of Teams

Teams are used in a wide variety of contexts. A growing number of companies are following the lead set by Dupont, Data General, Tandem Computers, and Digital Equipment in putting sales representatives, engineers, technicians, and production managers on teams to service customers and win new accounts.[13]

State legislatures are beginning to see the value of teams in improving organizational performance. There is a clear drive in many state legislatures to require companies to establish workplace safety teams since such teams, made up of equal numbers of workers and managers, not only reduce accidents but also lower workers' compensation costs, sometimes sharply. One reason for the success is the basic notion that the worker doing the work knows best about how that work should be done and can see potential safety conditions and issues before management can. Since both workers and managers are on the same team, closer consultation is possible on ways to reduce workplace hazards. Before teams were used, workers were likely to file complaints with OSHA, triggering inspections that could lead to fines. Now the workers, seeing their peers on the safety committees, are more likely to air their concerns to fellow workers, which can lead to more timely corrective action.

Product Ideas

Ideas for new products, services, or improvements in a process can come from anywhere. One source that is just beginning to be tapped is from teams at all organizational levels of the enterprise. Consider the case of the Rubbermaid company, an innovative and productive company that sat around for years among the ten most admired companies in *Fortune*'s most admired survey. For five or six years, the company was in second place. In 1994, the company won first place. The company's strategy in new products is to make small improvements to some 5000 unspectacular products: mail boxes, window boxes, storage boxes, toys, mops, dust mitts, spatulas, snap-together furniture,

---

[12] White, Joseph B. and Oscar Suris, "New Pony: How a "Skunk Works' Kept Mustang Alive—on a Tight Budget," *Wall Street Journal,* September 21, 1993, p. 1.
[13] "'Team Selling' Catches On, But Is Sales Really a Team Sport?" *Wall Street Journal,* March 29, 1994, p. 1.

and desk organizers. Most ideas for products flow from a single source—teams. Twenty interdisciplinary teams concentrate on specific product lines, such as bathroom accessories. According to one executive, the team approach to innovation has been so succesful that it would be fearful to contemplate a world without it. Rubbermaid's success rate in introducing more than 365 new products per year is remarkable, considering that the company does little market testing. Focus groups are used to evaluate new products, such as a new fishing tackle box. But no market testing is done—the products are put out quickly, which captures a market fast and reduces the threat of being copied.[14]

CONTINUED GROWTH

Teams will likely grow in use in the 1990s due to the explosive growth in technical information, which enables employees to know so much more about the technical and managerial nature of their work than their managers could understand. As highly educated specialists who are self-motivated and self-directed work together, their managers begin to know less of what the specialists are really doing. Managers become increasingly dependent on the specialized employees to make and implement decisions on the technical side of their work. For such specialists to work together, the team becomes an organizational design vehicle through which highly technical communication and interfacing can be carried out. As more expensive and exotic equipment and other resources are used in the workplace (such as the computer and technical information systems), the costs are so significant that people have to be able to work together and make real-time decisions and interventions on their own and solve technical and organizational interfacing problems without having to check with the boss.

Competitive pressures are causing companies to turn to the use of teams to get the work done sooner and at lower cost since the use of teams can reduce the need for traditional middle- and first-level managers—thus helping to get the product and process development and operating costs down. First-level and middle managers are becoming endangered species. A point often missed in considering the use of teams is how the leadership of the team is diffused among the team members. When such teams take on more of the functions of self-management, the manager and leadership functions do not disappear—rather, a moving leadership pattern emerges: Members of the team emerge as leaders as needed when their particular technical work tasks are developed and integrated into the overall team effort.

As the reader peruses the examples of the use of teams in this chapter, it should become apparent that teams have produced notable benefits. Table 1, in Chapter 1, provided a general summary of how teams have produced results.

---

[14] Alan Farnham, "America's Most Admired Company," *Fortune,* February 7, 1994, pp. 50–54.

In the material that follows, a more detailed profile of probable benefits is given.

TEAM BENEFITS

Experience has shown that the use of teams has helped to facilitate the introduction of new ideas in products and organizational processes. Workers who previously worked alone can now learn new knowledge and skills while serving as a contributing member of a team. Working on the team tends to reinforce the workers' abilities as well as provide the opportunity for synergistic thinking and action, which usually is not available when the team members work alone, out of the team environment. Communication ties are enhanced in a team, and when technological challenges emerge, the entire team can deal with those challenges and develop team-based remedial strategies.

Participation on a team usually means that the team members learn additional skills and trade off job duties. The team members, by developing multiskilled capabilities, can perform many different types of duties on the teams and learn additional skills while working on other teams. One important result of all of this is to reduce the number of job classifications, thus simplifying the hiring and assignment of people in their work.

There are important byproducts of using teams as instruments of organizational strategy. These include (1) enhancing people's technical skills as well as their appreciation of an organizational design that facilitates resource integration and (2) increasing opportunities for team members to assume meaningful leadership and management roles. Participation in both the operational and strategic affairs of the enterprise is enhanced, which helps people feel that they are worthwhile and can make meaningful and measurable contributions to the enterprise's destiny. Closer identification with the problems and opportunities facing the enterprise engenders understanding of what it takes to keep the organization on a successful path of producing results that have value to customers. Empowerment, properly given and used, unleashes a wave of heartfelt enthusiasm that improves morale, encourages risk taking, fosters creativity, and leads to innovation—all of which make people feel good about their job and their relationships with peers, superiors, and subordinates. People look forward to going to work every day. They begin to see the important link between individual effort and organizational efficacy.

LEADERSHIP

Leadership is critical in developing new products and processes. People on the teams, people in the functional departments, and people who manage the enterprise have the opportunity to develop enhanced leadership abilities as they work for each other and help each other and the enterprise move toward competitive organizational products and processes. When people develop leadership qualities as a result of teams, they realize the following:

- Leaders can come from any place in the organization, as people do the right things in improving the use of resources in creative and innovative ways.
- An important part of leadership in a team context is to build and maintain networks of interest with stakeholders and with higher organizational levels.
- There is ongoing questioning of the status quo and a belief that thinking about the future can help influence that future according to what is best for the enterprise.
- The ability to see a future that does not yet exist makes for provocative and fascinating thinking—indeed, the essence of strategic thinking.
- Foresight can link the future to a vision for the team's work and the enterprise's purposes.
- There are opportunities to enhance personal credentials in social abilities, communication skills, and interpersonal expertise, and there are enhanced abilities to work with and through other people to meet objectives and goals.
- Promotion opportunities are increased.

Table 6–1 indicates some of the many results experienced by contemporary organizations when they use teams. Table 6–1 provides only a brief overview of team results. In the final chapter of this book a more detailed discussion of the positive and negative results is provided.

VALUES AND TEAMS

Values in the context of management pertain to the usefulness or importance of those things that influence people's attitudes and the resulting development of an organizational culture that establishes general expectations for people's behavior. Values affect what people and the organization do and how well the company competes, and they have powerful influence over people's ways of thinking as they play out their individual and collective roles in the enterprise. To some degree, values influence everything that goes on in the enterprise.

The use of teams as instruments of enterprise strategy usually challenges existing values of organizational design and the relative importance of certain work in the enterprise and how that work gets done. Formal authority, responsibility, and accountability patterns will be affected when teams are used. Prevailing negative values that confront product and process development teams include the following:

TABLE 6–1 Team Results

• Lower costs	• Improved productivity, efficiency, and effectiveness
• Higher quality	• Greater learning
• Manageable strategic initiatives	• More teamwork
• Interdisciplinary focus	• Leader/manager development
• Feeling of contribution	• Self-destiny
• Improved career development	• More skills
• More enjoyment	• Identification with organizational purposes
• More creativity, leading to innovation	• Job enrichment
• Greater participation	• More fun
• Greater profitability	• Less parochicalism
• Interpersonal empathy	• Better communication
• Fewer managers	• Greater sharing of information
• Changed role of managers	• Greater organizational synergy
• Less bureaucracy	• Enlightened adversary viewpoints
• Enhanced responsibility/ accountability	• Empowerment
• Greater harmony of individual and organizational unit objectives and goals	• Improved culture
• Less command and control	• More consensus and consent
• Improved competition	• Improved organizational products and services
• Improved morale	• Improved organizational processes
• More association with winners	• More candid debate
• Cross-functional and cross-organizational fertilization	• Systems thinking
• Self-management	• Greater pride
• Improved labor–management relationships	• Greater dissemination of organizational performance information
• Flatter hierarchy	• Shared interests

- There can be a tendency for a given discipline to dominate the organization, as in the case of a public utility company's difficulties with the design, engineering, and construction of a nuclear power generating plant, which were caused in part by the values of senior managers, who were lawyers and who failed to appreciate the need for design completion before starting construction of the plant.
- There can be negative attitudes, such as those of design engineers in a manufacturing company, who believed that they were the elite members of the organization. This caused them to be cavalier about their role in product development and to view the manufacturing engineers as those people who were involved in "the dirty business" of manufacturing.

- There can be an uncompromising conviction to follow the unity-of-command management principle of having only one boss and thereby not accept the sharing of authority and responsibility among functional managers, the team manager, and members of the project team. For many years, organizations grappled with how a matrix organization used in the project management context apparently violated this principle. Today, acceptance of the matrix organizational design is more a way of thinking about reporting relationships than anything else.

- There can be a belief, as in an aerospace company, that marketing is less important than design engineering and manufacturing. The aerospace company's U.S. Department of Defense contracts did not require any real marketing effort because the company was not competing in a traditional marketplace.

- There can be strong opinions, as among senior people in a consumer products company, that it is impossible to predict the future and that the best strategy for survival is to watch competitors and their products and then imitate those products as soon as possible in the marketplace. Today, that consumer products company is in financial difficulties since its imitation policy on products has put it behind understanding changes in the technology underlying competitors' new products and organizational processes.

- There can be enchantment with past and current successes: Senior managers look at themselves and say, "We must be doing something right—look how much money we are making." The values of these kinds of managers do not include the belief that any successful product or service is already aging and will, without improvement, fail in the long run.

- Managers may believe that the current use of teams is a management fad that will go away in time, and the traditional vertical organizational design will once again hold forth.

- There can be a conviction that the design of products and services can be done in a sequential manner, in which design engineers do their work and pass the design on to manufacturing, on to marketing, and then on to after-sales service. Concurrent or simultaneous engineering is making the sequential manner of doing product development obsolete and noncompetitive. Chapter 10 describes the advantages likely to be found in using concurrent engineering through a team approach in developing new products and services.

On a more positive note, values developing out of the theory and practice of the strategic management of teams emphasize some of the following considerations:

- Teams for alternative uses in modern organizations are essential for bringing a focus to interfunctional and interorganizational efforts to capitalize on both operational and strategic initiatives.

- The person doing the job knows the most about how that job should be done and has an additional valuable insight into how the job should be managed. Given the chance, people can and will successfully manage themselves.
- Although the future cannot be predicted with absolute certainty, ongoing rigorous study of what the future may hold can provide meaningful foresight. Such study can lead to helpful insight into what likelihoods will create opportunities and problems for the enterprise.
- Product and process development teams are the best-known way of bringing a focus to the concurrent development of products, services, and the organizational processes needed to support future purposes. Furthermore, when such teams are used, employees receive valuable on-the-job training to enhance their technical and managerial knowledge, skills, and attitudes.
- The output of teams contributes to the operational competence, functional excellence, and strategic management of the enterprise. Accordingly, the outputs of such teams are building blocks in the design and execution of organizational strategies.
- An organizational and team culture characterized by trust, commitment, respect, conviction, and dedication will encourage people to contribute to their own well-being as well as to the fortune and culture of the company.

CREATION OF VALUES

There is increasing evidence that teams, properly used, can improve organizational productivity, efficiency, and effectiveness; increase quality; lower costs; and develop extraordinary competitive initiatives for the enterprise. The following values result:

- Teams engender synergy in the use of resources not otherwise available through the traditional organizational structure.
- The various disciplines represented by team members facilitate extraordinary oversight and a range of ideas through the dynamics of people looking at the problem differently.
- The people doing a job know the most about how that job should be done. When such people are put on an interdisciplinary team, they bring (both individually and collectively) an expertise that leads to enhanced knowledge and skills.
- Since team members are peers, there is a greater propensity to be adversial when inconsistencies or inadequacies are perceived, which improves the likelihood that useful team strategies will be developed and put forth.
- Delayers, debaters, procrastinators, and other people who can stop progress through the command-and-control nature of their bureaucratic posi-

tion have no place on a team, which typically would not tolerate such roadblocks to the team's work.
• Since team members are closer to the action, they have a better opportunity to identify with the team's objectives, goals, and strategies, which encourages self-motivation.

The emergence of teams has influenced the role and style of the traditional manager—who may even becoming something like a "nonmanager."[15] The nonmanager (or new manager, as labeled by this book's author) is described in Chapter 12.

CULTURAL CHANGES

Teams bring about cultural changes in the enterprise. The characteristics of a team-driven organizational culture include the following:

• Employees expect to participate in the development and implementation of strategies for the organization.
• Employees feel that their opinions are valued and that they are trusted in having access to key information on the performance of the enterprise.
• People are treated as thinking adults.
• The cultural ambience of the enterprise encourages creativity and innovation—it's OK to make mistakes on the road to positive results.
• Everyone in the organization tends to have a clear and close sight of suppliers and customers.
• The special perks—such as reserved parking places, executive dining rooms, and the like—formerly provided to senior and special people tend to be eliminated, thus adding to a culture of equality.
• Relationships among people in different specialities and at different organizational levels tend to improve as everyone recognizes that there is a high degree of interdependency among everyone and that everyone is important in making their individual contributions to the organization's success or failure.
• Everyone assumes responsibility for the quality of the processes involved in doing their work, the output of that work, and total customer satisfaction in that work.
• The crossing of boundaries within the enterprise becomes "simply the way we do things around here"—often leading to an increase in permanent

---

[15] The term *nonmanager* is taken from Brian Dumaine, "The New Non-Manager Managers," *Fortune,* February 22, 1993, pp. 80–84.

linkages with outside organizations through strategic alliances, partnerships, and joint ventures.

A key cultural characteristic of a company that uses teams is reflected in Honda of America Manufacturing, Inc., at Marysville, Ohio. Company policy encourages employees to "enjoy your work, and always brighten your working atmosphere and be ever mindful of the value of research and endeavor."[16]

CLASSIFICATION OF TEAMS

As indicated earlier, there are several types of teams found in contemporary organizations. A useful general distinction is to think of teams in the following contexts:

1. Those that create something new for the organization that did not previously exist. Project teams and product and process design teams fall in this grouping.
2. Teams that deal with problems and opportunities in the enterprise through analysis and recommendations. Task forces, audit teams, and quality assessment teams are examples of this form.
3. Teams that are not ad hoc but are a permanent part of the organizational design and exist to make or do things. Production teams, sales teams, and service teams are examples of this type of team.
4. Teams that are of a "plural executive" nature. These teams are usually found at the senior management levels of the enterprise and take the form of executive committees, management committees, or similar bodies.[17]

Although there is no such thing as a typical team, other authors have suggested that there are three broad categories of teams:

- Those that provide advice and involvement and that are essential problem-solving teams or quality circles.
- Production and service teams, which produce products or services, as in assembly, maintenance, construction, mining, and sales.
- Action and negotiation teams, usually of senior people in the organization, who deal with the top-level integration of organizational effort. Strategic planning teams, collective bargaining teams, and teams to study and make

[16] Tracy E. Benson, "Empowerment: There's that Word Again," *Industry Week,* May 6, 1991, pp. 44–52.
[17] I have added to the classification of teams suggested in Jon R. Katzenbach and Douglas K. Smith, "The Discipline of Teams," *Harvard Business Review,* March–April 1993, pp. 111–120.

recommendations for the restructuring and downsizing of the enterprise are examples of such teams.[18]

Within the context of strategic management of an enterprise, teams provide a focus for the transfer of technology in bringing about both operations and strategic change. Team management is integral to the continuous improvement of products and organizational processes, and it facilitates the resolution of organizational problems and opportunities. Teams are a transition vehicle to move from concepts (ideas) to operational and strategic initiatives, and they provide a practical means for dealing with the multidisciplinary nature of organizational change.

The continuing opportunities for team classification center around several purposeful applications of teams in the strategic management of contemporary organizations.[19] These applications and classifications include

Resource development
Development of strategic initiatives
Operational improvement
Product and process integration
Product, process, and facility capabilities

Resource development includes the creation of new resources, such as facilities or equipment, and improvement of human services for the organization. Construction projects are the best example of this type of project. Development of strategic initiatives includes those projects that promise to provide a long-term operational capability to the enterprise, such as basic or applied research projects, as in the following examples:

1. A chemical company is concentrating on new long-range international projects in small groups of technologies, among them engineering thermoplastics and pharmaceuticals. The company's strategy is to become the leading producer in the resulting products and services; the company expects each to yield market-beating earnings growth over time. The company invests heavily in projects that feed the pipeline with new projects and is prepared to absorb losses for five years or longer, at the expense of short-term gains, until profitability is reached.

2. A large systems company has found that the use of strategic alliances to share resources and technology has resulted in considerable payoffs in profitability and market share for its products. Project teams composed

---

[18] Eric Sundstrom, Kenneth P. DeMeuse, and David Futrell, "Work Teams: Applications and Effectiveness," *American Psychologist,* February 1990, pp. 120–131.

[19] This classification is paraphrased from David I. Cleland, "Project Management: The Strategic Trajectory," paper presented at INTERNET'92, Florence, Italy, 1992.

of specialists from the different disciplines of the company are used to carry out analysis of competitors. Intelligence gathering is done on competitors' products and processes and in any area of activity believed to give competitors advantages.

Operational improvement projects are initiated to improve the efficiency and effectiveness of current operations in the enterprise. For example, a team is dedicated to reengineering the order entry process of a company to improve operational effectiveness. In another company, a project is established to improve the knowledge, skills, and attitudes of salespeople to improve market penetration.

Product and process integration teams are designed to bring about the concurrent development of organizational products or services and the required organizational processes. Such projects include those described in Chapter 10, on concurrent engineering.

Product, process, and facility capabilities projects are similar to the previous classification but, in addition, concurrently provide for the total capability of designing a product and its supporting processes, including the design and construction of the facilities required to produce and support the product throughout its useful life cycle. For example, a lighting manufacturer that produces electronic ballasts (the transformers that run fluorescent lighting systems) used a product, process, and facility team to build a new $10 million plus factory in Illinois. Suppliers were awarded long-term, sole-source contracts. Working closely together facilitated the crucial element in moving fast—simultaneous design and construction of the product, the processes, and the factory. The use of a project team allowed redesign work that would have taken three weeks elsewhere to be done in two days through the project team.

SUMMARY

In this chapter, teams were described as a key means for improving the competitiveness of organizations. Examples were of teams use in contemporary settings to improve organizational performance and lead to improved competitiveness. Team benefits were described as including direct increases in productivity, quality, product/process earlier commercialization, and competiveness. In addition, teams were given credit for other improvements in organizations, ranging from enhanced motivation to improved culture in the enterprise. Finally, this chapter presented some ideas for team classification. This chapter presented the following key ideas:

• Teams are a direct and meaningful means of contributing to the efficiency and effectiveness of organizations.

- The many results that teams have produced in contemporary organizations make it clear that the use of teams is a necessary competitive strategy.
- Training is an important strategy in getting teams ready to produce meaningful competitive results.
- Unions can, and do, make important contributions to the development and implementation of a team-driven strategy in an enterprise.
- The results realized so far indicate that teams will grow in use in the future, resulting in team-driven organizational initiatives that produce important values for stakeholders.
- Teams contribute both direct and indirect results to the enterprise. While the direct results are measurable, the subtle results that improve the cultural ambience of the enterprise are important as well.
- Attitudes and the values held by people in the enterprise can inhibit or enhance the effectiveness of teams.
- Teams bring about cultural changes in an enterprise. The potential impact of these changes should be considered when evaluating a strategy to move to a team-driven organizational design.

How teams can be used in the reengineering process is the topic of the next chapter.

____7
REENGINEERING THROUGH TEAMS

People persist in believing that what has happened in the recent past will go on happening into the indefinite future, even while the ground is shifting under their feet.[1]

This chapter examines the basics of reengineering, including the use of teams as organizational designs in improving dramatically the organization's ability to compete in an unforgiving global marketplace.

Engineering may be defined as the application of scientific principles to practical ends in the design, construction, and operation of efficient and economical structures, equipment, and systems.[2] The term *reengineering* is defined by the pioneers of reengineering as "the fundamental rethinking and radical redesign of business processes to achieve dramatic improvements in critical, contemporary measures of performance, such as cost, quality, service, and speed." These pioneers also provide a quick definition of business reengineering as "starting over."[3]

The key words---*fundamental, radical, process,* and *dramatic*---have special meaning, according to Hammer and Champy:

- *Fundamental* refers to the basic questions to be asked, such as "Why do we do what we do?" and "Why do we do it the way we do?"

---

[1] George J. Church, "Forty Years of Nonsense," *Time,* January 30, 1995, p. 92.
[2] Morris, William, ed., *The American Heritage Dictionary of the English Language,* Houghton Mifflin Company, Boston, Mass., 1976, p. 433.
[3] Michael Hammer and James Champy, *Reengineering the Corporation: A Manifesto for Business Revolution,* Harper Business, A Division of HarperCollins Publishers, New York, 1994, pp. 31–32.

- *Radical* means to disregard existing structures, policies, and procedures and to invent new ways of doing work.
- *Process* is a collection of activities that takes one or more kinds of input and creates an output that is of value to the customer.
- *Dramatic* means not marginal or incremental, but quantum leaps in performance.[4] Reengineering is starting with a clean piece of paper and examining the organizational structures, departments, policies, procedures, and work processes to evaluate the efficiency and effectiveness with which work is carried out by the enterprise as it works with its key stakeholders, including customers and suppliers. Reengineering starts by asking key basic questions about the enterprise's mission, objectives, goals, and strategies:
  - What business are we in?
  - Why are we in this business?
  - Why are we working as we do?
  - Are there better ways to do our work?
  - What are the basic assumptions and policies that guide us in the work we do?
  - What can be changed in the way we do things to bring about major improvements in the way we work?
  - How can we analyze our organizational processes to gain insight into how things can be done better?

Some companies that have tried reengineering initiatives have reported success. For example, at Procter & Gamble, reengineering strategies in use since 1991 have simplified work processes and dramatically reduced the variety of its product offerings. P&G has also standardized ordering and billing across units. As a result of these reengineering strategies, the company is far out in front of an industrywide effort to take the costs out of the relationship between manufacturer and retailer.[5]

The focus of reengineering is to set aside the current ways of working and painstakingly examine the processes involved in doing the work, discovering new, innovative, and breakthrough ways of improving both operational and strategic work in the enterprise. Reengineering is a clean, fresh start—no preconceived notions, no limiting assumptions, no preexisting conditions or assumptions, no limiting factors, no shibboleths to limit imagination, creativity, innovation, and no precedents to inhibit the way people think and work. The following example of reengineering shows the potential benefits of a complete analysis of organizational processes.

---

[4] Ibid., pp. 32–36.
[5] Rahul Jacob, "Corporate Reputations," *Fortune,* March 6, 1995, p. 56.

During one of the largest process reengineering projects ever undertaken, GTE telephone operations management was stunned to find out that the administrative bureaucracy of the company was reducing productivity by as much as 50 percent. As part of its reengineering effort, GTE examined its own processes and benchmarked eighty companies in a wide variety of industries. Reengineering teams then created new concepts, approaches, policies, and procedures for the new processes. To provide incentive to the benchmarking teams, specific goals were set: (1) Double revenues while cutting costs in half; (2) cut cycle time in half; (3) cut product roll-out time by three quarters; and (4) cut systems development time in half. The company's reengineering efforts helped to integrate everything it learned into a customer value-added path.

One key result of the reengineering effort at GTE was the promotion of a cultural change—a change that promoted a sharing among employees so they would be open to any and all possibilities for improving the way they work.

At GTE, four critical components of reengineering were used:

- Executive support for reengineering through setting the example, promoting reengineering, and providing the required resources.
- Creation of a Process Reengineering department, which functioned as the owner of the methodology, assigned support workflow coordinators, and functioned as the corporate "cheerleading squad."
- Appointment and oversight of the process reengineering teams, including membership from front-line hourly employees and supervisors. In the first year, over 100 people were assigned to teams, with each team having responsibility for each process being reengineered.
- Establishment of teams of consultants to provide technical assistance and facilitation of the reengineering efforts through working with the teams.

During the five phases of process reengineering at GTE, the following were carried out:

1. There was a complete examination of how things were actually working at GTE. It was found that after investing hundreds of millions of dollars in computers, what GTE had put in place was a maze of functionally based systems that created rather than solved downstream problems.
2. The reengineering effort was carried out so that whatever savings and efficiencies existed could be harvested as quickly as possible from the process reengineering effort.
3. After identifying best practices among select U.S. companies, conceptual platforms for the new processes were created, followed by the integration of everything that had been learned during the benchmarking work.
4. The findings from the reengineering were put into practice.
5. It was recognized that full-scale implementation provides the payoff. An important part of the payoff was fostering a "mindset reengineering"

to support continuous improvement through ongoing reengineering. But the news from reengineering is not all good.

Reengineering according to Champy, is in trouble. Many reengineering efforts have fallen short of their goals; this has been caused by management. Operational work cannot be reengineered without changing the way managers do their jobs. Champy notes that radical change from reengineering is impossible unless managers know how to "organize, inspire, deploy, enable, measure, and reward the value-adding operational work."[6]

Reengineering is a relentless search for, and the implementation of, utmost changes in organizational processes to achieve bold, unprecedented results. It is not tweaking old policies and procedures, nor is it a rationale for continuous improvement. Reengineering asks the question: If this were a new organization, unfettered by traditions and established ways of doing things, how would we run the organization? Reengineering is needed for two reasons: (1) fear of competitors; and (2) a drive to do things better. Reengineering should be carried out against the major issues and organizational processes that are likely to have a major impact on the way an enterprise does business.

To reengineer is to struggle with first-hand, across-the-company changes. To initiate the process of reengineering, the strategy should be set first to avoid fixing processes that do not need repair. There should be a long, penetrating look at what business the enterprise should be in and what needs to be done to get into that business; this leads to customer-valued results. Reengineering is about the enterprise's operations, whether short term or long term.

Reengineering can have many objectives, such as cost reduction, consolidation of major functional areas, improvement of quality, faster development and commercialization of products, and strategic changes in the direction of the enterprise. For example, as part of U.S. Air's goal to achieve $500 million in annual cost reduction and revenue enhancements, a complete reengineering of the airline's maintenance, reservations, flight operations, and customer service departments is being carried out.[7] Reengineering can result in fundamental and radical redesign of major work processes. In general, reengineering will affect what the enterprise does and how it does it, and it will produce a new culture that emphasizes teamwork, the legitimacy of cross-organizational boundaries, and a philosophy of continuous process improvement. Reengineering cannot be done from the top down or from the bottom up. It must be done concurrently with top-down support and bottom-up use of teams to provide the interdisciplinary focus so essential to successful reengineering.

Reengineering of an enterprise is done in the context of making and executing operational and strategic decisions. By examining currrent operations,

---

[6] John A. Bryne, "Reengineering: What Happened?" *Business Week,* January 30, 1995, pp. 16–17. This is a review of the book *Reengineering Management* by James Champy, Harper Business, New York, 1995.

[7] *USAir Group, Third Quarter Report, 1994.*

decisions can be identified that will improve operations. The making and execution of decisions in the reengineering context is not limited to reinforcement of the conventional way of working, but rather extends to truly creative and innovative ways of doing things.

Teams take apart and rebuild every relevant process of the enterprise. As discussed elsewhere in this book, you cannot have effective teams without trust. Yet the use of teams on reengineering projects—which, by definition, evaluate and rearrange or even eliminate work—creates a paradox for workers. Means for dealing with this paradox include the following:

1. Keep the people informed as to the purpose, process, and potential outcomes—both positive and negative—of the reengineering effort.

2. Maximize the participation of as many people as possible on the reengineering team, during both the planning and execution phases of the effort.

3. Insure that those people likely to be displaced as a result of the reengineering will be provided assistance in finding other jobs either inside or outside of the organization.

4. Communicate continuously with organizational members to include careful empathetic listening to their suggestions, concerns, and viewpoints.

5. If possible, provide information on what competitors are doing on reengineering, and how their results could change market competitive patterns.

6. Tell people the truth, maintain open agendas, and share any information with them on how organizational performance will be impacted by the probable outcomes of the reengineering initiatives.

At Zeneca Agricultural Products, cross-functional teams of midlevel managers were appointed to work at getting working capital under control. In 1993, a dozen process reengineering teams drawn from the middle of the organization took the company apart—every business process from product development to order fulfillment—and converted the business from one organized along product lines to one structured by customers—corn and soybean farmers. The work of the teams was reinforced by the general manager, who spent "an unbelievable amount" of time with the teams urging them on and challenging them to do more by way of unconventional thinking about the organizational design of the company.[8]

Reengineering creates value—worth in usefulness or importance to the enterprise.

---

[8] Thomas A. Stewart, "How to Lead a Revolution," *Fortune,* October 28, 1994, pp. 54–55.

VALUE OF REENGINEERING

The powerful idea behind reengineering is that teams can be used to analyze how interdisciplinary and interfunctional processes can be assessed to determine how organizational boundaries and territorial imperatives impede the enterprise's ability to provide value to customers. Yet such teams can easily become orphans if they lack senior executive champions, who advocate the importance of organizational interfaces and integrated performance in managing the processes of value creation for customers. The use of teams means that organizational boundaries will be crossed—and this will create a modified culture. An atmosphere will prevail that it is not the work of defined organizational units per se that creates results, but rather the interfaces created out of working across disciplines and organizations. This means that the basic work of an organization takes place in two ways: (1) the technical excellence of organizational disciplines and functions, and (2) the ability to produce quality results across boundaries. Experience in successful reengineering strategies has shown that managing organizational processes without the restrictions or provincialism imposed by boundaries provides payoff in several ways:

- There will be improved customer satisfaction, for both internal and external customers.
- Problems and performance lags caused by interdepartmental barriers and problems will recede.
- There will be improvements in the enterprise's ability to attain its mission, objectives, and goals.

The payoffs to be realized through using teams for reengineering organizational processes and for managing those processes after the reengineering has been completed are meaningful. These potential payoffs are simply not available to the enterprise unless teams are used in the strategic management of the enterprise. In a sense, reengineering is a philosophy—a way of thinking about how to improve organizational performance.

REENGINEERING PHILOSOPHIES

Like other management systems and approaches, there are a few fundamental beliefs underlying the reengineering process:

1. It is recognized that the principal activities that are relevant to the delivery of value to the customer are contained in a gathering of organizational processes.
2. The development of a focal point to integrate this gathering of processes is best carried out through a team-driven organizational design.

3. Excellence in the ability to synergize and integrate business processes, including their continuous improvement, will be the critical success factor in global competition in the 1990s.

4. Teams used to develop integrated business processes, and the subsequent management of those processes through teams, will continue to be the creative and innovative way of improving quality, reducing costs, commercializing products and services sooner, and strategically managing the enterprise as if its future mattered.

5. Teams will be used as organizational design elements for operational and strategic purposes. This will cause fundamental rethinking of the perspectives of the business, eliminate departmental red tape, and focus process initiatives.

6. Computers and sophisticated information systems are creating innovative ways of providing information to decision makers that are more accurate, more timely, and more appropriate to the making and executing of decisions. Data based technology is eradicating traditional territorial attitudes about data, information, and the use of data as a strategic management tool.

7. The concept of concurrency—the ability to produce results in the development of new products and processes through the integration of organizational resources—is being translated into other enterprise initiatives, such as order entry management, inventory management, production scheduling, package labeling documentation, accounting and finance, and production flows (through the integration of equipment, tools, materials handling, manufacturing processes, and people into a paradigm of sustained superior performance).

Insight into the philosophical foundations of reengineering can be gained by a careful perusal of an article that appeared in the *Harvard Business Review.* This article described ten steps in a company's order management cycle (OMC). These steps, from planning to postsales service, are traditionally separated by departmental boundaries, whereby the order can sit unattended and the customer unattended. Ultimately, it is the order that ties the customer to the company. By examining the flow of the sales order as it moves horizontally from one functional department to another, insight can be gained into time lags and into the risk of the order "falling between the cracks." Each step in the OMC requires a bewildering mix of overlapping functional responsibilities. When the functional departments are crossed in the spirit of managing the processes of OMC, marked improvements in the efficiency and effectiveness of the OMC can result.[9]

---

[9] Benson P. Shapiro, V. Kasturi, and John J. Sviokla, "Staple Yourself to an Order," *Harvard Business Review,* July–August 1992, pp. 113–121.

Leadership of the reengineering effort is critical. It must be led by people who have the authority and visibility to oversee an organization process from end to end and from top to bottom of the enterprise. The ideal reengineering champion or advocate should be a senior executive at the business unit level. This advocate creates a first-class team of heavyweights from all relevant disciplines. Usually these heavyweights are the people whom their managers do not want to spare. Team members should also be chosen from human resources and information systems. Key leaders of the reengineering initiative can help dispel the fear, resistance, and cynicism that are inevitable as the reengineering teams begin their work—to unearth problems and opportunities and kick around strategies, often radical and bold.

The strength of reengineering is a philosophy that the process starts with a clean sheet of paper, which is then filled in by asking key questions about how and why value is created in the company. To reengineer means to wear the customers' shoes for a while. During the analysis phase of reengineering, one must be careful not to get caught up in the "analysis paralysis swamp"— spending too much time in the swamp analyzing data and procrastinating on making the hard, tough decisions about realigning organizational processes.

The point is that reengineering, properly planned and executed, holds many promises for doing things better in the enterprise.

PROMISES

The promise of reengineering is a successful search for new paradigms for the redesign and organization of work. Reengineering is not downsizing, restructuring, delayering, flattening the organization, or eliminating organizational units. Reengineering, properly carried out, can affect how the enterprise is organized, how it functions, what processes are carried out and by whom, and how certain work can be replaced with better ways of doing things. The traditional division of labor concept developed and published by Adam Smith in 1776 in his treatise *The Wealth of Nations,* which put forth the notion of breaking work into its simplest tasks and assigning each of these tasks to a specialist, lost sight of the larger objective of tracking the flow of tasks within organizational processes to create value for customers. The individual tasks and how well those tasks are carried out are important—but if these tasks are not done within the larger context of the effectiveness of the overall process, then performance and competitive abilities suffer. In the traditionally managed enterprise, processes are not emphasized; rather the focus is on specialized tasks, narrow jobs, single-skilled workers, and an organizational structure that reflects specialization and territoriality rather than processes and integration. Redefining who the customers are—both internal and external—and the nature of the integrated processes to satisfy these customers is the essence of reengineering. The promise of reengineering is inherent in the perspectives of its pioneers.

The key messages put forth by Hammer and Champy include the following:

- Managers need to abandon traditional organizational paradigms and operating policies and procedures and create new ones centered around the integration of organizational processes to do the job.
- The classical division of labor is a way of breaking work up into small units for assignment to specialists needs to be augmented with analysis of the relevant processes required to create value.
- The traditional, old ways of managing the enterprise do not work anymore. New paradigms are needed.
- The key to success in the modern organization is how the work processes and the people are aligned.
- Reengineering is a new journey, starting with a new road map.
- Reengineering asks such basic questions as "Why do we do what we do?" and "Why do we do it the way we do?"
- Reengineering is not continuous incremental improvement—it is major leaps in improvement.
- Organizational processes are the key to reengineering—traditional organizations focus on tasks, jobs, people, and structures.
- Reengineering requires that the following question be asked continually: "Who are our internal and external customers?"
- Reengineering is a new paradigm that goes beyond the traditional delayering, reorganizing, and flattening the enterprise strategies that worked in earlier days.[10]

Getting started in reengineering includes getting the teams and stakeholders organized.

GETTING ORGANIZED

The organization of the reengineering team is critical. The actual work of reengineering is done through the members of the team—both working alone and as members of the team. According to Hammer and Champy, two types of people are needed on the team. First are the insiders who currently work inside the processes undergoing reengineering. These people represent the existing processes, have been around long enough to know the ropes (but not so long that they think that the old processes make sense), and have credibility with their peers. Mavericks who know the rules and how to work the system are excellent team members. Second are the outsiders, who do not work in

---

[10] "The Promise of Reengineering," *Fortune,* May 3, 1993, pp. 94–97. This is a book review of Michael Hammer and James Champy, *Reengineering the Corporation,* HarperCollins, 1993.

the process and who can bring a higher level of objectivity to the team. These are the people who are not afraid to ask the tough and often controversial questions. Hammer and Champy suggest that a ratio of two or three to one is appropriate (insiders to outsiders). Both insiders and outsiders need to expect debate and conflict; be self-directed, creative, and innovative; be able to make discoveries; and be able to integrate and synthesize data, ideas, concepts, and processes. Team members must be comfortable with ambiguity, be able to work together in one place, and be fully committed without other jobs to be concerned about. Finally, the individual team members should be governed by their performance in contributing to the team's goals and objectives.[11]

The stakeholders involved in a reengineering effort are those who have some real or perceived claim against the things of value being created as a result of the design and execution of a reengineering effort. Although the reengineering effort is carried out through a team working with the stakeholders, other organizational units representing key principals in the reengineering effort are needed to improve the chances of the effort being successful. These principals include the following:

- *The champions:* A reengineering champion to provide leadership of an executive oversight team and to strengthen senior management's commitment to reengineering; provide the resources needed to do the job; and monitor, evaluate, and control the quality of the reengineering effort. This team does not do the reengineering but rather facilitates and coaches the reengineering team.
- *The facilitators:* Those functional and discipline managers whose cooperation and support is necessary for the reengineering strategy. Sometimes these officials will be formed into a reengineering facilitation team, whose purpose is to ensure that the teams doing the actual reengineering effort are provided the information needed, access to the people, and the general support and cooperation of the organizational units and people who are the objective of the reengineering.
- *The professionals and workers:* These people are the common denominator of the reengineering effort. Without their commitment and help, the effort will fail. Particular attention must be paid to these people, since realistically the reengineering effort will ultimately require them to rethink and redo the way they carry out their work processes. Some of these people will be reassigned, required to change the way they work, or even be a casualty and be let go from the enterprise.
- *The consultants:* Those experts who can help provide advice and counsel to the teams involved in the reengineering effort. Such experts can provide assistance to the process of reengineering—asking the right questions,

---

[11] Ibid., pp. 102–116, paraphrased.

suggesting work assignments for reengineering, and evaluating the efficacy with which the reengineering effort is being carried out.

- *The Chief Executive Officer (CEO):* This person's commitment and dedication to providing the senior leadership for the reengineering effort are paramount. The chances for any major change in the enterprise's success depend on the leadership provided by the CEO. Without such leadership, the reengineering will lose its impact or fail. The organization will be worse off for having tried to change and failed—this will be a blow to the morale and well-being of those people who sensed the need for change. James Champy believes that when you finish reengineering an organization, the few managerial jobs remaining will be (1) the process owner, (2) the coach, and (3) the leader.[12]

Using teams for reengineering promises a payoff in improvement not available through other organizational designs.

TEAM-DRIVEN REENGINEERING

First and foremost, process reengineering is a team endeavor. Since reengineering examines the manner in which products and services flow across organizational processes, an interdisciplinary team is absolutely essential that possesses the individual and collective credentials to know the technologies and key parameters involved in the reengineering of organizational processes.

The principal focus and system of operations in reengineering is the processes that must be carried out to conceptualize, design, and produce something of value for both the internal and external customers of the enterprise. In reengineering, examination of the work processes to produce something of value involves looking at both the cross-functional and cross-organizational work interfaces and what goes on in these interfaces to produce value. This is where most people begin to have reservations about reengineering—they have been educated and have worked in organizations in which their focus has been centered around work areas defined by specialization, by department, by organizational unit, and by boundaries and constraints represented in the traditional organizational chart. In fact, organizations have been able to produce results not only through the specialization of the people doing the work but through the informal working of people through the processes needed to get the job done. Reengineering has given a legitimacy to working through and across organizations to get the job done. Alternative teams provide the focus for working through and across organizational processes:

[12] Reported in "Managing Your Career," by Hal Lancaster, *Wall Street Journal,* January 23, 1995, p. 1.

- Project teams are used to work through organizational processes to design and build capital equipment and facilities.
- Concurrent engineering teams provide the means to work through organizational processes simultaneously in conceptualizing, designing, manufacturing, and marketing goods and services.
- Benchmarking teams work through processes to determine how well an organization is doing vis-à-vis its competitors and the best-in-the-industry producers.

Of the teams described in Chapter 1 (p. 10), all are characterized by their cross-functional and cross-organizational modus operandi. For the most part, reengineering efforts usually lead to the creation of teams to manage and work through interfaces to integrate organizational processes and improve operations. Many managers and workers are not literate in the knowledge and skills needed to work across lines of command and control typical of traditional organizations. Organizational processes are the collective tasks and activities needed to create value for customers. For example, the collective activities that are needed to take a customer's order, and that through organizational processes result in the delivery to a customer of the product or service and the payment for that order from the customer—all done in an orderly flow through different organizational units—are organizational processes. Traditionally, customers' orders would have been passed from department to department through a time-consuming handoff steps from one organizational unit on to other units—often with the order waiting for time and space at particular departments. As a result of organizing a team to manage the organizational processes to create customer value, several cultural changes come about: (1) Many tasks are combined into one process-directed task; (2) work is performed by those people who know best how to do the work—those people who are already doing it; (3) empowered people manage the processes and make and execute decisions; (4) since the experts are doing the work, that work tends to be done in its natural order; (5) since the teams doing the work are self-directed, checkup and monitoring and traditional control are reduced or even limited; (6) the team provides for a single point of contact to integrate the work across processes; and (7) the team leader is a single point of contact for the entire organization—a leader whose modus operandi is not restricted or limited by the territorial boundaries of disciplines, functions, or departments.

Teams established to plan for and carry out reengineering efforts are strongly committed to examining organizational processes through a philosophy of shared resources from the team member's speciality and common objectives and goals for making the reengineering a reality for the enterprise. The following are a few basics about the characteristics of reengineering teams:

- Specific and measurable goals must be established for the teams.
- The team must be committed to an overall objective for reengineering, which in turn supports the enterprise's mission and objectives.

- The team should be of a manageable size, represent the key disciplines involved, be easy to convene, and communicate and interact as a participative body of experts to evaluate organizational processes.
- The team should have a working philosophy that outlines how people will interact, how decisions will be made, how analysis will be done, and how results will be produced.
- Authority, responsibility, and accountability delineations are important and include a sense of both individual and mutual accountability to produce results. The team should have a clear consciousness of accountability and the creation of results that have meaning for the improvement of organizational processes.

To reengineer successfully means to do adequate planning for such work. An important part of planning for reengineering is to recognize the life-cycle phases of a reengineering initiative.

REENGINEERING LIFE-CYCLE PHASES

Set the Stage

The first phase is to set the stage. The team plan for reengineering is one of the most important documents in the reengineering effort. Essentials of the team plan include a document developed and signed by the CEO that establishes the rationale for the reengineering strategy, commits resources, and designates the authority and responsibility of the stakeholders (teams, champion facilitators, and so forth) who will be involved in the effort. An important part of the team plan is the documentation that sets the direction for the reengineering—an examination of the processes that will likely be reviewed in getting the effort underway. Since thinking in terms of processes rather than organizational units will be new to most people, the plan should define the rationale for reviewing processes, the scope of both individual and collective processes, and the desired and probable outcome of the reengineering initiative. Like any plan, the plan for reengineering is a road map that provides general guidance and approaches for how the reengineering will be carried out. Once the plan is developed—even in draft form—it will help put boundaries on effort and establish objectives and goals that will guide the subsequent reengineering initiatives.

Make Initial Forays

The team plan for reengineering is a living document that changes as the team's work is underway. An early first step, after the stage has been set, is to develop an understanding of how the enterprise currently operates, how it is organized, how the work is carried out, and what are the key characteristics of the existing processes. An early mapping of the existing processes is needed for the team to grasp the challenges in evaluating existing processes. In such mapping, carried out with the current experts in these processes, insight will be gained into some of the changes that might be instituted after adequate study and assessment. Another important activity to be carried out during the initial forays is to benchmark the competition and what the best practitioners in the industry are doing. Such benchmarking should get the attention of the reengineering stakeholders.

Develop the Mental Model

As the teams undergo their work in the enterprise, as they review existing processes and supporting organizational policies and procedures, and as they review the results of the benchmarking strategies and familiarize themselves with the flow of information, they can begin to visualize what the probabilities of future processes can be. The use of workshops to understand the strengths and weaknesses of the existing processes can be helpful. During this time, a lot of effort is expended to develop the databases, which provide insight into how things are currently being done in the enterprise. The mental model that is developed sets the stage for the next phase, which is to identify target project teams that will do further detailed and rigorous analysis.

Select Target Projects

In this phase, project teams are used to evaluate specific targets likely to hold promise for reengineering initiatives. For example project teams could be set up to examine the manner in which the following initiatives are currently being carried out in the enterprise:

- Order entry procedures
- Product and service development
- Procurement practices
- Design and construction of capital facilities
- Customer relations
- Manufacturing efficiency and effectiveness
- Accounts receivables
- Inventory practices
- Materials handling
- Marketing and sales management

The list of initiatives that could be examined by project teams can go on and on. Selection of the initiatives to examine depends on several criteria, including (1) potential for payoff, (2) importance to the business the enterprise is in, (3) gaps between the success of competitors and the best-in-the-industry performers, (4) known weaknesses in the enterprise, (5) relative priority in the use of enterprise resources, and (6) chances of successful implementation within a time frame consistent with operational and strategic schedules.

Contrive Strategies

After the reengineering effort has proceeded to a point at which insight into the likelihood of process improvements is possible, design strategies can be formulated for identified organizational processes that can be improved and have a good chance of being successful. This means that the analysis and insight gained by the project teams have developed to the point at which process design improvement plans can be developed. These plans are road maps or blueprints that outline the strategies and commitment of resources for producing integrated results in the reengineered enterprise. Two basic elements of these plans are (1) a design for implementation, and (2) the means for how the plans will be implemented (embellished with as much detail as needed so the chances of being successful in the implementation stage are enhanced).

Launch the Reengineered Enterprise

This phase involves launching and testing the reengineered processes and moving to full-scale implementation after the test results have been integrated into the processes. Full-scale implementation means that authority and responsibilities are changed and that new work processes have been learned and are able to produce the desired results. This period is the most dangerous time for reengineering because the enterprise is undergoing the change brought about by the reengineering of processes. Prior to this time, the impact on the people has been more conceptual than actual. The threat is real of acquiring new knowledge, skills, and attitudes and of having new authority and responsibility. People realize that things are not going to be business as usual as new personal relationships are forged and as new stakeholders, such as suppliers and customers, come into the organization. At this time, the risk is high for senior managers to falter, to fall prey to the idea that things are really not as bad as they had thought and that the current way of doing things, although in need of fine-tuning, is not so bad after all. It is easy and more comfortable for senior managers to drop the ball here. One way of avoiding this is to reexamine what the best performers in the industry are doing and how the competitors are faring.

Improve Continually

The final phase in the reengineering plan provides guidance on how the elements of benchmarking will be continued—how alternative teams will be used to augment the management of the enterprise, to reinforce the new paradigm of teamwork, and to move continually away from traditional management methods. In the reengineering enterprise, teamwork is a well-defined, effective way to conduct day-to-day management of the organizational process and make major contributions to the strategic management of the enterprise through new product and process development initiatives carried out concurrently.

Train, Train, Train

One of the major reasons for accelerated interest in training and education for employees is the need to improve the knowledge, skills, and attitudes of all employees in the new paradigm of doing business. The use of alternative teams in the enterprise, emerging new cultures, new work designs, different management styles, computer and information technology, and other changes require that enhanced training becomes a way of life in the enterprise. All employees need retraining, from the CEO to the employees who work at the lowest levels in the enterprise. As competitive changes affect the enterprise and as new paradigms of management and technical expertise come forth, training—and retraining—become critical success factors.

Successful reengineering does not come about because a lot of bright people get together and talk about how things can be improved in the enterprise. A disciplined series of phases are required to implement process reengineering.

THE RESULTS

The results of reengineering can be spectacular. At Aetna, the largest publicly traded insurance company in the United States, reengineering efforts were so successful that major changes were made in the way the company was organized and how it did business, and these changes set the stage for continual benchmarking and reengineering. Some of the major changes due to team-driven reengineering at Aetna eliminated business processes that had been followed devotedly for decades and engendered a new focus on customers. Specific changes included the following:

- There has been a reunion of personal and commercial lines of property and casualty so that sixty-five claim centers were consolidated into twenty-two regional centers, resulting in a savings of $100 million.
- A computer-based system links employees so they can order their own supplies from desktop terminals and have orders processed and paid for centrally, thus reducing the need for procurement (at a savings of $20 million). Laptop computers are now used to sign up customers on-site

and print out ID cards instantly, resulting in savings of $700,000 annually in productivity costs.

Aetna is emerging from a half century of bureaucratic gridlock. It had been organized into dozens of jealously guarded fiefdoms, some of which bore little resemblance to others. To tighten up the company's organizational design, fifteen new strategic business units were created, 5000 workers were let go, and the remaining 43,000 workers became believers in the benefits of reengineering.

The reengineering effort at Aetna was done through a mixture of team-managed small- and large-scale projects. Much of the reengineering was done around the focus of information technology, including image-processing software in Aetna's Health Plan Service Center. Aetna continues to evaluate establishing one mail center in which all claims will be opened, scanned and filed, and then sent electronically to the appropriate claim center. Customers will be able to call the center directly with their claims. In addition, Aetna is working toward having a lifetime contract with its customers.

Reengineering at Aetna has not been without pain. The technology vision to support reengineering and the company's future is clouded by technical and cultural barriers that prohibit rapid change.[13]

Union Carbide used reengineering to scrape $400 million out of its fixed costs in just three years. However, reengineering is not easy. It creates work and opens up plenty of possibilities. AT&T Global Business Communications Systems, which makes PBXs (private branch exchanges installed on the customer's premises), did the following in its two-year reengineering efforts: Rewrote job descriptions for hundreds of people, developed new recognition and reward systems, reconfigured its computer system, initiated massive retraining programs, and made extensive changes in financial reporting, proposal writing, and contracts. The company made major changes in its relationships with suppliers, its manufacturing processes, and its shipping, installation, and billing practices.[14]

A greeting card company set up over 100 people in ten cross-functional teams to review the critical parts and processes of the company that needed to be changed. Early examination by these teams established that once a concept for a new line of greeting cards was given to the creative staff for design, twenty-five hand-offs were required before the card was sent to the printing department. Ninety percent of the time, the prototype cards were resting in someone's in- or out-basket. A management committee would periodically review and pass on the work of the artists and editors. The work involved in moving from a concept to a finished product—a new line of greeting

---

[13] Glenn Rifkin, "Reengineering Aetna," *Forbes ASAP, Supplement to Forbes,* June 7, 1993, pp. 78–86.
[14] Thomas A. Stewart, "Reengineering—The Hot New Managing Tool," *Fortune,* August 23, 1993, pp. 40–48.

cards—was separated by disciplines, departments, floors, and buildings. The teams set out to reengineer the way the company did business by putting every business process under a microscope. The objectives established for the reengineering teams included the following:

- Discover how artists, editors, and other creative people work to conceive new products and how sales data are collected and used to influence new product development, marketing, and sales promotion campaigns. The teams also examined how the requirements of large, demanding retailers could be better satisfied.
- Consider how the proliferation of graphics production complexities and printing costs could be better managed with the current trend toward product proliferation. At the same time, consider how new products and promotional programs could be established that would win over wholesale buyers and retailers.
- Examine how the company could shorten the time for product commercialization to under one year from the existing two- or three-year cycle time, and at the same time develop strategies for reducing costs through continued improvements in process efficiencies and improvements in quality.

The reengineering efforts were particularly challenging to sell since the company faced no obvious crisis.[15] However, reengineering does not always work.

FAILURES

During 1994, it was estimated that American companies would spend an estimated $32 billion on business reengineering projects. Nearly two thirds of these efforts would fail. Citibank North America (N.A.) admitted that it wasted $50 million in a year-long effort to reengineer its back-office securities processing. Amoco Corporation experienced failure in its reengineering effort on two occasions—yet it learned its lessons and succeeded on the third try. The Chicago-based oil company reduced its capital-budget allocation process and staffing by a third and tied in the reengineering more closely with Amoco's business-performance planning. The earlier failures at Amoco were caused by not recognizing the interrelationship between management practices and processes. Success came when the teams working on the reengineering process projects included both line and staff managers.[16]

Most reengineering strategies fail because those doing the reengineering lack an understanding of what's involved or do not understand the true nature

---

[15] Robert S. Buday, "Reengineering One Firm's Product Development and Another's Service Delivery," *Planning Review,* March–April 1993, pp. 14–19.

[16] Bruce Caldwell, "Missteps, Miscues," *Information Week,* June 20, 1994, pp. 50–60.

of reengineering. Lack of a total commitment endangers the chances of success of reengineering. Sometimes failure can be attributed to trying to reengineer through some fine-tuning of organizational processes: The company fails to recognize that successful reengineering takes a dedicated commitment to analysis, evaluation, and selection of alternative ways of doing things. Reengineering requires that the basics of doing business are examined: organizational mission, objectives, goals, and strategies; organizational design; individual and collective roles; and management style. In addition, the company must analyze the work done, who does it, and how improvement in the performance of the work can be carried out.

At the American Express credit card division, 285 reengineering projects were initiated to move the company's credit card business closer to the goals of customers, employees, and shareholders. Of the 285 projects started, 100 were alive in the middle of 1994; the other projects were either completed or disposed of in various ways. Some projects were integrated into other projects, some were terminated because they had started with the wrong assumptions, and some had to be altered because of strategy changes within the company.

One reason for the failure of reengineering projects is that the process is used as a euphemism for downsizing or restructuring. People immediately sense that some jobs will be lost, reassignments will be given, and the organization will enter a period of change likely to affect the personal lives of the organizational members. In such situations, reengineering can lose its credibility. If senior managers waffle or fail to provide dedicated and committed involvement—passionate leadership—the effort will fail. If senior managers come across as not knowing what they are talking about or are perceived as not being committed or not knowing what they are talking about, then the reengineering effort will fail.

Reengineering undertaken at the Engelhard Corporation encountered unanticipated difficulties. Explaining the process and objectives of reengineering to the employees was easy—the hard part was getting their cooperation. People in the company were perceptive enough to recognize that the new processes and boundaries created likely meant the elimination of jobs. The work of the total quality management teams faltered when key employees became reluctant to suggest new ways of eliminating bureaucracy. The employees' reaction was understandable—they feared that their jobs would be on the line. If the reengineering suggests the use of empowered teams—as it usually does—such teams are endangered if the promise of empowerment and participation is not delivered. Employee disenchantment will follow. The most successful reengineering projects have been those that start modestly, with a small department or group that is organized properly and trained in the new approach and whose people are rewarded after reaching initial goals in the reengineering processes. Such success and consequent rewards will be recognized by the rest of the people and the chances of further successes in reengineering will be enhanced.[17]

[17] Fred E. Bleakley, "The Best Laid Plans," *Wall Street Journal,* July 6, 1993, p. 1.

Whatever the failures, persistence in planning and executing reengineering activities has rewards for the enterprise. But what about awards for the individual?

INDIVIDUAL REWARDS

Deciding to launch a team-driven reengineering strategy is the easy part. How to do it and how to win the full support and commitment of the people are major challenges. Motivating employees to encourage and support the effort depends on how much recognition and rewards the teams and the individuals who make significant contributions receive. In considering changes in the award system to recognize those teams and individuals who make significant contributions to reengineering, the following questions must be answered:

- Can the recognitions and rewards be handled through the existing compensation policies, or will a new incentive program need to be developed?
- How can the reengineering efforts—the progress that is being made—be measured? Would recognition programs rather than financial incentives make sense?
- Should all reengineering efforts be rewarded or just those that provide, or promise to provide, cost savings?
- How can a balance be kept between rewards for operational performance improvements vis-à-vis long-term improvements? Should cost reduction be a major driver of the reengineering effort? How can cost reductions that do not damage customer image and the future of the enterprise be encouraged?
- Should the reward incentives be contingent on the actual financial payback of the reengineering effort? What then are the appropriate measurements, the time frames involved, and the impact on the existing recognition and award systems?
- How will the size of the awards be determined? Will it be by a fixed percentage of salaries and wages or a flat dollar amount for all team members who have achieved overall improvements in processes?
- Who will be the decision maker regarding the awards? The line managers? The teams? Or a peer review schema?

When reengineering produces positive results for the enterprise and organizational performance improvement is realized, people will expect to share those results in some way due to their roles in formulating improved strategies. A conscious decision should be made regarding if and how individual and team awards are provided.

Once reengineering initiatives are launched, a wave of reverberations, or trigger effects, is likely to come about.

CONTINUED TRIGGER EFFECTS

As stated earlier in this book, the introduction of team-driven strategies in an enterprise has reverberations throughout the enterprise. Reengineering starts with the formation of a team to evaluate organizational processes—but it does not end there. A decision to use teams to manage the creation of products and services across organizational processes is becoming a way of life in organizations. There are profound implications in using teams for reengineering and for managing processes after the reengineering team's work is completed. After reengineering, the jobs move from being narrow work packages to work that is multidimensional. Accordingly, people must develop new knowledge, skills, and attitudes. The empowered people on the teams manage themselves—they plan for, make, and execute decisions. Traditional bosses become coaches, teachers, and facilitators—and the successful ones work hard at keeping out of the way of the empowered teams, who are making things happen in the enterprise. The organizational design centered around disciplines and functions loses its relevance—except as pertains to managing the strategic context of each discipline. Some of the more important outcomes of trigger effects include the following:

- Processes are emphasized and managed.
- Disciplines, functions, and departments become primarily organizations to maintain centers of excellence that provide a focus for operational strategic initiatives.
- Single-task jobs disappear and are replaced by multiskilled jobs.
- Training, retraining, and education become more critical and are success factors in productivity that exceed competitive standards.
- People become much less dependent on their supervisors and managers; they become empowered and think and act like managers.
- The ability to produce competitive results becomes the basis for the reward system in the enterprise.
- Organizations have much less hierarchy, are flatter, and more dependent on team-driven initiatives.
- Values change when people become empowered and work through teams; these values reduce provincialism and territory concerns and place a high value on creativity, innovation, and individual responsibility for results.
- The role of executives changes from managers to leaders, who empower, facilitate, coach, teach, and work hard at providing an environment in

which people are challenged and see a relationship between their work and the output of the enterprise.

SUMMARY

This chapter discussed the role of teams in bringing about the reengineering of an organization. Beginning with a definition of reengineering as set forth by pioneers Hammer and Champy, the following key messages were provided:

- Reengineering starts by asking several key questions about the enterprise and its mission, objectives, goals, and strategies. Reengineering seeks meaningful answers to these questions and reviews means to improve organizational performance through concentrating on organizational processes as the key to improved productivity.
- Reengineering is a relentless search for, and implementation of, the utmost changes in organizational processes to achieve bold, unprecedented results.
- Development of a philosophy of reengineering can be a valuable contribution to how one thinks and acts regarding the revolutionary potential of reengineering initiatives.
- Reengineering is a means of going from a traditional organizational design to one that emphasizes processes as the foundation of organizational performance.
- Teams can be used to explore reengineering strategies.
- Planning for reengineering initiatives can benefit from considering the likely life-cycle phases to be encountered in carrying out these initiatives.
- Reengineering is not all success and jubilation—sometimes there are failures, and those failures are often attributable to some common causes.
- Two important issues in reengineering are how individual awards are handled and how the likely trigger effects of reengineering can be felt throughout the enterprise.
- The focus of the reengineered enterprise is alternative teams as key elements in the strategic management of the enterprise. Reengineering starts—and ends—with teams.

How to design and operate self-managed production teams is discussed in the chapter that follows.

____8
SELF-MANAGED PRODUCTION TEAMS

A leader is best when people barely know that he exists.

LAO-TZU

This chapter discussed self-managed production teams. A self-managed production team (SMPT) is a team organized and dedicated to managing and creating the goods or services that are provided by an enterprise.

Another definition of SMPTs, according to the American Production & Inventory Control Society (APICS) *Dictionary,* is "generally a small, independent, self-organized, and self-controlling group in which members flexibly plan, organize, determine, and manage their duties and actions, as well as perform many other supportive functions. It may work without immediate supervision and can often have the authority to select, hire, promote, or discharge its members."[1] The term *production* is used in the sense of creating utility—the making of goods or services for human wants. SMPTs are made up of members from the same work area of the enterprise, and they have broad responsibilities and authority for planning, organizing, monitoring, and controlling the use of organizational resources to produce a product or service. These teams make decisions in such areas as task assignments, work scheduling, work design, training, equipment usage and maintenance, problem solving, worker counseling and discipline, hiring and firing of team members, and sometimes merit evaluations, promotions, and pay raises. Team members usually rotate task assignments, are paid for the additional skills in which they develop proficiency, and execute the principal functions of supervision

---

[1] *APICS Dictionary,* 7th ed., American Production and Inventory Control Society, 1991, p. 45.

formerly carried out in a traditional organizational setting by an individual called a boss.

THE ROLE OF SMPTs

SMPTs take raw materials and transform them into a product or service using hardware, software, and team members' labor. The materials include a facility, production equipment, individual and collective teamwork, and a process for creating value through the production process.

In traditional production work, management's role was to do the analytical studies needed to determine what was the best way to design the work and organize the workers. Management selected, motivated, and supervised the production workers so they followed the optimum production processes closely and competently. The workers merely executed the work and left decision making and other matters requiring judgment to the manager and staff professionals, such as industrial engineers. Production paradigms designed along these lines do not use teams. Teams are imcompatible with the philosophy of scientific management and with the command-and-control hierarchial approach.

The comparative advantage of a SMPT is in the team's diversity, capability, adaptability, and flexibility. Traditional production technology was designed to be operated by a person and not a team—hence the long production lines, on which time-and-motion strategies were developed to enable the single individual to do simple, rote work to assemble the materials coming down the production line, which led to completed products coming out at the end of the line. The existence of long production lines was an immediate and substantial obstacle to team performance, especially if the line distance was great and the noise of the machinery was substantial. The workers on the production line, like the production and the production equipment, ideally needed to be predictable and reliable and require maintenance. These linear models of equipment, facility, materials flow, and worker performance did not lead to teams as an option of organizational design choice.

Since SMPTs are from the same work area, they carry out limited cross-functional and cross-organizational work. Support from the enterprise's staff agencies, such as human resources, facilities management, procurement, logistic support, and so forth, does create the need for the SMPTs to function to a limited degree in a cross-functional context. For the most part, however, these teams are self-contained, with the members providing the knowledge and skills needed to work with the resources that are assigned to them. These teams are used in a wide variety of contexts:

- The use of self-managed production teams was instrumental in getting a plant owned by the Owens-Corning Fiberglass Corporation up and running after having been in mothballs for seven years. Seven hundred employees worked there at the height of the plant's activity in 1986, when it was closed. The plant was insufficiently automated and was closed because of high costs and the high debt taken on by the company to fend off a takeover attempt. In reopening the plant, for the first time in the company's operation, four teams consisting of fourteen people were initiated. Each team member had the same job classification, worked twelve-hour shifts, and was not unionized. The company reviewed 1480 applicants to select the teams. The selection process included having applicants write essays, take tests to determine their interpersonal skills, and attend classes to learn about Owens-Corning's vision for a high-performance organization. The teams would take over such work as security, minor maintenance warehousing, and shipping, in addition to their other responsibilities. The CEO of the company, along with the members of the board of directors, visited the plant. Senior management support for the plant included the demonstration that the plant would become a role model for manufacturing operations. Although there have been some minor start-up pains, the team-driven organization of the plant promises singular productivity records as well as greater worker satisfaction through membership on self-managed teams.[2]

- At one steel manufacturer's plant, employees are divided into 200 SMPTs. The initial objective given to these teams was to develop plans for the reduction of manufacturing costs by 40 percent. A major goal of the these teams is to eliminate 25 percent of the plant's jobs by 1995.

- At Lexmark International, Inc., a team of workers was formed to redesign the process of making a typewriter. The team produced an assembly line and process that required only an hour and quarter to make a typewriter, down from more than eight hours under IBM, which had previously owned the business. When workers need more parts, they can order them themselves. The organizational structure has been flattened so much that there are only four levels from the worker to the CEO; under IBM, the worker was eight or nine levels below the senior official. In another example of a team-driven initiative, a plan was created for a new laser-printer assembly line, and members of the SMPTs would not sign off on the new line until they worked with the industrial engineers and the line was designed to the team members' satisfaction.[3]

- At the Lyondell Petrochemical Company, managers and workers have been able to demonstrate what can be done by concentrating on speed and flexibility. The company has set new performance standards for the industry. The CEO runs an open company—teams of managers and workers tackle new undertakings and get bonuses if their ideas fly. Re-

[2] Fred R. Bleakley, "How an Outdated Plant was Made New," *Wall Street Journal,* October 21, 1994, p. B1.

[3] Paul B. Carroll, "Story of an IBM Unit that Split Off Shows Difficulties of Change," *Wall Street Journal,* July 23, 1992, P. A1.

search and development (R&D) is communal—the company has no central laboratory. Rather, teams develop R&D project initiatives and manage projects, farming out the technical details to commercial labs. A particular success story is that one team figured out how to build, at half the usual cost, a facility to make isobutylene, a chemical that will be used in the gasolines reformulated for the Clean Air Act.[4]

Teams are responsible for the whole work process in a work area of an enterprise as compared to specialized functional groups of a traditional organization. Teams are not the end but rather the means to the end of producing a product or service that will create value for the customer. Teams are managed and led by a member of the team, and often this role is rotated among team members.

One survey on the prevalence and practices of SMPTs in the northeast region of the United States found that the most frequently cited reason for team introduction was to facilitate product-quality improvement, enhance customer satisfaction, and improve productivity. The least important reason was to reduce staff and improve staffing flexibility. This same survey found that responsibility was shared between team members and the supervisor for employee discipline, performance appraisals, and budget preparation.[5]

SMPTs are like any other organizational forms: The mission, objectives, goals, strategies, organizational design, and individual and collective roles must be described. These teams are elements of a larger organizational system: the enterprise itself. Since SMPTs are an organizational unit within the enterprise, they require budgeting and funding support and access to information and other resources and must be held accountable for the results that they produce.

How teams are introduced is a critical element of organizational strategy.

INTRODUCING SMPTs

Preparing people and the organization for the use of SMPTs can be approached through several phases. The principal purpose of the first phase, called the **conceptual phase,** is to develop an information base on how such teams are used, where they are used, and the likely resistance and controversy that the introduction of teams can generate. A bibliography on the use of teams, developed at the local library, can provide insight into where and how teams are used. A visit to benchmark a few of the SMPT users will provide additional insight into some of the challenges likely to be encountered when teams are used. Additional work to be carried out during the conceptual phase includes

[4] Peter Nulty, "How to Live by Your Wits," *Fortune,* April 20, 1992, pp. 45–56.
[5] Sam T. John, "Work Teams: What's Ahead in Work Design and Rewards Management," *Compensation & Benefits Review,* March–April 1993, pp. 35–41.

the following: Senior management should communicate in clear terms to the workers that the change to SMPTs is needed to improve competitiveness; senior managers should assure the workers that every effort will be made to preserve their job security. Advising the workers that they will be expected to develop new knowledge, skills, and attitudes to serve on the teams, which will be handled through training programs in the company, should remove some of the threat inherent in the change to teams. Sharing the information about how SMPTs are used elsewhere can help soften the change to a team-driven organizational design. A final act in the conceptual phase is to organize the teams and provide them with an overall picture of authority and responsibility, duties, and where SMPTs stand in the overall production processes.

The second phase, **education and training,** is dedicated to the design of educational and training initiatives using team development that, in general, follow the examples discussed in Chapter 4. Additional instruction should be given in team building and in creating a climate conducive to teamwork by establishing a sense of common purpose among team members and by sharpening their interpersonel skills. During the team-building classes for the workers on a particular team, discussions can be focused around questions such as those indicated in Chapter 4. These questions can prompt a lively discussion of how the teams can be expected to work as an integrated, effective organizational design for improving production capabilities.

At the end of the education and training phase, the **gaining commitment** phase is entered. The teams have already been organized and have received training in the technical, social, and managerial context of their work. Although they have already started their work on the teams, they need additional guidance on how they will operate, how the work will be done, and how they will carry out both their technical and their managerial responsibilities. It is during this phase that they work together to become an integrated, effective, high-performance team that works as an integral production unit in the enterprise. During this phase the teams

- Build and maintain the communications networks and information systems required to do their job.
- Develop a high level of esprit de corps within the team through better understanding of how individual and collective roles can be carried out in a synergistic manner.
- Develop the policies and procedures needed to do the team's work.
- Solidify their roles as technologists and managers in the creation of value for customers.
- Develop and propogate a cultural ambience in the team that encourages ongoing improvement of production processes through the active participation of all team members.
- Work with the first-level supervisors in helping those individuals understand how their new role departs from the traditional boss role to one

of being a teacher, consultant, or mentor, whose principal purpose is to provide the resources and environment and then get out of the way of the team's work.

The final stage is one of **steady-state operation,** in which the use of teams becomes a permanent part of the strategy for the management and performance of production processes. The management system for the manufacturing organization has been fully integrated into the management system for the teams, and the use of teams has become sufficiently institutionalized—meaning that everyone accepts teams as simply "the way we do things around here." The teams are actively involved in a strategy of continuous improvement of their work and the management of that work. Performance evaluation schemas reflecting merit evaluation, promotion, and pay have been modified from the individual to some combination of both the individual's performance and the performance of the team. Other teams in the enterprise, used for such purposes as reengineering, benchmarking, capital project management, and concurrent engineering initiatives, are recognized along with SMPTs as key elements in the strategic management of the enterprise.

A common question that is raised is the issue of why the use of teams is being considered. In other words, what changes in production philosophies and processes make SMPTs an attractive organizational design for production excellence?

WHY SMPTs?

The primary reason for advocating the use of SMPTs is that the people doing the work know the most about how the work should be done. Employers are beginning to realize that an organization's real strength is not the equipment, buildings, or money but rather the people who, when empowered, can manage themselves and the work that they perform. The growing severity and complexity of global competition has prompted the need to develop new and innovative strategies for improving productivity, cutting costs, and improving quality. Companies that have initiated production teams have found that the people working on teams can make manifold improvements in the way manufacturing is carried out. Success in the use of advanced manufacturing systems technology depends on how well the people are integrated into the manufacturing operation. One study of the integration of people into advanced manufacturing technology found that failure in using such technology can be attributed to inadequate attention to the human element involved in technology implementation efforts.[6] A study of 160 *Fortune* 500 manufacturers indicated that seventy believed that the primary problem in implementing technology was people

[6] Christopher A. Chung, *Human Issues in Technology Implementation Management Simulator,* Ph.D. diss., University of Pittsburgh, 1995.

and organizational constraints.[7] In another study, 759 senior executives of manufacturing firms concluded that "world class companies understand that the major impediments to the adoption of technology in manufacturing are not technological, but are, instead, human related."[8]

The use of SMPTs provides an organizational design and the opportunity to develop a cultural ambience that encourages and facilitates the fullest integration of knowledge, skills, and attitudes in the production function. By using SMPTs, the chances are increased that an enterprise can take advantage of the creativity and innovative ideas that workers contribute toward improved manufacturing processes. Production teams are growing in popularity because manufacturing executives are recognizing that their use can facilitate more effective integration of people into manufacturing effectiveness and efficiency. Table 8–1 provides insight into the benefits of SMPTs versus traditional production systems (TPSs).

SMPTs are characterized by a team-driven culture, whereas a traditional production system's culture is driven by management using traditional bureaucratic command-and-control management philosophies and processes. Thus, moving from the traditional production systems operation to one using teams is a major and systems-related change. In some companies, the transition has been reasonably smooth. In others it has been a bumpy, emotionally wracked experience. Overly Manufacturing joined the growing numbers of companies

TABLE 8–1 SMPTs versus TPSs

SMPTs	TPSs
Team-driven culture	Individual-driven culture
Multiskilled members	Single-skilled workers
Team purposes	Individual purposes
Team commitment	Manager commitment
Shared resources, results, and rewards	Individual results and rewards
Focus on entire work area	Narrow specialization
Limited levels of hierarchy	Many hierarchial levels
Shared information	Information limited
Rotating leadership	One leader/manager
Team controlled	Manager controlled
Teams execute management functions	Managers execute management functions
Teamwork as a way of life	Limited teamwork
Process-driven	Function-driven
Continual self-appraisal	Limited self-appraisal
Customer-driven	Task-driven

[7] Anthony J. Frisca, "Systems Integration: What It Is. What It Isn't," *Automation,* October 1990, p. 38.
[8] John H. Sheridan, "The New Luddites?" *Industry Week,* February 19, 1990, pp. 62–63.

that were using SMPTs—the use of which caused major problems and challenges. Overly's managers recognized that the traditional authoritarian, nose-to-the-grindstone culture could not accommodate the growth needed to compete with foreign competition. The company broke with tradition and started giving workers monthly sales figures and quarterly financial reports to help them understand the deep trouble the company was in. An SMPT was appointed to develop and implement the company's new, low-cost method for making sound-retardant doors. Team members found ways to eliminate piles of metal that were taking up floor space. Suddenly everyone had ideas and suggestions—but managers perceived that the company was spiraling into self-managed anarchy. Problems that were blamed on the move to SMPTs included the following:

- Supervisors became critical of the teams' authority and responsibility.
- Relationships with the steelworkers' union became complicated—the union officials felt that they had been left out of the development of strategies for the change.
- Production planning got more complicated because of an increase in the number of people providing input to the planning processes.
- Little praise was given to those teams that were able to produce results—thus, team members began to believe that management did not care.
- Team members began to have doubts about the commitment of senior managers to teams, and they were vocal in expressing their doubts to anyone who would listen.
- Subtle warfare emerged—information that needed to be logged into computers on the production floor was not available. It took months for management to find out that the information was being hidden by disenchanted workers.
- Little or no feedback was provided to the teams on the suggestions that they had made for the improvement of operations.
- Older workers became open adversaries, resisting the pressure to learn several jobs in a team's area of work.
- Too many workers felt that a culture still existed in which people were told to "sit down, shut up and do what I tell you."
- The most vivid disenchantment came when team members realized that the chaos due to the unsuccessful attempt to install teams had no end in sight—that improvement of productivity and quality was not a one-shot effort undertaken by teams but rather was a long-term strategic challenge to be carefully initiated and orchestrated.[9]

An early task to be undertaken in the use of SMPTs is to develop an understanding of the organizational design for teams.

[9] Marc Levinson "Playing With Fire," *Newsweek,* June 21, 1993, pp. 45–47.

THE ORGANIZATIONAL DESIGN

SMPTs are not ad hoc, but are a permanent part of the organizational design of the enterprise and exist to make or do the things that support the enterprise's production function and thus deliver value to both internal and external customers. Production teams and service teams are examples of SMPTs. Other teams are ad hoc, such as benchmarking teams, reengineering teams, and concurrent engineering teams.

SMPTs typically consist of from five to fifteen workers from the same area of production. These teams are empowered for such matters as task assignments, scheduling, training, work methods, quality, maintenance, problem solving, and utilization of opportunities. Evaluation of performance, assessment of risks, and sharing of resources, results, and rewards are characteristics of the teams that are the most successful in bringing improvements to work areas.

The rationale for establishing SMPTs includes expectation of improved quality, productivity, service, and satisfaction. Greater flexibility in the use of people in the work area, reduced costs, faster response to change, and fewer, simpler job classifications are expected when teams are properly designed and used. Since individual members feel a greater sense of belonging and pride in the team's work, being a contributing member of an SMPT appeals to personal values, which helps attract and retain the best people.

The best SMPTs feel a strong sense of empowerment as they manage themselves, beginning with establishing their mission, objectives, goals, and strategies. As these teams manage themselves, they are expected to evaluate their own performance and coordinate with other teams and other organizational units across functions and organizations, such as suppliers and customers. The best teams develop themselves, encouraging individual members to seek technical, social, and leadership training as needed. Procurement authority is a key responsibility of the best teams in producing a product or service. Motivated and well-organized teams working in a supportive culture assume responsibility, seek new and ongoing challenges, and discipline themselves, winnowing out those persons that are not supportive or contributing to the team's purposes. In a growing number of situations, SMPTs hire and train new members.

Members of the SMPT should represent the disciplines involved in an area of production. An SMPT set up for continuously developing the planning for manufacturing could include the following work areas:

- Manufacturing or production specialist
- Manufacturing engineering
- Information systems
- Quality
- Procurement

- Human resources
- Industrial engineering
- Facilities
- Marketing/sales
- Computer technology
- Accounting/finance
- Union steward
- Scheduling
- Safety

Depending on the type of SMPTs, these functions could change.

SMPTs perform a wide variety of management and administrative duties in their area of work:

- Design jobs and work methods.
- Plan the work to be done and make job assignments.
- Control material and inventory.
- Procure their own supplies.
- Determine the personnel required.
- Schedule team member vacations.
- Provide backup for absentees.
- Set goals and priorities.
- Deal with customers and suppliers.
- Develop budgets.
- Participate in fund planning.
- Keep team records.
- Measure individual and team performance.
- Maintain health and safety requirements.
- Establish and monitor quality standards and measures.
- Improve communications.
- Select, train, evaluate, and release team members.

A few SMPTs do their own hiring. Prospective team members are interviewed by the professional from human resources, the manager concerned, and representatives of the teams. Other companies have experimented with having a team composed of representatives from the union, the SMPTs, and first-level supervisors do the hiring. However, having the teams do the hiring takes them away from their teams' work. Some companies allow the teams to interview job applicants and offer recommendations—with the final decision left to the managers and human resource specialists. Teams can be more concerned with getting immediate help and may tend to neglect the long-term suitability of the new hire. However, many companies that have tried hiring by teams believe that it is worth the efforts because it brings someone aboard who not only has the right qualifications but is more likely to fit into the social context of the team. Will team-based hiring grow in use? Perhaps, but not quickly because companies continue to experiment primarily with team-driven production strategies.

Asea Brown Boveri (ABB), a large multinational organization composed of more than 1000 companies, uses SMPTs as key organizational design units to improve production operations. At the company's plant in Vaesteras, Sweden, a center manufacturing team was established to be responsible for the entire order process of a product, from the first customer contact to invoicing. Supported by cross-functional training and contemporaneous electronic data processing (EDP) software, the team reduced order cycle time by more than 90 percent, resulting in higher levels of customer satisfaction.[10]

In cellular manufacturing, equipment and workers are organized by product or service rather than by similar skills needed and possessed. In production work, SMPTs are grouped by manufacturing cells of the production process. The team is organized to be cross-trained in the cell from start to finish, so the team's flexibility can help when production bottlenecks arise.

At Rohn and Haas in Kentucky, 10 to 15 percent of team members' time is spent in training. At the Saturn plant in Spring Hill, Tennessee, team members spend twelve days each year in ongoing training and education. At Saturn, the core courses for the teams are conflict management and team dynamics. Each of these core courses is designed to help people let go of their traditional thinking.

At the Packard Electric Division of General Motors, the design and development of self-directed management teams is shared between management and union representatives. The use of teams at this division has helped profitability because the production work is being done better and because costs that do not directly add value to the product (such as supervision) are being removed. At Packard Electric, a facilitator or team leader performs thirteen functions, which would have been carried out in a traditional area by nine different job classifications. Team leader responsibility rotates monthly, and each team member is required to accept the assignment.[11]

At the Somanetics Corporation, SMPT members vote on bonuses ranging from gift certificates to vacations for top-achieving peers. The company periodically provides group awards, including cash and company-sponsored events. At the Saturn Corporation, individuals are not evaluated individually; rather, team evaluations are given. Teams at Saturn can impose sanctions on problem workers, including three-day suspensions. At the Perkins-Elmer Corporation,

[10] "World Class Quality: The Challenge of the 1990s" (advertisement), *Fortune*, September, 23, 1991.

[11] "Minnesota Group Studies Social System," *Direct Connection*, Packard Electric Division, Warren, Ohio, March 4, 1993, p. 14.

peer pressure is sufficient to motivate team members. Corning, Inc. has found that team members judge each other more critically than managers would. At six hospitals managed by Quorom Health Resources Inc., employees collect feedback on their performance from customers and co-workers and then discuss the findings with supervisors.

Some organizations have always depended on SMPTs to do their production work. Mary M. Tjosvold, CEO of Mary T. Inc., a 600-employee Minneapolis company that provides residential social services for people with disabilities, believes strongly in the use of SMPTs because she realizes that employees have the most power in running a business. She has always managed with teams, has never had a hierarchy, and uses an organizational chart designed to put the clients in the center with the teams revolving around them.[12]

SMPTs cause changes throughout the production function.

THE CHANGE FACTOR

At Motorola, total customer satisfaction teams are empowered to make changes in production or other work procedures. Bonuses are paid when defect rates or cycle times are improved. SMPTs compete with one another for gold medals in companywide performance contests. Training has been extensive—Motorola spent $70 million teaching employees techniques for identifying and fixing production problems. Teams work with vendors— Motorola requires the same rigorous standards from vendors as are imposed on the company's own production work.[13]

The use of SMPTs causes many changes in the manner in which production activities are planned, organized, and controlled. Other changes brought about by these teams affect the culture of the production environment: There is an increase in the education level of the work force, and there are heightened expectations of working conditions and the manner in which the work is carried out.

Changes in an enterprise's production environment that affect the planning and execution of manufacturing systems technology include the following:

- Increased performance levels of workers
- Increased expectations of the work force in terms of added economic, social, and psychological benefits
- Growing use of strategies to encourage worker participation in the design and execution of their work—and increased worker influence over the cultural ambience in which work is carried out

[12] Bradford McKee, "Turn Your Workers into a Team," *Nation's Business,* July 1992, pp. 36–38.
[13] G. Christian Hill and Ken Yamada, "Staying Power," *Wall Street Journal,* December 12, 1992, p. A1.

- Added use of computers and information technology
- Changes in the role of the traditional first-level supervisor or boss brought about by the aforementioned factors

Traditionally, the first-level supervisor has been responsible for the following duties:

- Counseling and guiding employees
- Planning, scheduling, programming, and rescheduling
- Managing performance and evaluating worker performance, including merit assessments and changes in financial rewards for the workers
- Ensuring product quality
- Handling safety management
- Maintaining housekeeping of the production area
- Recruiting, selecting, and training workers
- Ensuring that equipment is operational
- Monitoring and facilitating production processing and product fabrication and assembly

However, in factories that use SMPTs, the first-level supervisor becomes increasingly dependent on the actions of teams. Developing communication networks with teams and with other stakeholders becomes a major responsibility of the supervisor. Other key responsibilities of the role of the new first-level supervisor include the following:

- Determining training requirements and providing for the training to be carried out for those people who need it
- Handling team and employee development
- Facilitating team problem solving
- Coordinating communication with team and other stakeholders
- Facilitating change at the production level
- Understanding enough of the technical side of manufacturing to be able to ask the right questions and know if the right answers are being given
- Facilitating meetings
- Resolving conflicts
- Providing an environment that facilitates motivation
- Providing leadership of people in their area of responsibility
- Monitoring
- Teaching

Not all teams work—some fail. SMPTs do not always work as intended. Failure is caused by lack of management commitment to the change process needed to go from a traditional organizational design to one using teams. Management impatience, inadequate empowerment, and the lack of an adequate budget and time allocation for training team members and team leaders are other reasons for failure. In addition, sometimes failure occurs if there are faulty management practices used in the enterprise, if the company faces a declining market, or if the team attempts to use too much technology or the wrong technology.[14] Other reasons for failure include the following:

- There is inadequate information to do the work.
- There is cultural resistance to the use of teams—people prefer to do things the way they have always been done.
- There is fear of an unknown outcome of teams in regard to the individual, the culture of the enterprise, and the ability of the enterprise to produce a product or service.
- Individuals are unable to change from the traditional style to the team way of doing things.
- Teams are perceived as a threat to existing managers since the teams are likely to undercut and devalue managerial responsibilities—with the threat of blurring authority, responsibility, and accountability.
- People believe that teams depreciate relationships between managers and subordinates.
- Unions may oppose teams since teams are likely to shift their allegiance from the unions to the company.
- Although the concept of teams may look great, major problems will arise in execution that cannot be solved without a major loss of production performance.
- Empowered SMPTs will not work unless the managers are willing to share control—an unlikely concession on the part of most managers.
- Teams often are launched in a vacuum, with little or no training or support, no changes in the design of the work of the team members, and no new supporting systems, like E-mail, to facilitate communication.

As one author has suggested, experience shows that some or all of the following are contributing causes of team failure:

- Lack of an articulated, clear work-team vision
- Lack of management commitment to make the rewards program work in the team ambience
- Lack of a champion to lead team development
- Insufficient employee involvement in the design of strategies for the teams

[14] Fisher, Kimball, *Leading Self-directed Work Teams,* McGraw-Hill, Inc., New York, 1993, pp. 10–28.

- Inability to overcome resistance to change
- Inadequate training resources
- Poor planning and execution
- Unreasonable expectations for a short-term payback
- Untimely initiation of pay-system changes[15]

Managers who envision designing, developing, and using teams should develop strategies that avoid the reasons for team failures.

The change in production strategies that calls for the use of teams is due in part to changes in the technology of production activities.

TEAMS AND TECHNOLOGY

American manufacturers that want to take advantage of the systems technology of the digital factory, where computers are linked to production equipment, have much of the stage set for them. The companies best suited for digital manufacturing techniques have broken themselves into smaller units or manufacturing cells, have flattened the bureaucracy, and have organized workers on the production floor into SMPTs with real decision-making and execution empowerment. In factories using digital manufacturing, the traditional steps of manufacturing—conception, design, tooling, manufacturing, distribution, and field maintenance—have been telescoped radically. The pioneers in digital manufacturing have insisted that product designers, process developers, computer specialists, and automation engineers all work together in the same laboratory. The SMPTs of knowlegeable and skilled workers are what is making the digital factory a success. The seminal thinkers in manufacturing are teams of people.[16]

At the IBM plant in Charlotte, North Carolina, SMPTs build twelve products at once—hand-held car-code scanners, portable medical computers, fiber-optic connectors for mainframes, and other products. Each member of the team is surrounded by kits of parts that people in a nearby parts cage have assembled to match production orders. Each team member has a computer screen hooked into the factory network that displays an up-to-the-minute checklist of the parts that will be installed on the product in front of him or her and will guide the assembly steps. When the team member finishes, he or she punches a button and the computer system moves the product via conveyor to the next team member's bench.[17]

---

[15] Sam T. Johnson, "Work Teams: What's Ahead in Work Design and Rewards Management," *Compensation and Benefits Review,* March–April 1993, pp. 35–41.
[16] Gene Bylinsky, "The Digital Factory," *Fortune,* November 14, 1994, pp. 92–107.
[17] Ibid.

Successful teams have increased expectations for changed performance awards.

MEASURING TEAM PERFORMANCE

As the use of teams grows in the enterprise, sooner or later it will become apparent that traditional pay programs based on a fixed hourly rate, individual piece-rate incentives, or individual merit will no longer function adequately in the SMPT environment. Alternative reward solutions will need to be examined, such as (1) profit sharing, (2) gains sharing, (3) skill-based pay, and (4) team incentives. There is substantial experience in administering the first three solutions. The use of team incentives is a pay method designed to deliver a uniform reward based on the achievements of the team as an entity. The interdependence of the team members, the opportunity for team contributions, the solving of problems, and the exploiting of opportunities provide the basis for a team-based compensation system. The challenges to using a team-based pay system include overcoming worker and supervisor resistance, finding the right performance standards, and measuring progress in attainment of that standard. It is important to assign accountability for work processes and results expected and reward both individual and team contributions. The basic differences between work groups and teams is that work groups emphasize individual performance and teams rely on the performance of the combined efforts of team members.

SMPTs need different performance measurement standards to evaluate their performance. Traditional measurement systems follow what goes on within a function or discipline, not what goes on across functions and organizations, or even between suppliers and customers. Team-based performance measurement strategies monitor and evaluate what goes on across organizational boundaries that produces a given result—usually the integration of organizational activities within a distinct process, such as order entry, sales management, production integration, and so forth. The means developed to measure team performance should help the team assess its performance—an important responsibility of the team leader and its members who belong to an SMPT. Whatever system is used, the teams should play a major role in its development, including the negotiations likely to be carried out in getting the system accepted by key managers. Since the team exists to deliver value across functions and organizations, means to track progress across boundaries that contribute to the delivery of a product or service must be developed. Usually these measures are few in number, directly related to the product or service being created. Management should create the context for the teams but not stipulate the measures. That is the job of the team, and when the measures are developed and approved by management, they will be better accepted by the teams.

Part of developing measures to evaluate team performance is to achieve joint agreement between management and the team regarding how and when the team's performance will be reviewed. The team and management should agree on the parameters of team review, including designation of those boundaries that would trigger further extraordinary review—such as increased costs, schedule delays, or quality problems with the output of the production process.

SMPT POTPOURRI

A clear advantage of using teams in the design and execution of initiatives for an enterprise is that such teams can effectively bypass the bureaucracy of hierarchial organizations. The evidence is clear that teams can enhance an enterprise's ability to remain competitive in the constantly changing global marketplace. Teams are rapidly on the increase as a form of organizational design for getting people to work together in the workplace. Teams that are effective exhibit several common characteristics regardless of the type of team or the organizational context in which they are used: a clear vision and mission statement, expected behavioral guidelines, specific objectives and goals, and performance standards. A clear definition of authority, responsibility, and accountability, coupled with means to develop and use feedback to evaluate performance, are key factors.

As young adults enter the work force, they will be expected to understand teamwork and serve as members of alternative types of teams. Concurrent with experience on these teams, they will be subject to different styles of management than their parents were. Since many teams are self-managed, there will be limited opportunities for entering the management career field— except for the opportunity to serve as a team leader or facilitator. Advancement for these young people will be based on their ability to develop multiple skills and to serve as contributing members of teams, as well as their individual competency and their contribution to the team's objectives.

As people from different disciplines with different backgrounds serve on these teams, creative and innovative team results will ensue—if such diversities are respected and welcomed in the organizational culture. People from different disciplines and backgrounds should be encouraged to conform to the team's needs, but at the same time they should seek opportunities to suggest improvements in the team's operation that spring from their diverse backgrounds. Team management philosophies will need to be as diverse as the team members yet still be directed to attaining the common objectives and goals of the enterprise. Team leaders and team members will have to recognize and overcome their personal prejudices and realize that being different does not preclude contributing to a team.

Trust is the single most important variable in creating an environment that facilitates team success. Trust is crucial because getting people with different backgrounds, morals, ethics, and characters to cooperate is a major undertaking.

At some companies, production workers are called associates or some such term, which distinguishes them from the traditional worker classification. Production associates are part of a unique culture that emphasizes team performance, equality, self-determination, and a sharing of authority, responsibility resources, results, and rewards. The hallmark of a team-driven culture includes the belief that lots of good ideas are needed to winnow out a few good ones that will improve the competitiveness of the enterprise. In such a culture, people are willing to put forth many ideas—even ones that seem strange—in the belief that a few ideas will survive analysis and help improve the enterprise. People believe that many diverse ideas will emerge, and they will gravitate to those people who are willing to listen and who can do something about the idea. An ambience of equality prevails, with managers and workers eating at the same tables in the cafeteria, with no reserved parking spaces (except for visitors), and with an abiding belief that the person doing the work on the production floor knows what is best for the production process at the time. A reduced number of managers often turns over significant decisions to workers—such as how production equipment is laid out to accommodate a production change. Although many of the workers on SMPTs are not classified as management, they are actually doing managerial jobs. Technical, managerial, and social training is provided to prepare workers to work on SMPTs.

The use of teams in the design and execution of organizational strategies is headed in the direction that all new innovations eventually go—toward institutionalization. Teams will become the dominant and natural organizational design and will be taken for granted in future organizations. Managing teams will be less challenging than it is today. Integrating team results into organizational results will continue to be a major challenge and responsibility for senior managers. The enterprise will become a constellation of teams, each having its particular purpose and tied together into a team-driven organization that manages change through team-driven strategies. Organizational managers will be caught up in facilitating and providing resources for the teams and in integrating the output of the teams in a strategy for the enterprise.

Any executive considering using SMPTs would benefit from reviewing the NUMMI Experiment—a remarkable change from a traditional to a team-driven manufacturing plant.

THE NUMMI EXPERIENCE[18]

In Fremont, California, a GM–Toyota joint venture called New United Motor Manufacturing Inc. (NUMMI) replaced what was once the General Motors

---

[18] There have been many studies of the NUMMI experience in turning a traditional plant into a world-class manufacturing facility. I have chosen to draw from one of these studies by Paul S. Adler, "Time-and-Motion Regained," *Harvard Business Review,* January–February 1993, pp. 37–107. This article is based on a two-year study of the New United Motor Manufacturing Inc. plant in Fremont, California.

Assembly plant at the same location. The original plant opened in 1961 and manufactured GM trucks and Chevrolet Malibu and Century cars. The original plant was organized along traditional lines, with more than eighty industrial engineers who established assembly line norms that were imposed on the work force. Over the years, the original plant became what one manager called "the worst plant in the world," for the following reasons:

- Productivity was one of the lowest of any GM plant.
- Quality problems were extreme.
- Drug and alcohol use was rampant both on and off the job.
- Absenteeism was so high that 20 percent more employees were employed just to have an adequate work force available on any given day.
- The local United Auto Workers (UAW) union had a national reputation for militancy.
- From 1963 to 1982, wildcat strikes and sickouts closed the plant four times.
- A backlog of 5000 unresolved grievances often existed.

Finally, in 1982 GM closed the plant.

In February 1983, GM and Toyota reached an agreement in principle to produce a version of the Toyota Corolla, renamed the Nova, at the Fremont plant. Toyota's production system and GM's marketing and sales system would be used, with Toyota taking on responsibility for product design, engineering, and daily operations. Called NUMMI, the two companies' objectives were complementary. GM wanted to learn the Toyota production system, and Toyota wanted to defuse the trade issue by building cars in the United States as well as learn about American union labor.

In September 1983, NUMMI and the union signed a letter of intent recognizing the UAW as sole bargaining agent for the NUMMI work force. Rehiring for the new plant would be from a majority of the GM workers that had been laid off. The UAW agreed to support the new Toyota production system and negotiate a new labor contract. Hiring procedures were as follows:

- Every applicant would go through three days of production simulation, written examinations, discussions, and interviews.
- Managers and union officials jointly evaluated applicants for the hourly jobs, team leaders, and team members.
- The union took part in selecting certain managers.

Over the next twenty months, 2200 workers were hired—85 percent from the old GM Fremont work force. The new work force was diverse—26 percent were Hispanic, 20 percent were black, and 15 percent were female. The first group of 450 team leaders and the entire NUMMI management team attended a three-week training program to prepare them for the new team-driven production management system, which included the basic philosophy of expecting employees to work harder and smarter. Early experience with the team-driven work force included favorable results:

- Absenteeism dropped to a steady 3 percent to 4 percent.
- Substance abuse dropped to a minimal problem.
- Participation in the plant suggestion system rose dramatically to 92 percent in 1991.
- Over the course of eight years, only 700 grievances had been filed.
- Morale surveys indicated that employees were either satisfied or very satisfied.

The cultural and production system at NUMMI changed so dramatically for a few reasons:

- Unemployment due to plant closure produced cooperation at the new plant.
- Troublemakers may have been weeded out in the rehiring process.
- NUMMI uses a comprehensive socialization process to instill a new set of values in the new work force.

The socialization process altered the attitudes of both workers and managers. Special parking spots and eating facilities for managers and workers were eliminated, and an identical dress code of uniforms for everyone was introduced. But something else happened as well. Workers were personally welcomed to NUMMI and became part of a finely tuned, superbly integrated production system that included the following:

- Just-in-time assembly line operation was initiated.
- Each assembly line station had quality assurance responsibility.
- A policy of *Kaizen,* or continuous improvement was instituted on the assembly line.
- Workers made suggestions to improve operations, and managers listened attentively and acted on those suggestions.
- Workers received cross-training for all production team assignments, which permitted them to shift from one task to another.
- Planned production leveling eliminated variation in assembly schedules.
- Management was committed to the social context in which work was performed.
- An atmosphere of trust and common purpose was sought constantly.
- Consensus around important decisions was established carefully.

The basic production organizational design at NUMMI was approximately 350 teams of five to seven people with a team leader. Four teams comprised a group, led by a group leader, who was considered the first level of management. Above the production teams were all the workers, team leaders, managers, engineers, and staff in the plant as well as NUMMI's suppliers. Toyota leadership wanted workers to know that the company was not the property of managers, but of everyone else—with the primary purpose of managers supporting production teams. Job classifications at NUMMI were only two, compared to eighteen at the original GM Fremont plant. At the GM plant, eighty hourly pay rates existed—at NUMMI, all production workers got the same hourly rate, except for the team leaders, who got an extra 60 cents. The Toyota approach to work standardization was done by team members, who used stopwatches and learned the techniques of work analysis, description, and improvements. Team members worked together in doing job design that would lead to standardization. Some of the benefits of work standardization at NUMMI include

- Improved quality standards
- Improved safety
- Easier inventory management
- Easier job rotation
- Flexibility, because workers began to act like industrial engineers
- Greater worker control, because they know best how to do the work
- Continuous improvement of production processes
- The development of each work station as an inspection unit and a center for innovation
- A cooperative and dynamic work force.
- A culture in which excellence is a way of life and trust and respect evoke a positive response from workers

As the cutural ambience at NUMMI improved and a world-class work force emerged, the trust and respect given to workers prompted them to find ways to reciprocate. Other characteristics of the culture included the following:

- Workers were able to order supplies without management approval.
- Decisions were made by a broad and horizontal consensus, which included widespread communication among everyone.
- The middle manager exercised authority, which was based on experience, mastery, and the ability to coach.
- Problems and opportunities regarding production became more visible.
- The power of workers and managers was increased in a rewarding, reciprocal manner.

Production capability became the business of everyone at NUMMI. The union served not only the workers' best interests, but also the larger strategic objectives of the business. The experiences at NUMMI highlighted the need to reinforce continuously a team-driven philosophy throughout the management hierarchy. An ongoing strong voice from the production floor was needed to keep the team-driven production system functioning properly. Finally, it was recognized that team-driven production strategies would fail if the teams and everyone else did not get the proper training and if there were not a cultural environment that supported the active participation of teams in both the technical and managerial aspects of manufacturing productivity.

SUMMARY

In today's globally competitive environment, manufacturers have experimented with innovative strategies to utilize people better in production work. SMPTs have brought about marked improvements in production efficiency and effectiveness. Today's factories require an organizational design that facilitates bringing people into a better focus for working together to produce products and services. SMPTs provide an organized focus dedicated to creating and managing the goods or services that are provided by the enterprise.

This chapter provided an overview of how SMPTs are organized and how they manage themselves to provide manufacturing systems technology for producing a product or service. Some of the major lessons of this chapter include the following:

- The comparative advantage of using an SMPT is diversity, capability, adaptability, and flexibility in using resources for the production function.
- The introduction of SMPTs in the production strategies of an enterprise requires careful preparation and prudent implementation.
- The basic reason for using SMPTs is that the people doing the production work are likely to know the most about how the work should be done— and, given the opportunity, they can manage themselves in doing that work.
- Specific methods need to be developed for measuring team performance and translating that performance into appropriate rewards for the teams and their members.
- The NUMMI experience is a remarkable story of how a traditionally managed auto plant failed and how a renaissance was fostered in this plant that made it successful. The use of teams, aided by a supportive culture, made NUMMI a hallmark of manufacturing excellence.

In the next chapter benchmarking teams will be presented.

___9
BENCHMARKING: USING TEAMS TO COMPARE

If you want things to stay as they are, things will have to continuously change.

THE LEOPARD, THOMAS DI LAMPEDUSA GIUSEPPE

This chapter discusses the essentials of the science and art of benchmarking. The purpose is to put benchmarking in the context of a process that can be carried effectively by a team—an interdisciplinary organizational design to facilitate the process of comparing the enterprise with competitors and with the best-in-the-industry performance. Only the key basics of benchmarking are discussed in this chapter. Footnote references in this chapter provide more detail on how these basics can be made operational in the design and execution of benchmarking strategies.

WHAT IS BENCHMARKING?

Webster's defines benchmarks as a surveyor's mark . . . of previously determined position . . . used as a point of reference from which measurements can be made.[1] Based on this definition, in this chapter benchmarking may be defined as an ongoing strategy of measuring organizational products, services, and processes against the most formidable competitors and industry leaders, resulting in the development of performance standards that lead to sustained superior output.

[1] *Webster's New Collegiate Dictionary,* G&C Merriam Co., Springfield, Mass., 1977, p. 103.

183

Benchmarking is a process for facilitating change, for filling the gaps between internal and external products and processes in the enterprise. Benchmarks, once determined, suggest what should be changed—they provide a model against which organizational performance can be judged.

Benchmarking accomplished through teams is used in several different yet complementary contexts:

- *Competitive benchmarking:* The five or six most threatening competitors are studied and evaluated to gain insight into their strengths, weaknesses, strategies, and performance capabilities.
- *Best-in-the-industry benchmarking:* The practices of the best performers in selected industries are studied and evaluated. Those selected for further study may or may not be in the same industry.
- *Generic benchmarking:* Business strategies and processes are studied that are not necessarily appropriate for just one industry.

Benchmarking has become an important initiative in the strategic management of organizations. For example, CEO John F. Smith, Jr., of General Motors is pushing his company into benchmarking in a big way. Every new operation must be benchmarked against the best in the class, including companies not in the car-making business. A core group of ten people from GM help coordinate GM's worldwide benchmarking strategies.[2] Benchmarking can reveal startling results. For example, when Digital Equipment benchmarked its manufacturing operations, it discovered that its costs were 30 to 40 percent too high.[3] Companies that have benchmarked their competitors have realized that no one knows their business better than their rivals.

Benchmarking used to be called competitive analysis—an activity that was carried out by successful companies to help them to judge the efficacy of their strategies. The term *benchmarking* is more appropriate because it requires not only the analysis of competitors but the study of the best in the industry in terms of both operational and strategic efficiency and effectiveness. But benchmarking is not a "silver bullet"—it is not a panacea for curing the operational and strategic ills of the company. The process of benchmarking is limited; it is part of other team-driven strategies that can improve organizational performance.

Benchmarking is used to prove that the objectives, goals, and strategies of the enterprise are appropriate and that competitors or the best-in-the-industry organizations have used these performance standards in improving their strategic and operational capabilities. Benchmarking can be used to get the attention of employees in developing and executing the strategies to make major forward thrusts in organizational performance.

[2] Alex Taylor, III, "GM's $11,000,000,000 Turnaround," *Fortune,* October 17, 1994, pp. 54–74.
[3] Stratford Sherman, "Are You As Good as the Best in the World?" *Fortune,* December 13, 1993, pp. 95–96.

Benchmarking takes its place as part of the monitoring, evaluation, and control function of the manager. To benchmark is to seek the answer to the question, "How are we doing in the business we are in?" The answer to that question cannot be found unless competitors and the best in the industry have been analyzed.

A philosophy of benchmarking encompasses the belief that ongoing comparison with the best and most threatening competitors makes sense. Moreover, comparing performance with those who are considered the best in the industry provides valuable insight into organizational capabilities. Benchmarks, once established, should be analyzed and compared with the enterprise's operational and strategic initiatives. Benchmarks and resulting comparisons should be used to further the ability to deliver quality products and services to customers.

WHAT SHOULD BE BENCHMARKED?

Those areas in the enterprise that are critical to success in the marketplace are the most likely areas to be evaluated. Taken in the broadest sense, this includes almost everything that goes on in the enterprise. Customer satisfaction, product and service quality, the reliability of the products and services that have been delivered, and organizational processes are all candidates for benchmarking. Process quality and efficiency, productivity, and timeliness of output are important considerations. Strategic effectiveness, employee morale, stakeholder satisfaction, and the ability of the enterprise to provide an environment in which creativity and innovation can flourish can be benchmarked. Virtually any area of the enterprise can be evaluated through the benchmarking process—what is benchmarked should have a strong linkage with current and future strategies.

At Ma Bell's Global Information Solutions (GIS), a reorganization of the company has reduced staff by 20 percent, has assembled several hundred cross-functional teams, and has emphasized that all objectives must clearly link to key results: customer or shareholder satisfaction and profitable growth. The CEO refers to the people reporting to him as the "16 people I support." GIS constantly benchmarks itself against rivals and surveys customers constantly, turning the results into a measure of "customer delight" on a scale of one to seven. Key characteristics of the culture at GIS include vision, trust, rewards, compassion—all the tools of enlightened leadership.[4]

Benchmarking should be a formal, continuous process for improving the operational and strategic capability of the company through an ongoing search for industry-best practices and assessment of competitors. Done properly, benchmarking is a measuring philosophy as well as a way to get ideas for product, process, and service improvements. It provides a way to see where

---

[4] Thomas A. Stewart, "How to Lead A Revolution," *Fortune,* November 28, 1994, pp. 60–61.

the enterprise stands in the industry and in its competitive profile. The idea for benchmarking can come from anywhere. At Texas Instruments' Defense Systems & Electronics Group (DSEG), an employee learned from a magazine article that the cosmetics company Mary Kay had managed inventory since 1985 with a 99.9 percent rate of completing its assembly and shipping of orders in twenty-four hours or less. DSEG sent sixteen surveys to companies with similar operations. Six sites were selected for a benchmarking visit. The team from DSEG created flow charts for each company visited, including one of their own, and constructed a best-of-best flow chart for its own operation. As a result, the assembly and shipping of orders was reduced from eight to four days. One of the key side benefits of the benchmarking was the realization that employees could be given additional empowerment for getting orders out to customers.[5] Another unit at DSEG decided to convert its processes from a traditional, functionally oriented assembly shop to flexible, cellular manufacturing. It benchmarked both internal and external organizations to garner the best way to design the manufacturing cells. As a result of findings in this benchmarking team, cycle time was cut from nine weeks to four and a half weeks; work-in-process inventory and scrap rate were reduced by nearly 50 percent.

Union Carbide's Robert Kennedy used benchmarking to find successful businesses, determine what made them successful, and then translated their successful strategy to his own company. The benchmarking team at Union Carbide looked to L. L. Bean to learn how it runs a global customer service operation out of one center in Maine. By copying L. L. Bean, Union Carbide teams were able to consolidate seven regional customer service offices, which handled shipping orders for solvents and coatings, into one center in Houston, Texas. By giving employees more responsibility and permitting them to redesign their work, 30 percent fewer employees were able to do the same work—including the analysis of processes to reduce paperwork to less than half. For lessons on global distribution, Union Carbide looked to Federal Express, and for tracking inventory via computer, Union Carbide borrowed from retailers such as Wal-Mart.[6]

All proposals at Union Carbide for significant financing at manufacturing require benchmarking information to accompany the proposal and its justification. In doing a study for a product design, a team with members from manufacturing and product engineering, finance, purchasing, marketing, and the shop itself is formed. The head of the manufacturing engineering department has executive responsibility for the team—for providing it with the resources needed and for facilitating the work that is being carried out. The team sets the performance standards and is responsible for designing the

[5] Nancy A. Hitchcock, "Benchmarking Bolsters Quality at Texas Instruments," *Modern Materials Handling,* March 1993, pp. 46–48.
[6] Sina Moukheiber, "Learning from Winners," *Forbes,* March 14, 1994, pp. 41–42.

steps involved in the benchmarking process and for recommending remedial strategies once the benchmarking project is completed.

INFORMATION SOURCES AND EXAMPLES

Information for benchmarking can come from a wide variety of public and private sources. Company records, site visits, interviews, customers, suppliers, regulatory agencies, periodical literature, seminars and symposia, investment bankers, and brokerage firms are a few of the key sources for information. A careful and ongoing reading of key periodicals such as the *Wall Street Journal, Fortune, Forbes, Business Week,* and similar sources can provide meaningful and insightful information on what competitors and best-in-the-industry players are doing. For example, two articles in the November 14, 1994 issue of *Fortune,* "The Digital Factory" and "Why to Go for Stretch Targets," provide insight into strategies used by companies that should prove useful for doing some general benchmarking, and they suggest areas and companies that should be studied further. Industrial intelligence plays a role in benchmarking.

CEO Wolfgang Schmitt of Rubbermaid Corporation manages the company so that it is able to produce more than 400 new products a year. A third of its annual sales of $2 billion comes from products that are five years old or less. A series of teams that replicate the management structure of the company are responsible for creating, improving, and marketing a series of new products. When a new line of products springs up, a team is put together to handle it. When a product line runs its course, the team is disbanded. At present, there are twenty-one teams, and Rubbermaid's goal is to have thirty teams consisting of five people each, from sales, marketing, finance, manufacturing, and R&D. Each of the teams can call on the parent company for support as they develop their own strategic and operating plans and conduct benchmarking. Each team is charged with profit responsibility, which gives them a sense of empowerment, entrepreneurship, and ownership.[7]

As part of its simultaneous reengineering efforts, GTE benchmarked eighty companies in a wide variety of industries. Self-directed work teams then created concepts for the new process gleaned out of the benchmarking process. In addition to the valuable information developed out of the benchmarking processes, the impact of the on-site visits on the benchmarking team was profound and did a great deal to establish the validity of benchmarking in the mindsets of team members. The imperatives that guided the reengineering efforts at GTE included the following: (1) Always begin with the customer; (2) aim for quantum improvements in performance determined by benchmarking against the best practices of the best companies; (3) develop an unassailable

---

[7] Marshall Loeb, "How to Grow a New Product Every Day," *Fortune,* November 14, 1994, pp. 269–270.

understanding of the existing processes as they really work, and not as they are supposed to work; (4) dare for breakthrough thinking and performance; and (5) listen carefully to the people who know the most about how the work is to be carried out—those people who are actually doing the work.[8]

At the Goodyear Company, a team approach to product and process development turned the corporate culture on its head. Extensive training for all of Goodyear's employees—from executives to workers on the shop floor—helped introduce and implement the team concept. The company's scientific and technical employees were tested to determine if they were right- or left-brained (in light of the assumption that left-brained people are logical, while right-brained people are creative). Goodyear felt that teams must have idea people as well as logical people who can implement the ideas. They also need people who can follow up and who can give good presentations. Teams are drawn from different quadrants of the company. Goodyear's teams are both cross-functional and cross-corporate and partner suppliers, customers, and other stakeholders. By using teams to include benchmarking initiatives, Goodyear has unleashed the power of the people and has moved away from the notion that managers are doing all of the creative and innovative work in the enterprise. A flatter hierarchy has been made possible by empowering people who are willing to assume risk, challenge the status quo, and develop innovative products and processes not discernible in the former traditional organizational structure and corporate culture. For Goodyear's corporate leaders, this has been an awesome challenge—from one of building stability to creating an environment that is capable of surviving and growing in a competitive world of continuous and unrelenting change.[9]

Benchmarking is carried out by nations. For example, it has been estimated that more than half the nations of the world—nearly 100 in all—are actively conducting industrial intelligence operations against U.S. firms. Their targets are the technology and trade secrets of U.S. high-tech firms. Information sought includes everything from laser research to rocket engine test data to marketing plans, contract bids, manufacturing cost analyses, and proprietary software. The Federal Bureau of Investigation (FBI) has more than twenty full-time agents working espionage cases in Silicon Valley, California; some of the cases being pursued by the FBI will likely surface in criminal courts.[10]

Sources of information for benchmarking are much the same as sources for competitive analysis. Information for benchmarking can come from searching through trade magazines and management/business journals, contacting trade associations, gathering intelligence at trade shows, and talking with industry

[8] David P. Allen and Robert Nafius, "Dreaming and Doing: Reengineering GTE Telephone Operations," *Planning Review,* March–April 1993, pp. 28–31.

[9] "American Industrial Dominance Will Depend upon Agility to Manage Change," *Focus,* National Center for Manufacturing Science, Ann Arbor, Mich., June 1993, pp. 1–5.

[10] For further insight into industrial espionage directed to steal U.S. technology, see Norm Alster, "The Valley of the Spies," *Forbes,* October 26, 1992, pp. 200–204.

experts and former employees. Chapter 5 of Robert C. Camp's book about benchmarking provides an excellent description of data collection methods and sources.[11]

ORGANIZATIONAL DESIGN

There are several alternative organizational designs to use in planning and executing benchmarking initiatives. Benchmarking carried out within just one organizational unit or function of the company could be done through a team or through the existing structure of the unit or function. If the benchmarking is to be done in an interdisciplinary context, then using a team to act as a focal point makes sense. A unit manager or a functional manager could have the benchmarking carried out through the existing structure, much like other activities are carried out. For example, a manufacturing manager could carry out benchmarking with other manufacturing units of the parent company. One advantage in using a team is that the benchmarking activity could be planned and carried out in an extraordinary manner, separate from the ongoing activities. If the team has been charged with the responsibility for doing the benchmarking, if an adequate plan has been developed to do the work, and if the team members have planned to devote adequate time to the benchmarking work, then there is a good chance that the work will be carried out adequately. One problem in having the benchmarking effort carried out as simply other tasks in the operational work of the organizational unit or function is that the benchmarking work can become a lower priority than keeping up with the routine work of the unit. People are usually reluctant to take time away from their normal work—particularly if they feel that their performance is being evaluated in doing that work.

When a team-based benchmarking effort is established that is apart from the unit or function's activities, two advantages can be realized: (1) Unit and functional managers can continue to employ resources to concentrate on the efficiency of their daily work; and (2) there will be greater synergy because there is an interdisciplinary focal point.

Benchmarking is carried out to evaluate the efficiency and effectiveness of products and organizational processes. Most often, when benchmarking is carried out properly, the organizational processes are improved, with an ultimate consequent improvement in the products and services offered by the enterprise. Organizational strategies typically involve interfunctional and interorganizational dependencies and considerations—an ambience that is known to and welcomed by team members.

A benchmarking champion is needed to lend credence and to provide leverage to the benchmarking team. The champion should be a member

---

[11] Robert C. Camp, *Benchmarking: The Search for Industry Best Practices that Lead to Superior Performance,* Quality Press, American Society for Quality Control, Milwaukee, Wisc., 1989.

of senior management or an individual who has the confidence of senior management. This champion, acting on behalf of the benchmarking initiative, offers several key benefits:

- Provides leadership within the enterprise for the planning and execution of the benchmarking initiative
- Ensures that the benchmarking results are integrated into the operational and strategic considerations of the enterprise
- Provides the required resources for the benchmarking effort, including designating the authority and responsibility of the people doing the work
- Keeps other key managers informed of the progress that is being made on the benchmarking initiative, including the probable outcomes and the potential use to which the information from benchmarking can be put.
- After the benchmarking work is completed, takes the lead in assessing the effectiveness of the work, including the lessons learned, so that future benchmarking strategies can be improved

In general, people who have a vested interest in the outcome of benchmarking should be members of the benchmarking team. Since these people would be expected to live with the results, they are key stakeholders and should influence the outcome, thus facilitating their participation in both the benchmarking activities and in implementing the recommendations of the effort. Such involvement will reduce the need to sell the resulting recommendations to them.

THE TEAM LEADER

The person selected to be the benchmarking project leader should have several capabilities:

1. The team leader should have a proven track record as a team leader, either in previous benchmarking efforts or as the leader of other teams.
2. The team leader should understand the technology that is involved in the benchmarking process. This understanding need not be extensive, but rather the leader should have sufficient knowledge to ask the right questions and know if the right answers are being given.
3. The leader should know what the management process is all about in terms of leaderhip, planning, organizing, motivation, direction, and control.
4. The leader should have the ability to sense and see the larger systems context of the benchmarking effort.

5. The leader should have the ability to make and implement decisions relative to the benchmarking process. The ability to communicate and strong interpersonal skills are also key attributes desirable in the benchmarking team leader. Knowing what data to look for and how that data can be used for insight into the benchmarking effort are critical. Credibility is an important asset of the team leader. After the team's work is underway, the leader will need to perform in a manner that reinforces that credibility. The team leader who has not had experience in benchmarking faces key challenges in developing credibility; however, successful experience as a leader of other teams should help build credibility.

Membership on the benchmarking team should include the principal stakeholders:

Team leader
Functional specialists
Customer/sponsor
Champion
Facilitator
Support people, such as legal, Management Information Systems, clerical support, etc.

STANDARD STEPS IN BENCHMARKING

People who have written books and articles about benchmarking processes usually cite several steps that are needed in carrying out the process. For the most part, these steps include the following, not necessarily in this order:

Determine what areas should be benchmarked.
Decide who the most relevant competitors are.
Decide who the best performers in the industry are.
Develop a benchmarking plan.
Organize the team.
Collect the information.
Analyze the information.
Determine the performance gaps.
Disseminate the findings.
Determine the relevancy of the findings.
Integrate the findings into strategies.
Prepare execution plans.

Execute the plans.

Maintain ongoing benchmarking.

Continuously improve the benchmarking process.

If benchmarking is not carried out, several conditions may impair the effective and efficient use of resources in maintaining competitiveness. An internal focus will likely come about, with its resulting "not-invented-here" (NIH) syndrome. Parochical attitudes will be reinforced, organizational myopia will come about, and there will be minimum commitment to improve operations. A closed-system mentality will permeate the organizational culture, the chances of obsolescence will improve, "catch-up ball" will be the name of the game, and there will be a high risk of the retirement of both people and the enterprise.

Using teams to perform benchmarking work involves several key phases in getting the team's work underway:

- Select the internal organizational units that will be the object of the study.
- Seek those organizations that likely qualify for the best-practices benchmarking initiatives.
- Develop a team strategy for how the benchmarking will be carried out, including key progress dates and how the work of the team will be reviewed and evaluated.
- Study and visit those organizational units and companies selected for the benchmarking studies.
- Keep the benchmarking customer(s) informed of progress.
- Translate the benchmarking findings into improvement strategies for the client organization.

BENCHMARKING PITFALLS

Benchmarking through the use of teams seems simple and easy, but there are pitfalls to be avoided:

- Organizing the team inadequately. There is no clearly understood statement of the team's performance standards, its objectives, goals, organizational design, and strategies. Failure to provide for these performance standards will seriously weaken the probable effectiveness of the team's work.
- Failing to provide synergy between what the team is likely to do and the client's organizational objectives, goals, and strategies. Too often the client's strategic and operational plans are not linked to the benchmarking

efforts underway. This lack of linkage causes the benchmarking effort to drift and move away from its original intended purpose.

- Providing too many people on the team, with resulting duplication of effort, overlaps of work, increased cost, and an inability for team members to see a distinct work area that is their responsibility. At Xerox, a pioneer in benchmarking, it was found through experience that six to eight people is just about the right size for a benchmarking team. Keeping the team small enhances the opportunity for increased communication, keeps logistics costs down, and makes site visits easier since a relatively small number of people are involved. The team should represent the disciplines or functional areas of work that are being benchmarked. The team members must be able to measure and assess what they are studying.

- Not keeping the client informed through regular briefings and assessments? This involvement should be proactive whereby the client takes an active part in designing strategies for the benchmarking, assessing continually how the work is being carried out, redirecting the work as needed, and assimilating the benchmarking results into the operational and strategic initiatives.

- Failing to concentrate on those specific performance standards and issues to be evaluated. This means that generic issues, whose assessments could be interesting but not likely to be relevant and applicable to the client's organization, must be avoided. These larger generic issues often are so broad—such as "improve manufacturing efficiency"—that they extend beyond the scope and abilities of the benchmarking team.

- Imposing unrealistic performance schedules for the benchmarking team's efforts. Too often, overzealous managers set a totally unrealistic time schedule—such as three or four weeks for the benchmarking work to be completed. Sufficient time must be allowed for organizing the team, planning data collection, collecting data, establishing contact with benchmarking hosts, assessing data, reaching conclusions, and providing a meaningful report. There should be enough time allowed to get the job done in a quality manner. Four to five months is about right—ten to twelve months is too long because the project will lose its appeal and priority as other issues come up in the enterprise.

- Selecting the wrong host organizations to benchmark. The organizations to benchmark in the context of the best in the class are those whose strategies and processes are outperforming the operations of the company doing the benchmarking. Identifying the best-in-the-class companies can be relatively easy to do, but getting into these companies to be hosts for benchmarking will likely be difficult since many other benchmarking teams are likely trying to do the same. It is better to make modest selections and find local companies or less well known companies that are excellent at what they do.

- Collecting too much data, and then trying to sort through all of it to find out what is truly relevant. It is better to carefully think through and build a mental model of what strategies and processes should be benchmarked, and then use the guidelines developed in this book to drive the data collection strategies.

- Becoming enamored with the numbers collected during the benchmarking process, and neglecting the qualitative data behind those numbers that explain the context of the numbers. The strategies and processes behind the numbers are critical, and translating those strategies and processes to the client's operations is the key purpose of benchmarking activities.

- The customer is the person or work unit that will make use of the benchmarking results. The customer is the sponsor—the person or organizational unit that intends to use the benchmarking results to improve operational and strategic initiatives.

If benchmarking is to be more than just the gathering of information, then the aforementioned pitfalls must be avoided carefully. In the initial meetings of the benchmarking team, these pitfalls and strategies for avoiding them should be discussed.

STRATEGIC OR OPERATIONAL

Benchmarking can be done to evaluate operational or strategic initiatives. For example, Bath Iron Works, the fourth largest shipyard in the United States, was totally unprepared for the end of the Cold War. The 108-year-old shipyard's business plan had assumed that the need for U.S. battle preparedness that had characterized the postwar years would continue indefinitely. As a result, the shipyard was a one-customer company. Lack of strategic planning caused by the comfort of getting recurring defense contracts led to a complacency in the company. With the end of the Cold War and the resulting cutback in defense contracts, the company turned to benchmarking to help set a future direction that did not involve defense contracts. Strategic benchmarking became an integral part of the company's strategic planning process. By benchmarking Germany's Thyussen for pipe bending, Walt Disney World for preventive maintenance, and L. L. Bean for such ordinary procedures as paper reduction, Bath Iron Works gained appreciation for what strategic benchmarking could do for its future. By analyzing its key skills and core competency in shipbuilding and by translating that competency to the design, manufacture, integration, and testing of complex structures, new opportunities were opened up for the company. Benchmarking and the tie-in of results provided new strategic opportunities, direction, and priorities for Bath Iron Works.[12]

Through the use of strategic benchmarking techniques carried out with successful global companies, Japanese companies are slimming down, delayer-

---

[12] Alexandra Biesada, "Strategic Benchmarking," *Financial World,* September 29, 1992, pp. 30–36.

ing management, and delegating more authority and responsibility to individual executives. Such entrenched practices as lifetime employment, promotion based on seniority, and avoidance of individual responsibility are no longer taken for granted. Japanese executives are determining the relevancy of consensus decision making and automatic promotion in the realities of global competition. Other changes in Japanese companies due to benchmarking of the best competitors include downsizing, reduction of the number of products, use of teams in a reduced number of work units, profit-center responsibility for organizational units, and a hard look at labor costs as a percentage of all costs.[13]

Using the need to make major improvements in the design and manufacture of airplanes, Boeing's CEO Frank Shrontz set goals to lower aircraft prices in part through paring the cost of manufacturing a plane by 25 percent by 1998. A second goal was to reduce radically the time needed to build the 747 and 767 from eighteen months in 1992 to eight months in 1996. To encourage his managers to adopt lean manufacturing techniques from other industries, the CEO Shrontz dispatched teams to study the world's best producers of everything from computers to ships. The result was performance standards that enabled Boeing to design and build each order of wide-bodied 747s and 767s in just ten months, and 737s and 757s in twelve months. The benchmarking process carried out by Boeing helped greatly in getting the attention of people who were enamored with the old, time-proven ways of designing and manufacturing aircraft that had been successful under former and different competitive forces.[14]

The use of teams to benchmark competitors and the best in the industry can avoid the comfort of success that has caused many dominant companies to grow complacent and neglect innovative strategies for developing new products and organizational processes. These companies acquired the usual encumbrances of success—arrogance, bureaucratic layers of authority that slowed down the making and execution of decisions, and the attitude that "we must be doing something right, look how well we are doing." The Xerox Corporation rode a wave of success in the 1960s and then stumbled in the 1970s—done in by arrogance, uncompetitive products, and the Japanese competition that it did not take seriously. Sears, IBM, and GM got to the top by outperforming competitors. Sears had the best store sites, GM the best dealer networks, and IBM a dominance in equipment that forced customers to go for other IBM machines. Sears and GM thought themselves protected by the economies of scale; GM by mass production; Sears by its purchasing power. The erosion of the positions of these big companies was so gradual that they were unaware that they were descending into a state of crisis. What threatened

---

[13] James E. Ellis, "Japan Inc. Finally Starts Its Diet," *Business Week/Enterprise,* October 1993, pp. 227–229.
[14] Shawn Tully, "Why to go for Stretch Targets," *Fortune,* November 14, 1994, pp. 145–158.

these companies were profound changes in their markets and the emergence of competitors who were doing things differently than the successful giants.

If these companies—and others that had similar fates—had done meaningful benchmarking, and if the results of such analysis had been accepted at face value by the entrenched executives, strategies might have been developed to initiate badly needed changes in their performance. It is true that these companies have survived at a considerable cost in lost business, financial losses, layoffs, and loss of market share. These companies are coming back as more efficient and effective organizations. If they had been doing adequate benchmarking on an ongong basis, it is quite probable that many of the difficulties that they encountered would have been eliminated or at least have been reduced. Benchmarking would have provided the senior managers with data bases on their competitiors, and the best performers in other industries, that could have been used as standards against which to judge their performance.

SUMMARY

This chapter discussed (1) the importance of benchmarking in determining the effectiveness and efficiency of existing performance standards in an enterprise; and (2) how the benchmarking process can be carried out through a team dedicated to that purpose. This chapter also discussed the following:

- Benchmarking makes sense as a key to gain insight into organizational performance through comparing an enterprise with competitors and with the best-in-the-industry performers.
- Benchmarking is integral to the management process of monitoring, evaluating, and controlling the use of resources directed to enterprise purposes.
- Deciding what to benchmark is an important decision to be made by those individuals in the enterprise who have the best knowledge of opportunities that exist for improving the performance of the enterprise. These people can include workers, managers, and professionals.
- Information useful for benchmarking can come from a wide variety of sources, both private and public domain. There is usually more information available than can be reasonably collected and analyzed; therefore, information needs and the collection process must be studied carefully.
- Benchmarking is a process that can be used to complement many team-driven initiatives in the enterprise, such as total quality management, concurrent engineering, project management, self-directed manufacturing, organizational designs, business process reengineering, and new business development actions.

- Several alternative organizational designs can be used to organize the benchmarking activities. Usually a team is used to gain the synergy of interdisciplinary effort and organizational focus.
- The benchmarking team leader is an important person who, when properly qualified and trained, can show how and when the benchmarking effort should be carried out.
- There are a series of standard steps that can be used to guide a benchmarking effort. These standard steps should be modified depending on the type of benchmarking to be carried out, the resources available, and the sources of information needed to build the benchmarking databases.
- There are pitfalls that should be avoided in the benchmarking process, and these pitfalls should be reviewed by the benchmarking team prior to the benchmarking process.
- Benchmarking can be used to evaluate both operational and strategic objectives, goals, and strategies.
- Benchmarking teams are important organizational design initiatives in the strategic management of an enterprise.

Concurrent engineering teams are described in the next chapter.

____10
CONCURRENT ENGINEERING TEAMS

Product development has been like elephant intercourse—much hooting, hollering, and throwing of dirt—and then nothing happens for more than a year.

JACK REICHER, CEO OF BRUNSWICK, A $3-BILLION-A-YEAR
SPORTING GOODS COMPANY

This chapter discusses concurrent engineering (CE), a recent innovation in the design and development of products and supporting organizational processes. CE is a systematic approach to the integrated, simultaneous engineering design of products and such associated organizational processes as manufacturing, procurement, finance, testing, and after-sales service for the delivery of maximum value to customers. In CE, a product—process design team represents all disciplines and interests of the product and its processes during the product's life cycle, from concept through use and disposal.

CE goes by different names, including the following:

- Simultaneous engineering
- Design for manufacture
- Parallel release
- Swarming
- Product–process integration
- Product–process teaming
- Design for value

Westinghouse defines its concept of design for value as "an integrated, systems approach to product and process development to produce designs with superior customer value using minimum resources." The company recognizes the benefits to be realized from design for value initiatives, including (1) improved customer value, (2) increased product quality, (3) reduced time to market, and (4) lowest possible cost.[1] CE can also be described in the context of a litany of expected outcomes or objectives, including

- Design for performance and quality
- Design for manufacturability
- Design for testability
- Design for marketability
- Design for compliance
- Design for serviceability
- Design for profitability

The current interest in CE can be attributed to the growing importance of continuously improving products and creating new products to compete in the global marketplace. CE provides the opportunity to commercialize products faster, at lower cost, with higher quality, and with greater customer satisfaction. Such opportunities enhance the chances of success in meeting the dynamic and rigorous competition that all companies face today.

Every small company has used CE to some degree. All that is required to start CE is a piece of paper, a pencil, and a willingness of people from the different disciplines to work together. In small companies, one individual often had responsibility for both design and manufacturing engineering. As the company grew in size and additional people were added, distinct disciplines were created with people assigned to these disciplines. The integration of effort that occurred when the company was smaller was lost. In large companies, new organizational designs are needed to bring about the focus and integration that are attained so easily in smaller companies—hence the emergence of product–process design teams dedicated to CE.

The use of product–process development teams in the CE context changes many things in an enterprise's operation. According to one periodical it promises to create the most wrenching cultural upheaval in manufacturing in a half century.[2]

There are clear reasons for CE to be adopted to meet the challenges that companies face today.

---

[1] *PQC Design for Value,* Brochure, Westinghouse Productivity and Quality Center, Product/Process Design, Pittsburgh, Pa., March 1989.

[2] John Carey and David Woodruff "A smarter way to manufacture," *Business Week,* April 30, 1990, p. 111.

THE CHALLENGES

Consider the challenges facing industrial enterprises:

- Between 50 and 80 percent of the cost of manufacturing a product is determined during the design phase.
- The total cost of a product is locked in at the end of the design phase of the product development effort.
- Well-designed products that were efficiently manufactured may not sell well.
- Overcomplicated designs can cause delays and lead to problems in manufacturing the product and may lead to costly engineering changes.
- By the time a product has left the initial design stage and key decisions about materials and processes have been made, about 70 percent of the cost has been locked in. This means that what happens beyond this point through manufacturing and marketing efficiencies will influence only about 30 percent of the product cost.
- Product life cycles are getting shorter.
- Simplicity in the design of a product is becoming a key factor in how well the product creates value for the customer.
- Efficiency and effectiveness in the manufacture of a product do not make up for poor product design or a marketing strategy that does not consider the customers' needs.
- The importance of product design cannot be underestimated, and the counsel and participation of key stakeholders—such as customers, suppliers, maintenance people, regulatory officials, workers, and others—can be valuable in creating a product design that will please customers, exploit supplier technology, and help after-sales personnel do their job.
- Since customers usually have a sense of their technological needs, their membership on concurrent engineering teams can help in finding innovative and user-oriented ways to design and package the product. In some industries, the majority of technological innovations come from customer insight and needs.

BENEFITS OF CE

Demonstrated benefits of CE include the following:

- Reduction of engineering change orders of up to 50 percent
- Reduction of product development time between 40 and 50 percent
- Significant scrap and rework reduction by as much as 75 percent
- Manufacturing cost reduction between 30 and 40 percent

- Higher quality and lower design costs
- Fewer design errors
- Reduction and even elimination of the need for formal design reviews since the product–process development team provides for an ongoing design review
- Enhanced communication between designers, managers, and professionals in the supporting processes
- Simplification of design, which reduces the number of parts to be manufactured, creates simplicity in fixturing requirements, and allows for ease of assembly
- Reduction in the number of surprises during the design process
- Greater employee involvement on the concurrent engineering teams, leading to enhanced development of their knowledge, skills, and attitudes

The potential benefits of CE can be significant. A more timely satisfaction of customer needs is reflected in up-to-date technology, and the presence of suppliers on the development team provides improved technology, higher-quality subsystems and components, and improved product design. The bottom line of CE is greater profitability and enhanced global competitiveness.

Getting to the market sooner is recognized as a distinct competitive advantage. Such speed pays off. For example, McKinsey & Company researched and developed an economic model that shows that high-tech products that come to market six months late but on budget will earn 33 percent less profit over five years. Alternatively, coming out on time and 50 percent over budget reduces profits by only 4 percent.[3]

SOME EXAMPLES

Companies that have tried CE have commercialized their products sooner. For example, Chrysler used a concurrent engineering team to develop the Neon, the small car that Detroit could not build. The Neon team mobilized 600 engineers, 289 suppliers, and blue-collar workers to meet the goal of delivering the new model in a speedy forty-two months and for much less than any recent small car had cost. The team started with an uncharacteristic willingness to borrow from competitors. The engineers drove competitive models such as the Honda Civic and Ford Escort. These models went through a reverse engineering process, in which competitive cars were analyzed to find the best—and the worse—features of their design. The team borrowed from Japan such techniques as quality management techniques, prioritization of customers' desires, and foolproofing of assembly procedures. Blue-collar work-

---

[3] Cited in Brian Dumaine, "How Managers Can Succeed through Speed," *Fortune,* February 13, 1994, pp. 54–57.

ers got more responsibility as members of the team. Workers suggested over 4000 changes in the car and in its production process, many of which were implemented. UAW officials were enlisted full time on the team. The development time for the Neon avoided Chrysler's—and other automobile manufacturers'—weakness: glacially paced product development.[4]

At Ameritech, a concurrent engineering team was established to evaluate and plan a $1 billion fiber-optics installation in the company's five-state region. The team set technical specifications, bid the project, and took care of regulatory problems in just three months. If the company had used traditional management of the development effort, approval up and down the organizational hierarchy would have taken much longer—at least three years, by some estimates. A financial reporting team was also organized and was comprised of the chief financial officer, controllers, and accounting members. By visiting sites around the United States, talking with subsidiary people, and analyzing reporting procedures, the team was able to eliminate 6 million pages of reports.[5]

Inside Motorola's walkie-talkie plant in Penang, Malaysia, in all-Malaysian research and development team of 200 engineers helps develop next-generation radios and cordless phones. Workers are actively involved in recommending improvements in product design and in quality initiatives. In 1993, employees submitted 41,000 suggestions for improving operations. One of Motorola's key objectives is to get employees at all levels to forget narrow job titles and work together in teams to identify and act on problems that hinder quality and productivity.[6]

Part of CEO Michael H. Spindler's revitalization strategy for Apple Computer, Inc., includes the Apple New Product Process, which requires two phases of rigorous review—concept and investigation—before any project is given the green light. All development projects have been scrutinized and priorities set. The importance of maintaining overview of product development in the company is underscored in the CEO's pledge to the board of directors that 50 percent of his 1994 annual compensation would be pegged to getting it done right. Part of the philosophy of the company in product development is "Don't throw technology over the wall"—this is a way of focusing attention on the importance of concurrent development of products and organizational processes to support those products.[7]

The key overall elements of CE include (1) the use of product–process design teams to integrate product and process considerations in developing new products; (2) the use of CAD/CAE/CAM (computer-aided design,

[4] David Woodruff and Karen Lower Miller "Chrysler's Neon: Is This the Small Car Detroit Couldn't Build?" *Business Week,* May 3, 1993, pp. 116–126.

[5] Brian Dumain, "Times Are Good? Create a Crisis," *Fortune,* June 28, 1993, pp. 123–130.

[6] Engardio and Gail DeGeorge, "Importing Enthusiasm," *Business Week: 21st Century Capitalism,* 1994 Bonus Issue, pp. 122–123.

[7] Kathy Rebelolo, Ira Sager, and Richard Brandt, "Spindler's Apple," *Business Week,* October 3, 1994, pp. 88–96.

computer-aided engineering, and computer-aided manufacturing) to support design strategies through shared product and process information; (3) the use of appropriate analytical methods to optimize a product's design and its supporting organizational processes; and (4) the use of team management and leadership initiatives to produce meaningful results in the design of new products and processes.

DISADVANTAGES OF SERIAL DESIGN

In the serial design process, product and process design work proceedes from one functional department to another in the enterprise. In this design process, work starts off with establishing the requirement for the product or service, design and development work on the product is then undertaken as the next step, prototype development is carried out, then on to manufacturing and finally to marketing as part of the serial process of design. In concurrent engineering, the design, development, manufacturing, and marketing is started and continued in a simultaneous manner for all the functional input required for the product and organizational processes.

Serial product design has several major weaknesses and outcomes. Compared to CE, serial design causes increased costs and schedules, which leads to untimely product commercialization. Using engineering changes to improve product design or to manufacture the product causes additional cost and schedule delays. Poor design leading to quality problems as a result of serial design requires that a rework of product and process be carried out—additional planning of resources is needed. Since the people working on the design are in different functions of the enterprise, there is limited communication; there is a compartmentalization and resulting parochialism of organizational disciplines with regard to product and process development. Design goals become limited, and there is lack of common design goals. Scrap, reworking or parts, poor quality, and wasted effort in replanning, reprogramming, recycling, and redoing work continue to increase costs and delay schedules. The impact of serial design on an organizational culture includes a continuation of bureaucracy compounded by organizational fragmentation, power struggles, overspecialization, and an ongoing risk of work falling between the cracks of the organizational departments. The behavior patterns of people involved in serial design tend away from the development and acceptance of the systems nature of concurrent product–process development—there is little sharing of a common objective in the organization's culture. In addition, there tends to be a limited perspective of the life cycle of the product, which results in a failure to plan adequately for keeping customers satisfied during the after-sales service phase of the product. Serial design tends to be viewed as an operational, short-term activity rather than a strategic initiative directed to improving the enterprise's competitive performance. In serial design, a greater number of parts and components is likely, as is the risk of compromising the state of the art in both design and manufacturing. In summary, a failure to designate, work toward, and achieve common objectives and goals through a product and process strategy results. Customers and suppliers are not part of the design process, limited feedback occurs across organizational walls during the design work, no one is accountable for both product and process design, and the time to commercialization is often so long that the original market research is antiquated.

Serial or over-the-wall design has been likened to the old game of telephone. People sit around in a room and whisper something into the ear of the person sitting next to them, and this message is passed around the room from ear to ear. By the time the message gets to the last person in the room, it is much different from what was said to the first person.

People embarking on a new CE initiative are the most comfortable when the initiative is at the conceptual and philosophical level. At that level, everyone thinks the initiative, makes good sense. It is when they begin to realize that new roles and reallocation of authority and responsibility will be required—and that some people will lose their right to make decisions without any input from other people—that resistance begins to set in. CE has a better chance of being implemented if it can be linked and meshed with other strategic initiatives in the enterprise, such as total quality management and the use of alternative teams in the enterprise (e.g., self-directed production teams, benchmarking teams, or reengineering teams).

ADVANTAGES OF CE

In product design and the supporting organizational processes, CE has many advantages:

- It simplifies the design, making the product easier to manufacture.
- It reduces the number of parts, which reduces product cost, improves reliability, and makes after-sales service easier.
- It improves productivity and quality through a greater standardization of components and reduction of inventory.
- It reduces development cycle time, which facilitates a quicker response to changing markets.
- It eliminates redesign work—the design is done right the first time.
- It improves the maintainability and testability of the product.
- It improves competitiveness because of lower costs, earlier commercialization, higher quality, and better satisfied customers (particularly when customers were brought into the design activities).
- It allows for greater introduction of improved technology, particularly from suppliers who became part of the design teams.
- It reduces warranty claims on the product.

OBJECTIVES OF CE

CE's general objectives are to determine the character and configuration of the product and supporting organizational processes. This includes investigating the form, fit, and function of the product through executing design-for-productivity and supportability studies to determine product improvements without compromising form, fit, or function. Design of appropriate manufacturing and assembly proceses is a key objective, as is working with customers and suppliers. Value engineering determines product and process suitability.

In the process of carrying out CE, other objectives have to be established and met as well:

- Appropriate and cost-effective assembly processes must be determined and designed.
- Interfaces must be established with customers and suppliers to ensure their input into the concurrent engineering effort.
- Relevant value engineering initiatives must be conducted.
- Value must be delivered to the customers.

STRATEGIES

Plans to launch CE initiatives should start with a background search of business literature to find examples of how CE is supposed to be carried out and examples of companies that have tried such initiatives (including both successful and unsuccessful efforts). This literature should be distributed to the key people in the initiative. After these people have had an opportunity to study this literature, a series of workshops should be conducted to answer questions about the initiative, particularly how it is envisioned that CE will be carried out in the company. During this training activity, the logic and rationale for CE should be explained.

Key and successful competitors should be identified and benchmarked regarding their CE strategies. The findings of such benchmarking are bound to get the attention of key people in the initial CE activities. Early in the initiative, the objectives, goals, and strategies of CE should be developed by working with the newly appointed team. In addition, the following need to be done:

- Identify the individual and collective roles of team members.
- Develop policy documentation stipulating the authority, responsibility, and accountability of the principals involved.
- Determine the decision context of the team's operation—what limits of authority team members will have in doing their design work.

- Determine how individual and team performance and rewards will be handled.

INTERFACE WITH SUPPLIERS

Companies that launch CE projects find that recasting design and process work in cooperation with customers and suppliers has a high payoff value. Using fewer suppliers favors developing strategic alliances that encourage suppliers to improve their offerings continually, and bringing suppliers, actively into design activities improves product development.

Japanese automakers, who did some of the pioneering work in CE, assign suppliers varying levels of responsibility for product development. Only about a dozen first-tier suppliers enjoy full-scale alliance with their customers. In part, this is because few suppliers can make the investments in personnel, computer-aided design (CAD) systems, prototyping facilities, and R&D capabilities that a true alliance with the original equipment manufacturer (OEM) requires. World-class Japanese auto manufacturers set clear and understandable objectives and goals with suppliers. Targets and prototypes are used to discipline the suppliers to perform. Because of their strategic relationship with the OEMs, the suppliers are able to offer meaningful new design ideas.[8]

Cooperation with suppliers on CE teams has become one of the characteristics of successful companies. When representatives of the OEMs and the suppliers work together, success in global competition is more assured. At the John Deere company, suppliers have worked alongside their counterparts at Deere right from the product concept and design stages of new tractor production. Deere, by policy, is involving suppliers earlier in concurrent engineering efforts. In addition, a key supplier was asked to help design the most advanced facility and manufacturing processes for building the 5000 Series tractors for Deere. Three key objectives were established for this effort: (1) Save time on production and delivery, (2) reduce costs, and (3) find innovative ways to eliminate waste.

One such example of eliminating waste was to provide an efficient way for supplying the 35–40 Parker fluid connectors and assemblies that go into each tractor on the John Deere assembly line. All of these parts are put in one reusable container and are packaged according to how they are used on the assembly line. The containers are put right alongside the Deere tractor as it travels down the line. After use, the containers are returned to the supplier's service center for a fresh supply of parts and another trip down the line. This system simplifies and reduces the need for reordering; the kit number replaces

---

[8] Rajan R. Kamath and Jeffrey K. Liker, "A Second Look at Japanese Product Development," *Harvard Business Review,* November–December 1994, pp. 154–170.

35–40 part numbers. Use of the kits has saved assemblers as many as 28,000 hand motions.[9]

PROTOTYPES

The use of prototypes in CE as working models and mock-ups can help provide insight into the forces involved in testing and driving the innovation process. For example, Bosch, the German electronics giant, used a prototype to help marketers and designers develop a common design vocabulary to facilitate better communication in the design of a new high-tech helmet. The prototype became an economical way to evaluate product and manufacturing risk. At Sony, the popular line of consumer electronics for kids, "My First Sony," was a byproduct of intensive interaction (not market research) between Sony's designers and their young customers. When 3M's Post-It notes first appeared, customers had few clues about how the first prototypes of this sticky paper could be used. Eventually the designers and marketers, working with the prototypes of the notes, discovered a wide variety of uses for the new Post-It product. Today we wonder how we got along without these Post-Its.

Valuable feedback can be obtained from using a prototype. In addition, the prototype can be used as a sales tool for evaluating continued investment of develoment funds. Prototypes can be considered as a form of "dress rehearsal."[10]

GETTING STARTED

In launching a CE initiative, the characteristics of successful initiatives should be reviewed, and such characteristics should be shared with the new CE team. Senior management support and commitment are essential and include providing the resources, facilitating the organization of the teams, regularly reviewing the work of the teams, and continuing to communicate the reasons for the change in the way products and processes are designed. Having information available on competitors and how they handle design can be convincing. If a link between the way that competitors do their design work and their success in the marketplace can be established, it will get the attention of even the most stubborn skeptics. A clear distinction should be made between the policies and procedures of serial design vis-à-vis concurrent design, and the ways that concurrency can improve competitive postures should be discussed. It is paramount to give the teams clear authority and responsibility and to

[9] "John Deere and Parker Build Value in World-Class Tractors" (advertisement), *Wall Street Journal,* February 17, 1994, p. A7.
[10] Michael Scrage, "Prototypes: Building Blocks for Entrepreneurs," *Wall Street Journal,* September 9, 1991, p. C16.

expect their acceptance of accountability. In addition, it is essential to provide training in the philosophy and procedures of CE. Anything that can be done to get people to accept ownership of CE and the results that it produces will have a favorable impact on how the integration of design and processes is carried out in the enterprise.

The first CE initiatives that are started should be those that are likely to be successful. Such success can be used to convince people that the new way of doing design makes sense and should be continued.

As the initial initiatives are completed, they should be assessed to develop a database on what will be required to make the new design initiatives successful.

One company developed a postassessment model to determine lessons learned from its initial venture into CE and to guide future work in simultaneous design. This company learned the following from the new design approach:

- Senior management support was absolutely essential to set the stage, prepare the culture, and make unequivocal commitments to providing the resources needed to carry out the new process.

- A competitive crisis, which came about when the company found out that one competitor was about to launch a new product that embodied major improvements in technology, substantially motivated managers and professionals to embrace CE. Investigation into the practices of this competitor caused the company to conclude that the competitor was getting its products to the marketplace sooner, at a lower cost, and with higher quality. By reverse engineering the competitor's product, the matter of higher quality became markedly apparent. Finding out about this competitor's technology advantage was serendipitous and led to a formal benchmarking of other competitors. The result was that the company was soon playing "catch-up ball" without an accelerated product development initiative.

- The sequential method of product and process design had served the company well as long as competitors were using the same traditional approaches. However, with the new game of CE, competitive survival required that the company continue to embrace its new way of product and process design.

- A greater commitment was needed to provide future teams with the authority, responsibility, and resources to do their job. A major commitment to education and training was needed in the future, as well as a policy of continuous improvement in the manner in which future design efforts were undertaken.

- Further enhancement of concurrency in product and process design could be done if care was taken to develop a sense of ownership among the team members.

- Greater attention needed to be placed on more frequent and comprehensive review of the progress made in future concurrent engineering initiatives.

- A commitment was needed that each design effort would go through a postappraisal effort. The lessons learned from this appraisal would be integrated into the training curriculum of the enterprise so new teams could review and discuss these lessons in future design efforts.

Learning about how other companies do CE can help get an enterprise's team ready to do CE. At Ameritech, a new concurrent engineering project called Looking Glass was initiated through a team of engineers, marketers, and purchasing agents, who planned a $1 billion fiber-optic installation in the company's five-state region. The team set technical specifications, bid the job, and took care of regulator problems in just three months. If the company had used traditional serial design strategies, the effort would have required managers to get approval up and down the organizational hierarchy and would have taken an estimated three years. In another first step, a financial assessment and reporting team made up of the chief financial officer, controllers, and accountants was launched. By roaming the country and talking with subsidiary people and doing analyses of reports, the team was able to eliminate 6 million pages of reports.[11]

BARRIERS TO CONCURRENT ENGINEERING

There are cultural and other obstacles to the successful development and operation of CE. A major obstacle is the different background of design and manufacturing engineers—two principal players in the operation. These principals have their parochial backgrounds and technical languages and lack a common language and perspective required for CE. Design engineers tend to view themselves as being creative—a viewpoint that is correct, since design engineering is both a science and an art. Manufacturing engineers are often viewed as doing the planning for the "dirty work" of engineering. Design and manufacturing engineers are usually located in different buildings and in different places in the organizational design of the enterprise.

There are other pitfalls to be avoided in using CE strategies. A lack of interdisciplinary appreciation and expertise on the part of the designers can compromise the effort. If there is an inherent bureaucratic bias in the enterprise, leading to built-in inflexibility in how the organization works, interaction among the members of the design team can be impaired. If manufacturing cost information is unavailable, the input from manufacturing into the design phase will be imparied. Ineffective communication among the members of the product–process development team can inhibit creativity and innovation in designing better products and supporting processes. If the team members are not qualified in their technical fields or if they lack the interpersonal skills to work together in the team culture, the design may be compromised. Finally,

[11] Brian Dumaine, "Times Are Good? Create a Crisis," *Fortune,* June 28, 1993, pp. 123–130.

there is the danger that a design team will arrive at premature compromises on designs too early and negate the benefits of CE.

When CE is launched in the enterprise, reverberations or trigger effects occur.

TRIGGER EFFECTS OF CE

When a CE initiative is launched, a series of trigger effects are set in motion that eventually lead to significant changes in the way in which product and process design are carried out in the enterprise. Changes in the role of people—including managers, professionals, and workers—come about. The way in which decisions are made will be modified, and individual managers and professionals will see some of their decision authority being modified to include more decision making by team members. Power relationships within the enterprise are changed. Cross-functional and cross-organizational activities start a modification of the organizational culture. Conflicts over design, which were formerly hidden between the boundaries of the organization, tend to come out into the open, with better resolution strategies and results. Design becomes an enterprisewide activity, and the results of this evolution stretch throughout the life cycle of the product. Since design becomes more of a competitive and profit issue, senior managers will become more involved and committed to supporting design activities. Cultural changes will come about as the way people work together changes. There will be expanded opportunities for development of leadership skills for more people—those who serve on the product—process design teams. More training in both technical and social skills will be required for people, and there will be a greater need to communicate.

Other trigger effects of CE include using organizational changes to put design and manufacturing engineers together. At one company's decentralized business unit, the entire manufacturing organization reports to one individual. This includes procurement, configuration management, piece-part engineering, design and manufacturing engineering, and manufacturing planning. At General Motors's Truck and Bus Group in Pontiac, Michigan, manufacturing engineering lives side by side with product engineering during design, development, and testing. Further integration of disciplines is used through the form of a product–process design team. Better coordination of design and manufacturing activities is made possible by having people work together up front so that customers are better satisfied. At General Electric's Industrial Circuit Breaker Division, design and manufacturing engineers are under a common manager. A position of productivity czar was created (with the rank of vice-president) for engineering, production, and sourcing to facilitate a synergy of the disciplines involved in product and process design. At Xerox's decentralized business unit in Webster, New York, the entire manufacturing organization reports to one individual (this include procurement, configuration management, piece-part engineering, and manufacturing planning).

In many companies, the distinction between designer and manufacturer is becoming less clear. Some companies are seeing a distinct advantage in putting shop floor employees on product design teams. A lesson can be learned from the Japanese, who do not have separate design and engineering functions.

The growing integration of design and manufacturing engineering through various organizational designs highlights the importance of communication and the development of useful coordinating mechanisms. Throughout the experience of product design, several alternative ways of integrating disciplines have been tried. These include a policy of manufacturing sign-off of design, the use of an individual as an integrator–coordinator to pull together the efforts of design and manufacturing, and the use of product–process design teams. Finally, as experience in the use of such teams demonstrates the value of further integration of the disciplines in product development, product–process design departments have been set up. For example, continued integration of activities at Eastman Kodak reduces the distinction between the designer and the manufacturer. When benchmarking was carried out against Japanese companies, it was found that separate design and manufacturing functions did not exist.

At the Ford Motor Company, a matrix design recently installed is more product driven. Most of the self-contained country units have been eliminated along with the separate vehicles, engineers, and components that they produce. Ford wants to make cars for the global market. Similarly, Texas Instruments has worldwide product development teams that weed out parochial ideas and support ones that have global appeal.

IMPROVEMENT IDEAS

Here are a few ideas drawn from industry on how to get a company ready for more global competition:

- Hierarchies should be flattened, leading to fewer bureaucrats, faster decisions, and a freer flow of ideas. For example, ASEA Brown Boveri has only one layer between the top ranks and the business units.
- Companies like Unilever, GE Appliances, and Texas Instruments all use special teams to set up new operations. L. M. Ericsson used teams to beat out rivals by developing digital mobile-phone systems for Europe, the United States, and Japan. At Texas Instruments, a team combs its operations for ideas that have a global potential.
- Unilever sent a team of Chinese-speaking troubleshooters from the company's 100-country operations. The team helps to build detergent plants, market shampoo and other personal products.

- The CEO of L. M. Ericsson introduced a matrix system, with unit managers reporting to both product divisions and corporate headquarters. Executives now spend more time building consensus, but the matrix has been effective for sharing information among forty R&D labs around the world and for getting products to market faster.
- At Chrysler, the general manager of the large-car platform team explicitly rejects the traditional product development processes of his U.S. competitors in favor of simple milestones and aggressive target dates. Chrysler outsources about 70 percent of its parts to a greatly reduced number of suppliers early in the development cycle. Supplier bidding has been virtually eliminated, and some suppliers have full-service responsibilities for coordinating the development activities of other lower-tier suppliers. Following dramatic reductions in the number of suppliers as well as other concurrent engineering strategies, Chrysler compressed development time by about 25 percent of more and produced world-class vehicles with state-of-the-art components at lower costs.[12]

The use of product–process design teams brings about a systems perspective of product development. The use of such teams changes the pace and thrust of design, changes the role of people, and realigns the sequence of decisions involved in the design of products and processes. The cross-organizational and cross-functional operation of concurrent engineering changes the power and influence relationships and helps bring conflict over substantive issues into the open. Design becomes an enterprisewide activity, stretching throughout the life cycle of the product. As senior managers become involved in setting the stage for the operation, they gain a greater appreciation of what is needed to pursue competitive product development initiatives.

Concurrent engineering costs money—but so do serial design activities. More important, managers considering the use of concurrent engineering need to know what the cost would be of not starting the effort to do things simultaneously in product development—what would be the impact on competitiveness?

Finally, setting up and operating design teams may require more up-front commitment of funds and time but will ultimately lead to reduced time and costs when concurrent engineering is carried out efficiently and effectively.

WHY NOW?

Since the potential benefits of concurrent engineering are so important to improved competition, why has it taken so long for the activity to gain acceptance and popularity? Earlier attempts to implement CE were thwarted to a large degree by hierarchial organizational cultures and their strong parochial-

---

[12] Rajan R. Kamath and Jeffrey K. Liker, "A Second Look at Japanese Product Development," *Harvard Business Review,* November–December 1994, pp. 154–170.

ism reinforced by strong middle-management fiedoms. Managers did not want to give up control to a team that crossed functions and organizations to do its job. The serial over-the-wall approach used in traditional product design reflected the prevailing organizational philosophy, which reinforced the existing bureaucratic hierarchial and layers of specialized jobs around each department. People resist change—and when forced to accept change, they take plenty of time to change their ways of working.

In the early days of project management, the use of a matrix organizational design, with its dual reporting relationships, made people uncomfortable. Many people resisted having a reporting relationship with two people. As the use of matrix organizational designs accelerated, people became more comfortable with the matrix. The use of product–process design teams activates a matrix system, and people can feel discomfort, particularly due to modification of traditional design and manufacturing work in addition to the fear of dual reporting relationships.

As computer and information technology advancements occurred and as the role of middle managers came into question, the issue of territoriality in an organizational culture came into question. Nonetheless, the serial approach endured simply because the cultural message continued that "this is simply the way we do things around here." As long as traditional organizational philosophies prevailed and the existing organizational hierarchy was reinforced, innovative ways of using teams to bring a focus to cross-functional and cross-organizational activities were stifled.

SUMMARY

A distinct technological competence in manufacturing and other processes required to get a product into the hands of customers provides considerable opportunity for gaining and maintaining a competitive edge in the global marketplace. Products can be reverse engineered, but it is difficult to determine the specific strategy of a competitor in its manufacture of a product.

Product designers are not the only ones likely to have creative insight into the design of a product. Customers who use the product know what works and what does not work. Members of a product–process design team, representing different disciplines and having different experiences, can provide a source of innovation not usually tapped in serial design. They can be from the marketing staff; they can be users, suppliers, and after-sales service people; and they can be those who maintain the product. When a suitable culture is developed in the design team, there will be more communication and a greater exchange of information among team members—there will be synergy in considering the suitability of the design.

In today's unforgiving global marketplace, decisions concerning a freezing of a design must be made in a timely manner. There is simply not enough time to bring about timely decisions using traditional and antiquated serial design strategies. As the product–process design team works together, there will be a heightened awareness of the importance of product design to improve effectiveness and efficiency, and there will be an appreciation of the costs of not doing design in a timely manner (particularly as competitors' design strategies are benchmarked and their products are reverse engineered). Customers usually know what they want the product to be—what technology it can offer them, and how it can create value for them. Their presence on the product team can help in finding ways to adapt and package the technology to their needs. In some industries, the majority of technological innovations come from customers.

This chapter presented an overview of concurrent engineering. As a systematic approach to the simultaneous design of products, services, and organizational processes, CE provides opportunities for reducing the time required to commercialize new products and services. Since the cost of manufacturing a product, as well as the total expected cost of the product, is determined during the design stage, the importance of CE as a competitive strategy cannot be underestimated. Some of the major points discussed in this chapter are as follows:

- The benefits of CE make it clear that any company that wishes to remain competitive must embrace the concept and practice of CE.
- Getting products and services to the market sooner gives a distinct competitive advantage.
- The use if CE is growing, as evidenced by the number of leading companies whose experiences with CE were discussed in this chapter.
- Traditional serial product design has several major weaknesses, such as increased costs and schedules leading to untimely product commercialization. Manufacturing and marketing considerations of product and services are not adequately considered until after the product or service design is completed, which creates the need to modify the product or service through engineering changes. Competitive advantage is often sacrificed as a result.
- The key objective of CE is to deliver value to the customer on a more timely basis. CE enables the full consideration of manufacturing, marketing, after-sales service, and financial issues early in the design stage, thus providing more time to evaluate and design better strategies for delivering value to the customer.
- Launching CE activities is similar to launching other team initiatives. Objectives, goals, strategies, and organizational design considerations must be dealt with early in the life cycle of CE.
- Customers and suppliers play important roles in any CE effort. When these key stakeholders are brought into the CE process, the benefits of CE are leveraged and can lead to global competitiveness.

- There are barriers to CE, such as attitudes, nonsupportive cultures, territorial issues, and an unwillingness to depart from "the way we have always done things around here."
- CE is an idea whose time has come—its arrival was delayed because of a fixation with the traditional hierarchical approach to management, parochial thinking, and satisfaction with the over-the-wall approach. When global competitors began using CE, the competitive dimensions of global business changed and interest in CE grew.

There are several other types of teams used as elements of organizational strategy. These teams are discussed in the following chapter.

____11
SUNDRY TEAMS

The results produced by many different types of teams contribute to the well-being of the enterprise.

This chapter discusses several alternative types of teams: (1) task forces, (2) plural executive teams, (3) product management teams, (4) quality teams, (5) audit teams, and (6) crisis management teams. In many respects, these teams are similar to the other teams presented in this book. The fundamentals of team management—planning, organizing, motivation, leadership, and control—apply to these teams as well as to the other types of teams discussed in this book. In some contexts, the results produced by these teams contribute outputs that become building blocks in the design and execution of operational and strategic initiatives in an enterprise.

One way of looking at the different types of teams is to review their reason for existing. A useful distinction is to think of teams in the context of (1) teams that create something new for the organization that did not previously exist (project teams and product–process design teams fall in this grouping), (2) teams that deal with problems and opportunities in the enterprise through analysis and recommendations (task forces, audit teams, and quality assessment teams are examples of this form, (3) teams that are not ad hoc but are permanent parts of the organizational design and exist to make or do things (production teams, sales teams, and after-sales service teams are examples of this type of team), and (4) teams that are of a plural executive nature and are usually found at the senior management levels of the enterprise (executive committees and management committees are examples).

TASK FORCES

Task forces are commonly used by organizations to deal with temporary problems and opportunities that cannot easily be handled by the existing organizational structure. Usually the solutions or approaches to these problems or opportunities require cutting across organizational boundaries. A task force can be a powerful mechanism for bringing people together to focus on both simple and complex matters, usually for a specific purpose for which the other types of teams described in this book would be inappropriate. When the objective for which the task force was organized is satisfied, the people on the task force go back to their permanent assignments in the organization.

A procurement task force at H. J. Heinz Company was appointed to find and work out partnerships of the most efficient suppliers around the world and consolidate purchasing across all of the company affiliates. So far this team has saved Heinz $100 million on an annualized basis. The team's efforts with suppliers in value-engineering packaging and raw materials will provide additional opportunities for cost reductions in the years ahead. The pace of the task force was remarkable; it took less than four months from the time the task force team was launched until the contracts with suppliers were signed. Traditionally, the company had negotiated purchasing agreements on an annual basis. The long-term contracts gave the suppliers security to work with the task force team on value-engineering processes and generate savings for both sides of the relationship. The cost savings are due to reduced product costs in the suppliers' factories and in the Heinz production facilities—a real "pulling costs out of the system."[1]

Another major food processor appointed several task forces that were used to conduct ad hoc studies and recommend strategies to senior management for improving performance of the company:

- Purchasing practices
- Overhead costs
- Commercialization of products and services
- Corporate downsizing and restructuring
- Upgrading manufacturing practices to reduce production costs
- Benchmarking of competitive products

Preliminary results from the output of these task forces were provided to another corporate task force that was engaged in reviewing the strategic direction of the company.

A task force composed of persons drawn from the appropriate units of the organization is usually used to deal with short-term problems or situations.

---

[1] "The Power of Change," *The H. J. Heinz Company 1993 Annual Report*, p. 3.

People can be assigned on either a part-time or full-time basis to work on the situation. In effect, an informal matrix organizational form exists on task forces: The people serving on the task force have to satisfy two "supervisors"— their regular supervisor, and the task force leader. Since each member of the task force comes from different functional elements of the enterprise and brings different viewpoints, goals, loyalties, purposes, background credentials, and attitudes to the task force, the integration of human effort to produce positive results on the task force is no small challenge for the leader.

The task force approach is a rather simple concept and certainly not a new one. When managers perceive real or imagined organizational boundaries or that the existing organizational design is not equipped to handle a problem or opportunity, a task force can be used. Sometimes the problem or opportunity does not fit the existing organizational structure or is something so new that managers do not know how to handle it; and sometimes the effort requires such a departure from established policies and procedures that it simply cannot be dealt with by the existing organization.

People who are nominated to serve on a task force should have the knowledge and skills needed to contribute to a high-quality solution and should have the organizational power and influence to see that their contributions to the task force effort will produce usable returns. Task forces are appropriate when organizations face temporary challenges that contain some of the following characteristics:

- Several different parts or disciplines of the organization are or will be affected.
- The solution of the problem or opportunity has a high priority, and organizational managers should commit resources as soon as possible.
- There is not an existing organizational unit that is qualified or equipped to address the situation.
- The nature of the solution is highly uncertain, and a database of potential solutions is needed to support the decision makers in the enterprise.
- The solution is likely to result in significant changes in organizational mission, objectives, goals, or strategies.

More often than not, task forces serve as preliminary initiators or organizational changes. Task force leaders and people who serve on task forces can improve their performance by following the general instructions provided in this book for the other types of teams used as instruments of organizational strategy. Task force leaders have a major opportunity to practice the fundamental skills essential to general management or the management of a functional entity:

- Exercising judiciously the knowledge, skills, and attitudes needed to design and execute the management functions of planning, organizing, motivating, direction, and control

- Planning for and leading effective meetings
- Conducting ongoing communication with the task force members and with other stakeholders of the task force initiative
- Planning for and conducting rigorous analytical studies to develop the databases required to make and recommend implementation strategies
- Planning for, obtaining, and distributing financial and other assets for the task force
- Identifying and negotiating the individual and collective roles of the task force members
- Developing the proposals and briefings needed to fulfill the task force's objectives and goals
- Keeping a balance between the analytical and political considerations involved in recommending a course of action for the task force's output
- Meeting budget, schedule, and task force output goals

Task forces are an organizational unit in every sense of the word. Although they are temporary in nature, their success depends on how well the leader and the task force members are able to work together within an assigned mission to produce an output that is useful to the enterprise.[2]

PLURAL EXECUTIVE TEAMS

The management of large, complex organizations presents many pressing issues, such as market changes, product development initiatives, advances in technology, and global business. These issues have created major serious time and intellectual challenges for senior executives. As organizations continue to be buffeted with political, social, economic, competitive, and technological changes, the overall management of these organizations will continue to be complex and demanding beyond the capabilities of the most qualified and energetic single manager. Faster reaction time is required for both operational and strategic initiatives.

The major theme of this book is to present alternative teams as a means for managers to delegate authority and responsibility for key operational and strategic problems and opportunities. Each of the teams discussed in this book holds the promise of an effective organizational delegation process to manage the use of resources, provide specific and measurable initiatives that will improve productivity, and position the enterprise for adapting those future strategies that will ensure its survival and growth in both current and future

[2] Readers who wish to find additional material on task forces are encouraged to read the chapter by James P. Ware, "Making the Matrix Come Alive: Managing a Task Force" in *Matrix Management Systems,* Van Nostrand Reinhold Company, New York, 1984, pp. 112–131.

markets. Consider the awesome challenges of contemporary managers in selecting short-term and long-term strategies for the following:

- Concurrent development of products, services, and supporting organiza-
  tional resources that will lead to faster commercialization of products
  and services
- Intensity of global competition
- Reduction of costs through reengineering, restructuring, downsizing, and
  out-sourcing of generic services
- Continuous improvement of organizational products, services, and organi-
  zational processes
- Higher quality of products, services, and processes
- Growing stakeholder interest in and influence on the affairs and fortunes
  of the enterprise
- Higher productivity demands
- Growing influence of product/service and process technology
- Increasing participation of people in the management of the enterprise
- Increasing tendencies toward more local, state, and national regulation
  of products and services and the conditions under which organizational
  purposes are fulfilled

The strategic management of a large enterprise requires a focused, integrated assessment of the organization's ability to perform its mission through
satisfying its objectives and goals within the construct of a meaningful design
and implementation of strategy. Various organizational roles have been tried
with varying degrees of success to help a one-person manager cope with the
complexity and breadth of running a major enterprise:

- Assistant to the manager
- Chief of staff
- Special assistant
- Executive assistant

The authority and responsibility delegated to these individuals vary depending
on the ability of the incumbent to assume some of the workload of the chief
executive officer (CEO).

Early, unique experimentation with a multiperson CEO was carried out
by the E. I. DuPont de Nemours Company in 1921 in the form of a ten-person
"committee-line" group devoted full time to company affairs.[3] The idea of a
team managing the affairs of an enterprise was not confined to the United

---

[3] William H. Mylander, "Management by Executive Committee," *Harvard Business Review,*
May–June 1965, p. 51.

States. In Germany, a team known as the Vorstand was used to provide collective management of a company. Many different names have been used to describe a top-level team:

- Office of the chairman
- Office of the president
- President's office
- Corporate executive
- Management committee
- Executive office
- Executive committee

Throughout this section, the term *plural executive* will be used to describe a senior-level team that collectively provides integrated management of an enterprise.

Reluctance to use the plural executive can be attributed to the unity of command principle, which states that a person should receive orders from only one individual. Conventional management theory and wisdom have held that a violation of Fayol's principle would create ambiguities in the authority and responsibility patterns in an organization, leading to compromise of the organization's ability to attain its purposes. In today's team-driven enterprise, the authority, responsibility, and accountability patterns are complex, ever-changing, and based as much on a team's or group's ability to manage and lead other people and elements of the enterprise as the traditional formal designated authority of a single organizational position.

Normally, the members of the plural executive are from the senior-level positions in the enterprise, although sometimes specialists such as legal, R&D, or manufacturing representatives will be included. Most of the literature on the subject identifies several required capabilities of the members: (1) interpersonal skills; (2) intellectual maturity; (3) proven track record; (4) demonstrated judgment; (5) A systems appreciation; and (6) the ability to evaluate risks, uncertainties, and organizational purposes in making strategic decisions for the enterprise, as well as the ability to maintain oversight of the enterprise's strategic direction.

As both a policy-making and oversight team, the members of the plural executive have authority and responsibility for making and executing decisions within the context of the enterprise's strategic purposes. An effective plural executive cannot be leaderless—the CEO has overall responsibility for leading the team. In theory, plural executive team members have equality in making decisions, but the CEO has the residual responsibility and accountability to see that the right decisions are made at the right time, or to overrule the decision of the team if he or she deems it prudent. Should the plural executive be unable to come to a full consensus, then the CEO, as the plural executive team leader, must make a decision. A decision made as a result of the team's inability to come to a consensus should be weighed carefully to understand why the team members have not been able to come to an agreement on a decision leading to a course of action. After careful examination of the risk, uncertainties, alternatives, and probable and possible outcomes as a result of the pending decision, the CEO has the residual responsibility to make a decision.

A plural executive is the most senior team in the enterprise. In a real sense, a corporate board of directors is a plural executive. Boards of directors have been used in the business community for over 150 years. State general corporation laws require that all business corporations have boards (they typically stipulate that the corporation "shall be managed by a board of at least three directors"). An effective corporate board of directors reviews pending major capital projects to determine their "strategic fit" in the overall strategic direction of the enterprise. Once a major capital project is funded, it becomes an important responsibility of the board to maintain surveillance over how well the project is progressing toward meeting its objectives and how the corporate strategy is likely to be affected when the "deliverables" of the project take their place in the "business the company is in."[4]

The board of directors is usually one level above the plural executive. If the plural executive team does its work well, the job of the board of directors should be made easier and more meaningful—*if* the board acts prudently in its fiduciary responsibilities to the corporation.

The advantages of using a plural executive team are much like the advantages of using any of the teams described in this book:

- Multidisciplinary review of major organizational strategies
- Intellectual expansion of the capabilities of the individual members as they work in synergy in making and executing decisions
- Reduction of parochial viewpoints of the individual members as they come together to merge their viewpoints and represent their functional areas of responsibility
- Greater flexibility in the use of resources as they enter into the give-and-take characteristic of teamwork
- Built-in checks and balances to monitor the actions of the individual executive working alone
- Greater opportunity for a systems integration of resources as the team members work together to meet the enterprise's mission, objectives, goals, and strategies
- Insight into the abilities of the individual members of the team and sharpened perception into which executives have the best leadership capabilities for further promotion in the enterprise

---

[4] For further reading, see Chapter 5, "The Board of Directors and Capital Projects," in David I. Cleland, *Project Management: Strategic Design and Implementation*, 2nd ed., McGraw-Hill, New York, 1994, pp. 105–132.

The plural executive is like any other organizational form: Its purpose should be established and described in appropriate documentation, such as a charter that delineates its authority, responsibility, and accountability. A team leader should be established, and the plural executive's operational effectiveness should be evaluated from time to time. How well the plural executive is doing its job can be assessed by examining how well the enterprise's purposes are being realized and how well the alternative teams in the enterprise are doing what they set out to do.

The plural executive, like other teams in the enterprise, is not a panacea. Yet any method of increasing the probability of a more integrated, synergistic approach to the management of large, complex organizations will bring a greater understanding of the enterprise, its emerging strategies, and the actions needed to satisfy its stakeholders. Greater integration of resources (leading to greater organizational synergy) will likely increase the probability of the enterprise outperforming its traditionally organized competitors.

Product management teams, used in product marketing strategies, have been around for some time.

PRODUCT MANAGEMENT TEAMS

Product management is generally considered an early form of project management. As the marketing of goods and services has become more complex and demanding, senior managers have searched for organizational designs that are adaptive and better suited to marketing single- and multiproduct lines. Marketing specific product lines, meeting the demands of specific groups of consumers, and at the same time remaining competitive demand innovative organizational designs that will focus the use of resources to accomplish product marketing aims.

The origins of product management can be traced back to the Procter and Gamble Company in 1927. A new product, Camay, soap, was not meeting sales projections; one individual was assigned as a product manager to bring a center of interest to marketing the soap. The product manager worked across organizational boundaries in the company to improve product marketing. The idea of a product manager caught on in other companies, such as Colgate-Palmolive, Kimberly-Clark, American Home Products, and Johnson and Johnson. In some companies, the product manager is referred to as a brand manager. Regardless of the title, one individual is designated as responsible for managing a product or a group of products. In so doing, the individual operates across organizational boundaries, much like the matrix management context of the project manager in the 1950s and 1960s.

Although the concept of the matrix organization was first put forth by Professor John F. Mee in 1964, its use has to some extent always existed—at least in the informal sense of an individual charged with a specific responsibility to deliver results. This individual had to cross organizational boundaries to get the job done.[5]

The product manager may be granted considerable or little documented authority—in either case, the individual's ability to exert personal authority through knowledge, experience, interpersonal skills, negotiation abilities, and so forth usually constitutes the major thrust of his or her authority. Regardless, the product manager becomes the organizational convergence for planning the control of the resources used for products. The product manager and the formal or informal team that helps that individual become visible in the enterprise. The individual and the team, however formal, will be held accountable for the success or failure of the product. A product charter for the product manager is a useful policy document so everyone understands the role that is expected in the management of a product or products. A product charter should include policy guidance regarding the following:

- A description of the product or products to be managed
- The delegated authority and responsibility and the context in which the product manager and the team members will be held in their roles
- Proposed target markets for the product
- Cost estimates for product marketing
- Schedules for marketing strategies
- Supporting organizational resources, as well as the responsibility of functional and other units of the enterprise in providing resources to the project manager
- The decision context of the product manager: a citation of those decisions that the product manager can make, followed by an enumeration of those product-related decisions that must be referred to higher authority for resolution
- Suggested marketing-mix considerations, if relevant
- The basis on which the product manager and the team members will be evaluated and rewarded

The evaluation criteria for the product manager and the team are an important matter. A number of factors can be considered that suggest the parameters of the evaluation and subsequent reward system. Some of the factors are beyond the direct control of the product manager. Nevertheless, he or she is still likely to be held accountable for the performance of the product. As a minimum, the evaluation criteria should include the following:

- Financial performance of the product
- Awareness of the market conditions and the development of a product

[5] John F. Mee, "Ideational Items: Matrix Organization," *Business Horizons,* Summer 1964, pp. 70–72

marketing plan to position the product for its best possible performance in that market

- Competitive assessments, including the benchmarking of major competing products
- Profile of the marketing mix that best positions the product.
- Awareness of the likely performance of the product, including the need for further development of new or improved products to meet anticipated competition
- Ability of product planning to produce results
- Adequacy of the ongoing review of the product performance, and the communication of such performance to senior level managers
- Ability of the product manager to work effectively in the matrix context in the enterprise

Products go through a life cycle. In the 1930s product managers came about for the planning and execution of product marketing. Today, product managers are expected to manage all aspects of a product throughout its life cycle. Marketing changes when competitive conditions change, when customers tastes vary, and when the market composition changes.

The product manager's job, working through the product management team, can be viewed as consisting of several major work packages:

- Planning for the product marketing, including linkages with enterprise strategic and operational plans and the development of operational plans for managing the product
- Careful description of the product, including specifications, operating characteristics, and physical characteristics (e.g., form, fit, and function)
- Detailed description of target markets and distribution matters, which can become the basis for executing marketing strategies
- Description of competing products, including ongoing benchmarking and reverse engineering of competitive products
- Description of the life cycle concept for the product
- Pricing strategy, including an understanding of market information that will enable the company to practice competitive price discrimination
- Promotion strategies, including when, how, where, and why certain advertising, sales promotion, and other promotional initiatives will be undertaken
- Distribution channels, including suitable inventory levels, customer responsiveness, and measurement of the firm's ability to meet customers' needs on a timely and quality basis
- Financial strategies, including estimates of revenues, costs, and likely profit contributions

• Overall schedules for how resources will be planned and committed to support the product

The product manager's early emergence in the late 1920s was one of the first signs that an alternative organizational design was needed to bring focus disparate functional activities in an enterprise. The individual appointed as a product manager, working within a product management team, creates an informal matrix context. All of the things that are done in modern organizations to enable alternative teams to function across organizational boundaries should be done for the operation of a product management team. As in other teams, as planning and control become more complex, subject to changes, and buffeted by the demands of global competition, the product management team will become more important as a way to find customers, get to them with quality products and services, and provide linkages to the strategic management of products and services within the enterprise.

QUALITY TEAMS

The use of teams in total quality management (TQM) has gained considerable acceptance in contemporary organizations. Quality circles, properly used, can facilitate quality management and productivity improvements, improve labor–management communication, and improve job satisfaction and the quality of worklife for employees. In addition, quality circles and quality teams can help in the planning and implementation of technological changes in the enterprise. Quality circles and quality teams are like other types of teams: They are highly participatory and integrate decision making and implementation for the improvement of quality to maximize customer satisfaction. Quality teams are especially valuable for helping improve complex and multifaced product, service, and organizational process design and execution. Quality teams play an important role in total quality management.

Much has been written about total quality management. Even the term *quality* has received many definitions. In a general sense, the term *quality* means that (1) the product or service provided by an individual or an organization is free of defects and performs its intended purpose according to specifications; (2) the product or service specifications are as close as possible to what the customer requires; (3) when the product or service is used by the customer, it performs in a reliable fashion with minimum downtime; and (4) the product or service provides value to the customer. TQM has emerged in recent years as a major new strategy in many enterprises. These strategies are driven by intense global competition characterized by an increasing market demand for better-quality products and services at competitive prices. The increasing cost of product design and production has motivated managers to find innovative ways to improve productivity, cut costs, and get to the marketplace sooner— and do all of these things in a quality manner. Both internal and external customers are aware that the quality expectations of product and service users have increased. In short, when the customer uses the product or service and it works as intended, that is quality.

Quality means many things. One authority in the field has described the eight dimensions of quality:

1. *Performance,* which refers to the product's functioning or operating characteristics. For an automobile these would include acceleration, handling, cruising speed, and comfort.
2. The *product features,* which are secondary characteristics that supplement the product's basic functioning, such as free drinks on a plane flight.
3. *Reliability,* which refers to the probability of the product's failing within a specified period of time.
4. *Conformance,* or the degree to which a product's design and operating characteristics match preestablished standards.
5. *Durability,* which is basically a measure of the product's life.
6. *Serviceability,* or the speed, courtesy, and adequacy of product repair.
7. *Aesthetics,* which relate to how a product looks, feels, sounds, tastes, or smells—clearly a matter of personal judgment that reflects individual preference.
8. *Perceived quality,* which recognizes that perceptions of quality are subjective and are evaluated less on their objective characteristics than on their images, advertising, or brand names.[6]

Quality improvement success can be seen in the products of many companies. Two excellent examples are L. L. Bean and the Caterpillar Tractor Company. L. L. Bean executes a customer-driven quality program through

- Conducting regular customer satisfaction surveys and sample group interviews to track customer and noncustomer perceptions of the quality of its own and its competitors' products and services
- Tracking on its computer all customer inquiries and complaints and updating the file daily
- Guaranteeing all its products to be 100 percent satisfactory and providing a full cash refund, if requested, on any returns
- Asking customers who are returning an item to fill out a short coded questionnaire and explain their reasons for returning the merchandise
- Performing extensive field tests an any new outdoor equipment before listing it in the company's catalogs[7]

---

[6] David A. Garvin, "What Does 'Product Quality' Really Mean?" *Sloan Management Review,* Fall 1984, pp. 25–40, by permission of the publisher. Copyright 1984 by the Sloan Management Review Association. All rights reserved.

[7] Hirotaka Takeuchi and John A. Quelch, "Quality Is More Than Making a Good Product," *Harvard Business Review,* July–August 1983, pp. 140–141. Copyright 1983 by the President and Fellows of Harvard College; all rights reserved.

The Caterpillar Company is fully committed to a quality program that includes

- Conducting two customer satisfaction surveys following each purchase, one after 300 hours of product use and the second after 500 hours of use
- Maintaining a centrally managed list of product problems as identified by customers from around the world
- Analyzing warranty and service reports submitted by dealers, as part of a product improvement program
- Asking dealers to conduct a quality audit as soon as the products are received and to attribute defects to either assembly errors or shipping damages
- Guaranteeing delivery of any part in forty-eight hours to any customer in any part of the world
- Encouraging dealers to establish side businesses in rebuilding parts to reduce costs and increase the speed of repairs[8]

The Texas Instruments Defense Systems and Electronic Group formed its first pilot quality teams in 1983. Teamwork, strategic planning, concurrent engineering, and strong supplier links have worked synergistically and have created impressive results. Since 1987, customer-conducted quality audits have declined by 72 percent. Since 1988, formal customer complaints have decreased by 62 percent, and the Group has topped competitors in eleven customer satisfaction categories. Revenues per worker went from $80,000 in 1987 to $125,000 in 1991. Teamwork within the team-driven organizational design at the Group has been the primary moving force to bring about these impressive improvements.

At a major electronics firm, quality teams called total quality teams (TQTs) have residual authority and responsibility for changes in production processes by working with industrial engineers and manufacturing engineers and specialists. The quality standards set in the company's plant are the same stringent standards put on vendors who wish to earn and retain a preferred vendor long-term contract with the company. Teams earn bonuses that are linked to defect rates and production cycles. The company has an aggressive training and education program designed to improve the knowledge, skills, and attitudes of all employees. People who have the tenacity to stick with the educational program can, over a period of several years, earn a degree through part-time study at a local university.

The concept of TQM has spread beyond industrial use. The mayor of Madison, Wisconsin led the city government into the quality movement. He recognized the crucial importance of the top executive getting personally and visibly involved in the change to a TQM culture. A key strategy in the design

[8] Ibid.

and implementation of the quality initiative in Madison was the recognition that problem solving to improve the delivery of city services requires teamwork and breaking down barriers between departments. Team members were front-line employees in problem solving. The fact that these employees were being consulted and enlisted rather than being ignored resulted in "huge improvements in morale and productivity." After the employees became involved, they expected feedback about the things they were doing well and verbal and written notes of appreciation from the mayor. In short, the TQM teams performed as teams and wanted to be recognized as teams. By the end of 1988, seventy-five quality team leaders had been trained. Team leaders were those individuals who had a stake in the outcome of team decisions and who led the teams. Facilitators were also appointed who came from other divisions or departments, who had no stake in decisions, and who took special responsibility for maintaining group processes.[9]

Most of the literature about TQM emphasizes giving customer concerns top priority and studying and continually striving to improve every work process so that the final product or service exceeds customer expectations. By building excellence into every process in an organization and by bringing quality initiatives together in products and services, customers will find their expectations exceeded. Quality leadership in products, services, and organizational processes can be done without using quality teams. While teams can be a crucial organizational design for quality improvement, TQM requires the commitment of everyone in the enterprise—from the CEO to the workers—as salespersons selling quality products and services to customers.

At the Boeing Defense & Space Group of the Boeing Company, the mission of satisfying customer needs provides the basis for a definition of the word *quality* as it is used in the quality improvement process: "Quality is providing our customers with products and services that consistently meet or exceed their needs and expectations, at a cost that represents value." To meet the expectations of internal and external customers, more and more dependence is being place on teams of people to work across organizational boundaries to get the job done.[10]

Quality teams—sometimes called quality project teams—are only one dimension of TQM. Such teams are an important dimension of TQM. The success or failure of a quality team will have a great impact on the organization because of the visibility of the team. As the challanges for improving quality become discernible, the benefits of having people at levels of the organization working on quality teams become apparent. The objective of quality teams is to improve work processes that have been identified as important to a positive change toward quality products and services. The multidisciplinary

[9] Joseph Sensenbrenner, "Quality Comes to City Hall," *Harvard Business Review,* March–April 1991, pp. 64–75.

[10] *Desktop Guide for Continuous Quality Improvement,* Boeing Defense and Space Group, Continuous Quality Improvement, Seattle, Wash., 1992, pp. 3–16.

quality team can study the organizational processes methodically to find ways of improving the use of resources and integrating those resources into the enterprise's products and services. Quality teams bring a focus to quality improvement initiatives in a manner that traditional organizational design is not able to do. Managers who advocate quality teams, and often work on these teams, will learn about and how to plan for quality. They will identify multiple problems and opportunities that can remain hidden in the parochial "silos" of the functional elements of an enterprise.

Once a quality problem or opportunity has been found, the team brings an interdisciplinary, methodical approach to finding a permanent solution or exploiting an opportunity. Quality teams, as they work on quality initiatives, have the means to solve problems and exploit opportunities—and in so doing become missionaries for TQM education and training and for the development of a culture in which TQM simply becomes "the way we do things around here." The contribution of the quality team to a culture that supports TQM is just as important as the solution of a quality problem.

Quality teams, properly organized and managed, provide meaningful opportunities for workers to get involved in improving organizational performance. For example, at the Allen-Bradley plant in Twinsburg, Ohio (which makes circuit boards, programmable controllers, and other electronic devices), employees had to cope with a pile of manuals, work orders, and memos, most written in "engineeringese." Workers, frustrated with the blizzard of paperwork, resorted to their own methods of doing things—like taping up crude crib sheets on their work benches. The plant manager pulled seven assemblers off the floor, some for as long as seven months, and put them on teams with engineers and supervisors. Their task was to devise procedures comprehensible to everyone. Now paper and envelopes have been replaced by electronic mail, which delivers new instructions and purges old ones.[11]

At one Hewlett-Packard factory a decade ago, four of every 1000 soldered connections were defective—not a bad record for those days. Engineers were able to cut the defect rate in half by modifying the process. When quality teams of workers were brought in, they practically rebuilt the entire operation and slashed defects to under two per million.[12]

At two Exxon plants near Houston and Baton Rouge, workers and managers were organized into quality teams to find ways to streamline the plants. From 1988 to 1990, plant operations cut its working capital needs from 18 to 8 percent of its $400 million yearly sales. Changes that were accomplished to bring about these improvements included the labeling of thousands of gauges so they could be read by both experts and workers. In addition, maintenance on a huge compressor that usually failed three times a year brought down the plant for three days each time. Since the plant's maintenance crew was

[11] Ronald Henkoff, "The Hot New Seal of QUALITY," *Fortnue,* June 28, 1993, pp. 116–120.
[12] Otis Port and John Carey, "Questing for the Best," *Business Week/Quality,* 1991, p. 16.

increased from eight to thirteen, the compressor has not failed in nearly three years.[13]

Eastman Chemical, a Baldridge Award winner in the large manufacturers category, culminated in the realization of TQM objectives first set forth in 1980: To be first in quality. The company's interlocking team structure links all employees and provides a direct link from operators to senior management throughout the company. Through these teams, driven by the highest of quality standards, individuals are able to improve processes and manage their teams' efforts. Multiple strategies are used to drive a continuous improvement process through all of the interlocking teams, which brings virtually every employee into the teaming and quality improvement process.

TQM has two applications in the strategic management of teams. The first is a direct application, in which teams are set up for the specific purpose of improving quality in products, services, and processes. The deliverables of such teams are TQM-directed strategies to improve quality throughout all elements of the enterprise. The second application is simply the use of TQM concepts, techniques, and processes in the work of alternative teams, reengineering teams, benchmarking teams, concurrent engineering teams, and so forth. The demarcation between the two types of teams is somewhat blurred, depending on the purpose of the teams. Whatever the application, TQM is an attitude, intellectually conceived, that includes the reasoning and capabilities of all members of the enterprise as they analyze, decide, implement, and review the quality of their work in delivering value to both internal and external customers.

Can TQM initiatives be set up successfully without using teams? Probably not, since the opportunity for quality improvement rests within a given unit of the enterprise, such as a function, office, or business unit—as well as in improvements in cross-functional and cross-organizational work. TQM is everyone's work—individuals, groups, teams, organizational units, and the enterprise as an entity.

Five principles are suggested to live by in TQM:

- *The CEO must be involved* (e.g., taking the lead in setting up teams).
- *Customer focus is critical.* Pepsi-Cola surveyed 10,000 customers to develop sixteen priorities for its new quality effort. Fed Ex lives by its Service Quality Indicator, which tracks how often customers experience the annoyance of late deliveries and misplaced packages, among other things.
- *TQM must be linked to a few clear strategic objectives.* Ask "Just what am I trying to achieve?" Johnson and Johnson's redesigned TQM has three objectives—boosting customer satisfaction, reducing product intro-

---

[13] Thane Peterson, Kevin Kelly, Joseph Weber, and Neil Gross, "Top Products for Less Than Top Dollar," *Business Week/Quality,* October 25, 1991, p. 68.

duction time, and cutting costs. A cross-functional team reduced the expense and time it takes J&J to develop customized retail displays for chain drugstores and supermarkets. Motorola has two key objectives: (1) defect prevention, and (2) cycle time reduction (including reducing the time it takes to get jobs done).

- *A financial payback is required.* Clear TQM objectives are important, and payback should not be put on hold forever. At Rubbermaid, before a TQM team is formed, proponents must answer three questions: Who is your customer, what service are you providing, and what business strategy are you satisfying? Tenneco took a hard look at how quality failures were piling on extra costs. These included the cost of internal failures (unscheduled downtime), external failures (a flood of warranty claims), prevention (project planning), and appraisal (testing, inspection).
- *Any outsider's new TQM program must be considered.* However, companies should not negate their uniqueness by adopting an off-the-shelf quality program.[14]

There are a few other suggestions that can help make TQM work:

1. The senior executive must make a clear demonstrated commitment to the design and implementation of a TQM program in the enterprise, including active involvement in the design and development of the program.
2. A few key objectives and goals should be selected for the program that have a high probability of being attained.
3. Customers should be the focus—what do they want and need by way of products and services and what will they hold in high esteem?
4. TQM must be linked to a clear financial reward system that employees understand and trust.
5. Companies should not take a "canned" program from off the shelf—they should benchmark competitors and the best in the industry and develop a program that has an operational, strategic, and cultural fit for the organization.
6. Companies should use teams as the basic organizational design through which TQM initiatives will be developed and implemented.

A key aim of any TQM program is to improve the quality of products, services, and organizational processes; deliver ehnanced quality to internal and external customers; and improve morale and productivity by making employees' jobs more meaningful and encouraging their participation in the management of the organization (and thus eliminate supervision and quality inspection staff).

---

[14] Rahul Jacob, "TQM—More Than a Dying Fad?" *Fortune,* October 18, 1993, pp. 66–72.

The International Quality Study, conducted by the American Quality Foundation and Ernst & Young, examined the quality management practices of four industries in Canada, Germany, Japan, and the United States. A major finding of this study was that business in all four countries (except Japan) expect to increase the involvement of employees in quality-related teams. The Japanese expect little change in their use of quality teams.[15]

AUDIT TEAMS

Audit teams, which perform independent performance audits on some aspect of an organization, can provide valuable insight with which managers can develop strategies for improving deficiencies. An independent audit may be defined as an in-depth process that involves analysis of an organizational work element's performance: finance, marketing, manufacturing, R&D, project, and so forth. Usually an audit covers both the technical and managerial aspects of the work. The intent of the audit is to evaluate the success of the unit—its ability to produce meaningful results toward meeting its mission, objectives, and goals. Audit of a project is best done at key points in the project's life cycle, or when the project is being buffeted by important problems or changes whose effects managers may not fully appreciated.

Audits are used at all levels of an enterprise. At the board of directors level, an audit can be done to determine performance of major units or the entire corporation. A board of directors may order an audit and, through one of its subcommittees, make sure that the audit is appropriately executed and followed up with the most relevant and timely remedial action.

An audit was conducted of a large water pollution abatement system project prior to the initiation of detailed planning to turn the completed system over to the project owner. This audit disclosed several contract modification changes that were being unduly delayed and that could have had an adverse influence on the operational availability of the system. By discovering the delay in these changes through the audit, the project manager was able to initiate remedial strategies to get the project back on schedule and meet its operational date.

The process used in the audit of a project can give insight into how an audit team should be managed and what should be expected in the successful pursuit of an audit.

Project Audits[16]

Project audits provide an independent appraisal of where a project stands and the efficiency and effectiveness with which the project is being managed. A project audit should do the following:

[15] "The International Quality Study," *Quality Progress,* November 1991, pp. 33–37.
[16] David I. Cleland, *Project Management: Strategic Design and Implementation,* 2nd ed., McGraw-Hill, New York, 1994, pp. 295–298.

- Determine what is going right, and why.
- Determine what is going wrong, and why.
- Identify forces and factors that have prevented or may prevent achievement of cost, schedule, and technical performance goals.
- Evaluate the efficacy of existing project management strategy.
- Provide for an exchange of ideas, information, problems, solutions, and strategies with the project team members.

A project audit should cover key functions, depending on the nature of the project, in both the technical and nontechnical areas:

- Engineering
- Manufacturing
- Finance and accounting
- Contracts
- Purchasing
- Marketing
- Organization and management
- Quality
- Reliability
- Test and deployment
- Logistics
- Construction

An unplanned audit may be called for during the project life cycle if principal managers sense that the project is in trouble or is heading for trouble. If there is uncertainty concerning the project's status, or if there has been a change in the strategic direction of the organization, a project audit may be in order. When a new project manager takes over a project, he or she should order an audit, both to become familiar with an unbiased view of the project and to come up to speed with the key issues and problems that are facing the project.

An audit team is much like other forms of teams. It must be organized so team members know their individual and collective roles on the team. Many of the planning initiatives undertaken on any team can be applied to an audit team, such as development of a work breakdown structure; establishment of schedules, scope of work and deliverables, objectives and goals; development of a review process; and provision of details on when, where, and how the audit will be done. A financial strategy to cover the costs of doing the audit is also needed. Matters of confidentiality and to whom the final audit report will be given should be stipulated.

CRISIS MANAGEMENT TEAMS

A crisis can arise at any time in organizations. Aircraft crashes, oil spills, fires, tornadoes, hostage-taking situations, product liability suits, computer viruses, earthquakes, loss of key personnel, and so forth: An endless list of potential crises could be developed. In a few moments a stable situation could deteriorate, leaving an enterprise fighting for its life. How well an organization responds to crises will be reflected in the timeliness and thoroughness of its response. How well the resolution of a crisis is led by a responsible and competent individual will affect the outcome. In any event, preplanning for potential crises should be carried out. How well a crisis leader deals with the stress, public relations, decision making, and damage control is important as well. Swale has suggested a crises control model for team crisis management as the basic organizational design for dealing with crises.[17]

SUMMARY

This chapter discussed several types of sundry teams. These teams are used as organizational designs to focus the use of resources in dealing with both operational and strategic initiatives. These sundry teams require careful management: They should be properly planned, organized, motivated, led, monitored, evaluated, and controlled to ensure that their objectives and goals are properly and economically attained.

Some of the key messages contained in this chapter include the following:

- Sundry teams are formed to deal with such initiatives as short-term, unique problems and opportunities.
- Plural executive teams provide a synergy of major organizational considerations in the strategic management of an enterprise.
- Product management teams have been with us for several decades and are used to bring together marketing matters in products and services.
- Quality teams help to improve organizational products, services, and processes, leading to total quality management success in the enterprise.
- Audit teams are used to evaluate the ability of an organization, or one of its units or functions, to produce efficicious results.
- Crisis management teams are used to deal with crucial periods and issues in an enterprise.
- Since sundry teams are much like other types of teams in an enterprise, their management parallels many of the management ideas and processes suggested for other teams.

[17] See W. Stephen Swale, "Crisis Project Management," *pmNETwork,* January 1991, pp. 25–29.

The strategic implications arising from the use of teams to focus operational and strategic initiatives are many. The trigger effects go beyond improvements in quality and productivity. They range from an impact on the organization's management to the personal management style carried out by managers and workers as they go about their work in the enterprise. Once teams are used in an enterprise, things are never the same again. Everything about the enterprise is changed, and the organization's competitiveness in the global marketplace is improved.

When teams are used many changes impact the organization. An especially important change is in the role of the manager—the subject of the next chapter.

_____12
THE NEW MANAGERS

> *O brave new world, that has such people in't.*
> THE TEMPEST, WILLIAM SHAKESPEARE (1564–1616)

This chapter deals with the new managers—those individuals who occupy positions of responsibility in contemporary organizations and whose roles have changed markedly since the use of alternative teams has arisen. The people occupying managerial positions today cannot function effectively in a traditional managerial manner. The emergence of team-driven organizations has brought along with it a different type of manager, one called the "non-manager" by *Fortune* magazine.[1]

A HISTORICAL PERSPECTIVE

The idea of using teams as elements of organizational strategy was put forth early in the development of management theory in this century. An early advocate of the use of teams and their benefits was Mary Parker Follett, who advocated flatter organizations, extolled the benefits of teams and participative management, and stated that leadership comes from a person's ability rather than from a designated formal organizational position. She recognized and promoted the now popular idea of empowerment. During her period, in the

---

[1] "The New Non-Managers," *Fortune,* February 22, 1993, pp. 80–84. The term *new manager* is more descriptive of this changed role (hence its use in this chapter).

1920s the management community was still caught up in Frederick Taylor's command-and-control style of management carried out through the military model of a hierarchial organization. (Frederick Taylor is recognized as the father of scientific management.)

Follett believed and wrote about the popular notion today that the "person doing the work knows the most about how that work should be done." She advocated cross-functioning in a horizontal rather than the vertical authority that prevailed in her time—a harbinger of the alternative teams used in today's organizations. She recognized the importance of leadership by stating that "the leader makes the team" and that knowledge and experience should decide who will lead at any particular moment.[2]

The evolving new managers are a different type of manager—one who must earn the right to "manage" other people in changing organizational environs.

NEW-MANAGER ENVIRONS

The new managers are leaders, mentors, facilitators, coaches, sponsors, advocates, chaplains, comforters, trainers, teachers, team players, entrepreneurs, problem finders, and problem solvers—many things, but certainly not the traditional manager who exercises supervision over subordinates. These traditional managers have become a part of the history of management theory and practice. The new manager is a Socratic manager who asks questions that will get people thinking about their work and moving in the right direction. Some of the challenges facing these new managers include the following:

- Lifetime learning will be required of everyone. Each organization will be a learning organization as it tries to develop in its people the knowledge, skills, and attitudes needed to cope with changing environmental and competitive conditions. People in the new organizations will expect to be treated as equals who are not told what to do but are given intelligent choices of what to do and then have the freedom to make the best choice—the one that best suits the purposes of the organization to which they belong. People will become both specialists and generalists in several different areas of technology, including the management of that technology.

- Openness will be a strong predisposition of the new manager and those team members who serve as leaders of their teams. Crucial information, like organizational performance, sales, profits, costs, operating plans, organizational finances, new products, competitive practices, pending policy initiatives, and even wages and salaries will be made available to people.

---

[2] *Mary Parker Follett—Prophet of Management: A Celebration of Writings from the 1920s,* Harvard Business School Press, Boston, Mass. Taken from Danba Wechsler Linden, "The Mother of Them All," *Forbes,* January 16, 1995, p. 75.

Experience has shown that when given access to such information, people can be trusted. They will respect the confidentiality of such information. Traditional managers can have a difficult time reengineering themselves to the new managerial philosophy of openness. The transition will be easier for people who have had experience operating under a team-driven culture.

- The new managers will not be the traditional watchdog, controller, bureaucrat, police officer, or slave driver. Today's employees want a more caring, emphatic, supporting management style and will be willing to forego other aspects of their employment (and even salary) to get it.
- Growing flexibility in the use of contract services and temporary employees means that employees will be more likely to leave and find another work environment more in sync with their values. The new values reflected in a recent National Study of the Changing Workforce conducted by the Families and Work Institute in New York confirmed this. The variables that people considered to be most important when deciding to accept their current jobs were open communication, effect on personal/family life, and the nature of the work.[3]
- As stated in this book, the person doing the work knows the most about how that work should be done. The new manager explicitly recognizes this and works to respect, trust, and empower those individuals.

NEW-MANAGER CHALLENGES

The command-and-control management style of the traditional manager will have to change. The older management style primarily called for people who were very focused, structured, analytical, and action oriented. As we move into the information and team-driven age, managers will have to develop adaptive, flexible, multilateral thinking and recognize that change is underway at all levels and all disciplines of the enterprise. The new manager must use information, go where necessary to get the job done, pull together the use of resources in an integrated manner, and maximize the participation of people from cross-functional and cross-organizational environments to pull everything together. Some of the challenges facing these new managers include the following:

- The single-focus job as we know it today will likely cease to exist. A regular set of duties, with regular pay, work hours, and fixed workplaces, will likely change and people will be assigned to teams for a particular area of work. When the work is completed, the people will move on to

[3] Cited in Ken Blanchard, "The Changing Role of Managers," *Quality Digest,* January 1994, p. 17.

another team, perhaps within the same organizational unit, or move elsewhere in the enterprise.

- Working units, whether a company or a department within a larger company, will be smaller and stem from the downsizing and restructuring that is underway in most enterprises. The old, vertically integrated huge corporations, with their hundreds of thousands of employees, will eventually be reduced in size. Those that will survive will have decentralized authority in smaller work units, tied together with the corporate headquarters through information and computer networks.

- Managers have historically enjoyed higher pay and fringe benefits and perks or special privileges, such as reserved parking spaces, executive dining facilities, and first-class air travel. With the increase in the number of leaders and managers in self-managed, team-driven enterprises, managers will find that they will have to give up many of their pay and fringe premiums and share these with their peers, subordinates, and superiors.

- All managers and professionals will have to become conversant with the converging telecommunications and computer technologies.

- Increasingly more work, in both manufacturing and the service industries, will be done by teams working on ad hoc projects and other teams initiatives, from the senior level of the enterprise down through the worker level.

- Although there will be fewer traditional managers, the opportunity to serve in a de facto leadership management position will become more widespread. Hierarchy will have lost its meaning, and people will gravitate to work on alternative teams in many different enterprises—moving both within a specific company and then to other enterprises when their services are needed. Managers who believe that their sole responsibility is to manage and coordinate the work of subordinates are in for a brutal shock when they find that such a management philosophy is badly outdated. Process skills will be required of these people: to lead process-management teams, to communicate, to integrate, to provide resources, to mentor, to coach, and then get out of the way and let the people manage themselves and do the technical work that is required. Managers and leaders will become generalists who are able to work with different functions and organizational levels and with outside stakeholders.

- The hallmark of success as a professional, a manager, or a leader will be the ability to be a team player—to be recognized as such and have a demonstrated track record of doing so across geographic and regional boundaries. People skills will be a major requirement of the multilevel-multifunctional, multiorganizational, multiregional manager—the new manager.[4]

---

[4] Some of this material has been gleaned from Walter Kiechel III, "A Manager's Career in the New Economy," *Fortune*, April 4, 1994, pp. 68–72.

HORIZONTAL DESIGNS

The new managers, buttressed by distinct strategies calculated to reinforce an organizational design that is characterized by both horizontal and vertical forces, are becoming the dominant means of assigning and using resources in contemporary organizations. Several key strategies are used to increase the influence of the horizontal forces in such organizations.

Work is organized around processes rather than tasks. Functional departments will exist to provide a home base for special resources, such as engineering, marketing, manufacturing, and finance. Members from these functional departments serve on teams that have specific performance objectives and goals. These teams are used to focus the management of core processes across functional departments that produce products and services for internal and external customers. Managing across functional and organizational boundaries becomes as critical as managing up and down in the organizational hierarchy.

Since there are fewer managerial and supervisory personnel required, downsizing of the organizational hierarchy can be carried out. Flatter organizational hierarchies, are needed, and the management of a key organizational element in the hierarchy will change. For example, a chemical company replaced several of its senior functional managers with work teams. Instead of having a single manager for marketing, the company uses a senior-level team to carry out the marketing function. This arrangement is working well—the managers and professionals take off their functional hats and put on their team hats, which gives them a broader perspective of the function and brings about a more consensual decision-making process. Fragmented individual tasks that add little or no value to organizational objectives and goals can be integrated into the teams' work; if it adds no value, the work can be eliminated. The number of teams used to perform on and manage the core processes is reduced to the minimum needed. Teams, which for the most part manage everything in the enterprise (as well as themselves), become the building blocks of the organizational design. First-level supervisory roles undergo major modification since the teams manage themselves. The supervisors that survive any downsizing or restructuring become facilitators, coaches, teachers, counselors—basically working on providing the environment, the resources, and the coordination of resources for the teams and, most important, keeping out of the way of the teams' work. Each team has its objectives and goals, develops its strategy, and is held responsible and accountable for measurable performance goals.

Experience in companies that have changed their organizational design to accommodate the use of teams has shown opportunities for enlightening management changes. For example, General manager Doug Cahill of Olin Pool Products, which controlled more than half the market for dry sanitizer (a chlorine-based treatment for swimming pool water), created a new model for his organization. He described the new organization as being "so flat that you could stick it under a door." Fourteen departments became eight process teams, with names like "fulfillment," "new products," and "resources," centered around a core titled "customer." The general manager's job was not there at all. By eliminating titles and departments, Cahill wanted to force people to be responsible for their work, not for their jobs. Bonuses would be based on the division's profits, not departmental goals. Bonuses became predicated on team performance, and Cahill made a commitment—approved by his manager—to remain around for at least three years so the transition to a new paradigm in organizational design would be complete before he left for another assignment.[5]

Other changes with which the new manager must deal center around the idea of organizational values stemming from new relationships with organizational stakeholders.

VALUES

The creation of value for internal and external customers is done through strategic partnerships with suppliers and customers. Suppliers and customers participate in the design and development of new and improved products and services through membership on concurrent engineering teams, self-managed production teams, project teams, reengineering teams, and task forces that are used to evaluate problems and opportunities cutting across the boundaries between suppliers and customers. Since the customers have representatives involved on these teams, the likelihood of customer satisfaction with the final products and services that are delivered is enhanced.

The creation of value for both internal and external customers becomes the name of the game to improve organizational performance, attain objectives and goals, and bring a greater satisfaction to those stakeholders that affiliate with the enterprise. Teams are rewarded for their performance through changed appraisal and pay systems. Technical and social training to enhance the knowledge, skills, and attitudes of team members and other organizational members is essential so everyone understands and accepts the new paradigm of organizational life, in which the new managers take on striking new roles that depart markedly from the role of traditional managers.

The team-driven organizational design that helped spawn the new manager largely eliminates the hierarchy and functional boundaries of an organization. Senior executives of the enterprise assess the strategic probabilities and possibilities of the enterprise's future and are likely to be organized themselves into a plural executive team. These senior executives, in their responsibility for the strategic management of the enterprise, still depend on specialized staff services, such as human resources, legal, public relations, and so on, to help them in their oversight responsibilities. The senior leaders of the enterprise are becoming more multiple skilled rather than narrow specialists, and

---

[5] Thomas A. Steward, "How to Lead a Revolution," *Fortune,* November 28, 1994, pp. 48–50.

they exist to facilitate the strategic direction of the enterprise, allocate resources, and ensure the overall coordination and integration of teams, processes, and coherence in strategic direction. However, below the senior level,
the use of teams has taken over the performance of technical work and the
management of that technical work. The use of teams, with oversight carried
out by a team of senior executives, affects every aspect of organizational life.
Teams are the building blocks of the new organization facilitated by the
new managers.

The organizational model formally held by the neatly arranged boxes on
traditional organizational charts has given way to linear responsibility charts
(LRCs), which depict the individual and collective roles of team members.
The development and use of these LRCs can be a complex and painful exercise
as team members must choose their individual and collective roles *and* defend
those roles with other team members. Definition of these roles becomes particularly challenging when viewed from the perspective of the cross-functional
and cross-organizational processes of the enterprise. Despite the complex and
painful development of LRCs, their development will reduce to a minimum
ambiguities, duplication, and opportunities for things to fall between the cracks
in an enterprise.[6]

The collaboration of activities across different boxes on traditional organizational charts was difficult at best in traditionally organized enterprises. Often,
this collaboration was done through the informal organization and was usually
accepted by traditional managers, since no formal alternative existed (such
as the use of teams in new organizations). The matrix organizational form
was a compromise over the traditional vertical model since the hierarchy was
kept in place, and most of the formal authority and power of the vertical
hierarchy was left in place.

The new managers strive to develop and propogate a culture whose values
support teams, the management of core processes, and effective work with
suppliers and customers. These new managers stay away from the details of
day-to-day activities (they expect the teams to do this), and they concentrate
on their new responsibilities of facilitating teamwork, allocating resources,
maintaining oversight, and ensuring that decisions are made and implemented
at the right times and in the right places. Performance evaluation of new
managers is done by the several constituents that these managers serve: team
leaders, team members, peers, and associates. For example, at one large and
successful company, training appraisal and compensation systems involved
assessment by peers and others above and below an employee to evaluate
the individual as a contributing member of the team and the organizational
unit to which the team belongs. Employees, including managers, are evaluated
based on the results of their organizational unit, such as the team.

To be successful as a new manager, individuals will have to be able to work
with and serve on teams, know how to cross boundaries to get the job done,

---

[6] See pages 67–68 for a description of LRCs in defining individual and collective roles.

satisfy a new and demanding group of stakeholders, and develop the best possible interpersonal skills. In short, they must be team players who are respected by many other people—peers, associates, superiors, subordinates, suppliers, customers, and so forth.

NONSUPERVISION PHILOSOPHIES

Successful companies today are characterized by their use of teams to manage and work on cross-functional and cross-organizational initiatives. The use of teams to make small improvements in existing products and to reach out for the development of products that currently do not exist in the company's inventory of products means that the managers who maintain oversight of these teams need to have a distinct management style much different from the traditional command-and-control mentality that worked in earlier times. Most ideas for new products flow from two sources: individual and teams. Teams made up of different disciplines, dedicated to work across functions and organizations, focus on specific product lines. Some managers who have become so dependent on the use of teams believe that a world of management without the use of teams is unthinkable. They do not supervise these teams in the traditional sense of supervision, but rather they provide the following environmental support for the teams:

- Provide adequate resources to do the job, and facilitate processes to ensure that those resources are available when needed, in the right quantity and quality.
- Work with team leaders to ensure that team members have the needed knowledge, skills, and attitudes to be a contributing member of the team. Members who need additional training to enhance their individual and team contributions should be scheduled for appropriate training in a forthright manner.
- Counsel team leaders in their roles as leaders and managers in working with team members and with other teams in the enterprise. This counseling could lead to the opportunity for team members to learn new knowledge, skills, and attitudes in the science and art of management and leadership.
- Schedule and conduct meetings to review the progress that teams are making and to compare the teams' results with the operational and strategic needs of the enterprise.
- Conduct a postevaluation of each team's work at the conclusion of the team's effort to develop information and to gain insight into what has and has not worked. The information collected should be synthesized and integrated into a "Lessons Learned" document that can be used to orient and train future team members.

- Work with other senior managers to bring synergy to the individual team effort that is underway in the enterprise so organizational objectives and goals are met.
- Recognize that creative people tend to be restless and need time to brainstorm, to step back and look at their work differently, and to think through the probabilities and possibilities of doing creative things differently in their jobs.
- Know that creative people working on teams in a cooperative mode can become passionate about their ideas and about seeing them developed and implemented. Yet managers should know that any idea, however brilliant and initially promising, is just the beginning of the creative process. The idea must be developed, packaged, and "sold" to team colleagues and to managers of the team.
- Know that when a manager does have an idea, it should be passed on to someone on the team, who should be allowed to think that it was his or her own idea. In this way, the idea will have a better chance of receiving due evaluation and consideration by the team. Team members do not like to have ideas forced on them.
- Give the team leaders and the teams considerable freedom to operate within the broad boundaries of the team and the other organizations that are involved.
- Know that creative people working on teams in a cooperative mode can become passionate about their ideas and about seeing them developed and implemented. Yet managers should know that any idea, however brilliant and initially promising, is just the beginning of the creative process. The idea must be developed, packaged, and "sold" to team colleagues and to managers of the team—and to customers.
- Know that when a manager does have an idea, it should be passed on to someone on the team, who should be allowed to think that it was his or her own idea. In this way, the idea will have a better chance of receiving due evaluation and consideration by the team. Team members do not like to have ideas forced on them.
- Give the team leaders and the teams considerable freedom to operate within the broad boundaries of the team and the other organizations that are involved.

NEW-MANAGER COMPETENCIES

New managers will be able to use teams in moving the organizational products and processes together and will be able to cross boundaries and reach into the heart of the organization to produce results. The new managers will abandon the command-and-control model of management and embrace the consensus-and-consent way of leading and managing the organizational unit for which they are responsible. They will do the following:

- Facilitate the technical work and management of the organizational units for which they have responsibility.
- Find ways to help people work across organizational boundaries and functional territories to get the job done.
- Have unassailable credentials to serve on teams (specifically, to manage teams) and to see the logic of teamwork in the overall strategic management of the enterprise.
- Be willing to empower people to give up control, to trust, respect, be committed, and be loyal to other team members and the new manager.
- Follow with passion and dedication the golden rule: Treat others as you would like to be treated.
- Forget the titles of controller or director because those titles are anachronisms in a team-driven organization.
- Remember that the people doing the work know the most about how that work should be done and, given the opportunity, will make meaningful contributions regarding how that work should be led and managed.
- Follow a careful path between being a leader who sets the vision and a manager who uses resources efficiently to take the organization toward attaining that vision.
- Become a role model by having the ability to teach, mentor, coach, and help people prepare themselves to do better and more satisfying work in the enterprise.
- Think like a strategist—one who works diligently at getting information about the probabilities and possibilities of the future and the design and execution of strategies to make that future a reality for the enterprise.
- Become an avid reader of those journals and periodicals that report on new management concepts and processes and how and where these new ways of doing things are being carried out. Select the most meaningful of these concepts and processes and pass them out to constituents to improve the breadth and depth of their managerial and leadership capabilities.
- Recognize that the opportunities for leadership in a team-driven enterprise are almost without constraints. People of all disciplines and at all levels in the enterprise have the opportunity to become leaders.
- Set the example that a good leader is also a good follower, and that leaders are role models for other people in the enterprise.

The new paradigm of organizations operating under the leadership of new managers can result in extraordinary savings in managerial and staff personnel. For example, at Nucor Steel, twenty-five corporate staff members oversee a mini-empire of seventeen operating units, producing 3.9 million tons of steel products per year. Between 1986 and 1991, the company's sales more than doubled; its marketing, administrative, and other expenses remained virtually flat at $67 million. During 1992 its ratio of managers to production workers stood at a rock-bottom of 1 to 300. In an industry noted for its administrative and bureaucratic bloat, that is incredible. The secret: Individual operating units become self-sufficient businesses, and a sales manager at each operating unit charts and forecasts monthly production schedules. Teams are used to bring a focus to operating business unit work processes.[7]

NEW MANAGERS-TO-BE

Young people today—new managers-to-be who envision becoming part of the management ranks in their future careers—should recognize that the prize is going to those people who have a track record of using their effective cooperative talents in being a team player rather than just a competitive individual. In the team society that is becoming characteristic of today's competitive world, individual contribution will count as well as the individual's ability to work as a team player and a collaborative member of a team, who learns new tasks needed on the team and shares information with other team members. Team players have their individual capabilities, but they know how to grasp how a team works and how a team goes through several stages before it finally works effectively. These individuals also know what knowledge, skills, and attitudes they need to become an effective new manager and when to seek the help of human resource counselors to begin a personal program of self-development through formal training classes, on-the-job training, and varied experiences in working with different teams in the enterprise. People who get noticed as valuable team members and who are always looking for ways to enhance the team's performance will stand out as potential future new managers in the enterprise.

THE NEW-MANAGER ORGANIZATION

What does a model organization look like in which new managers are flourishing? The first thing that comes to mind is that the culture is one in which the basic management philosophy of consensus and consent prevails. A company operating in the new-manager environment has its factories and offices filled with empowered and well-trained employees whose employment expectations, wages, and living standards are rising continually. Real estate and banking organizations are thriving, supporting the business infrastructure of the com-

---

[7] Robert Wrubel "Lean Management—Nucor," *Financial World,* September 29, 1992, pp. 50–51.

munity. Advanced corporate and university R&D initiatives are underway, adding to the opportunities for new product development and growing businesses. The community, however defined, is a paradigm for collaboration among teams, organizations, functions, organized labor, local government, civic, education, and religious and cultural leadership.

Within the organization, there is an effective working commitment to total quality management led by knowledgeable leaders who have developed and propogated a culture of trust, loyalty, commitment, and respect. People care about each other and work together in empowered teams. Teams continue to proliferate in the enterprise, and strategic partnerships have been built up by teams with suppliers and customers. An ethic of hard work prevails, reinforced by training, communication, recognition, and leadership strategies to encourage the participation of all employees on the team. The key to employee satisfaction and productivity is having employees on teams that focus on what the customer needs, on eliminating waste and nonadded value in the utilization of resources, and on making work meaningful and rewarding. Organizational people are aligned and are pulling together. End-user customers are happy, and employees are developed to their fullest potential through training, caring, and listening. Key decision makers in the enterprise are long-term oriented, and quality is a way of life in the enterprise.

SOME COMPARISONS

Table 12–1 shows an empirical comparison of changes in management and leadership philosophies. This comparison is done in the context of the old world of command and control and the new world of consensus and consent.

Table 12–1 indicates that the new managers operate in cultural settings different from the traditional culture of earlier times. Some of the differences in the new culture are subtle. Nevertheless, the influence of this new culture has changed markedly the operational and strategic behavior of contemporary enterprises reflected in their cultures.

The new manager shows the right balance of both leader and managerial competencies. The next section presents a few ideas about the meaning and process of leadership.

LEADERSHIP

The successful new manager is a leader, and leadership opportunities pervade the team-driven organization and its stakeholder world. The CEO of a large, successful company sent an important message on leadership throughout the

TABLE 12–1. Changes in Management/Leadership Philosophy

The Old World: Command and Control	The New World: Consensus and Consent
Believes "I'm in charge."	Believes "I facilitate."
Believes "I make decisions."	Believes in maximum decentralization of decisions.
Delegates authority.	Empowers people.
Executes management functions.	Believes that teams execute management functions.
Believes leadership should be hierarchical.	Believes that leadership should be widely dispersed.
Believes in theory "X."	Believes in theory "Y."
Exercises *de jure* (legal) authority.	Exercises *de facto* (influential) authority.
Believes in hierarchical structure.	Believes in teams/matrix organizations.
Believes that enterprises should be organized around function.	Believes that enterprises should be organized around processes.
Follows an autocratic management style.	Follows a participative management style.
Emphasizes individual managers' roles.	Emphasizes collective roles.
Believes that a manager motivates people.	Believes in self-motivation.
Stability.	Change.
Believes in single-skill tasks.	Believes in multiple-skill tasks.
Believes "I direct."	Allows team to make decisions.
	Believes that a manger leads, as opposed to directs.
Distrusts people.	Trusts people.

company. He stated that "we know without leaders who 'walk the talk,' all of our plans, promises and dreams for the future are just that—talk."[9]

Some of the key values about leadership at the General Electric Company include the concept that the only way to gain more output from less input, to grow and to win, is to engage every mind within the company—to excite, energize, involve, and reward everyone. GE bets everything on its people—empowering them and giving them the resources, and then getting out of their way. Part of the GE's strategy to empower people is to reduce the organizational layers and walls between them and others. Within GE, there is a strong belief that these layers and walls cramp people, inhibit creativity, waste time, restrict vision, smother dreams, and slow things down. Senior management at GE is looking for leaders at every level who can energize,

[9] Chairman of the Board John F. Welch, Jr., *1991 Annual Report,* General Electric Company, February 14, 1992, p. 5.

excite, and coach rather than enervate, depress, and control—and be rewarded in their souls as well as in their wallets. Leaders at GE are rated by those above them, by their peers, and by their subordinates as well. "This has become a powerful tool for detecting and changing those who "smile up and kick down." Stock options, once awarded to just a few senior executives, are given to over 15,000 employees whose contributions have become visible because of teamlike work environments and flatter organizations.[10]

Table 12–2 describes the more specific elements about GE's values. Throughout the roles performed by team leaders, a concept of changes in leadership philosophies is pervasive.

KEY STRATEGIES

The key strategies that new managers can use to provide leadership for a team-driven enterprise reflect the culture of such an organization. The enterprise is organized around both functions and processes rather than tasks. The core work of the enterprise centers on using teams as focal points for pulling together the resources across functions and organizational boundaries to produce a product or service. Managers have dual responsibilities for providing resources and keeping oversight of the technical work being performed and for integrating that work into and through organizational boundaries. The ability to do the technical work and to integrate that work into organizational processes becomes the principal means for creating organizational value. Per-

TABLE 12–2.   GE Values . . . GE Leaders throughout the Company[11]

- Create a clear, simple, reality-based, customer-focused vision and be able to communicate it straightforwardly to all constituencies.
- Understand accountability and commitment and be decisive. Set and meet aggressive targets, always with unyielding integrity.
- Have a passion for excellence. Hate bureaucracy and all the nonsense that comes with it.
- Have the self-confidence to empower others and behave in a boundaryless fashion. Believe in and be committed to Work-Out as a means of empowerment. Be open to ideas from anywhere.
- Have, or have the capacity to develop, global brains and global sensitivity and be comfortable building diverse global teams.
- Stimulate and relish change; do not be frightened or paralyzed by it. See change as opportunity, not just a threat.
- Have enormous energy and the ability to energize and invigorate others. Understand speed as a competitive advantage and see the total organizational benefits that can be derived from a focus on speed.

---

[10] Ibid. pp. 1–5.
[11] John F. Welch, Jr., *1991 Annual Report, General Electric Company,* February 14, 1992, p. 5.

formance objectives and goals are linked to internal and external customer satisfaction. Teams and not individuals are the focus of organizational performance. These teams combine individual technical performance and managerial performance to create customer value. The members of the teams develop dual competencies: first in several work tasks; and second, in the leadership and management that work. Team members are able to perform these dual competencies through formal training courses, on-the-job training opportunities, and access to information on the performance of their team, their assigned functional areas, and the overall integrated performance of the organization to which they belong—the profit center, the division, or the entire organization itself. An important part of developing employees' competencies is through their exposure in working with customers, suppliers, local communities, and other stakeholders. Individuals are awarded for skill development and contribution to the team's efforts; teams are awarded for the ability of the team to produce valued results.

SUMMARY

This chapter discussed the idea that the traditional manager is an anachronism—behind times in providing executive oversight in the design and execution of team-driven organizational strategies. Those people who have oversight authority and responsibility in modern organizations, whether at the senior level of the enterprise or in decentralized units (including the team level), require new knowledge, skills, and attitudes. The people that occupy these new positions are different from the traditional managers and leaders. They are new managers who work within the traditional boundaries of management and leadership but bring much more to their roles.

New managers are leaders, facilitators, coaches, mentors, teachers, sponsors, chaplains, comforters, trainers, team players, team leaders, and entrepreneurs—many things that enable people to attain their personal and organizational objectives and goals. Some of the major characteristics displayed by these new managers include the following:

- An openness in working with people, providing them with key information on the performance of the organization
- Behavior unlike that of traditional managers, who served as watchdogs and controllers
- Appreciation of and respect for people, recognizing that such people move around in new organizations—from team to team, from specialized skills to multiple skills, from temporary to permanent organizational positions, and even from one career to new careers in their professional lives

The new managers work in a highly decentralized culture, so their success will ultimately depend on how good they are at being a team player, whether as a member or leader of a team. Organizations that support and develop careers for new managers exhibit strong values, including a predisposition toward horizontal and multilateral relationships and the building and maintenance of networks with suppliers and customers. The new managers are not supervisors and are not considered bosses in the traditional sense of the word. They develop competencies beyond what was considered acceptable for traditional managers. Young new managers-to-be have a better chance of taking on the skills of this new type of manager since they have likely been exposed to such managers in their early professional careers.

Organizational designs change to accommodate the new managers. There are altered authority patterns and structures, reduced staff, different interstaff relationships, and greater opportunities for organizational renewal.

Teams can create negative results, as discussed in the next chapter.

PART IV
NEW DIMENSIONS

____13
THE NEGATIVE SIDE OF TEAMS

Make much of negatives.
"THE REAL WAR," WALT WHITMAN (1819–1892)

Teams are not a panacea for all of the operational and strategic problems and opportunities likely to be encountered by an enterprise. An indicated elsewhere in this text, teams do provide certain key advantages and benefits in different contexts to the organizations that use them. But there is a cost and a potential negative side to the use of teams in the organizational design of contemporary enterprises. This chapter discusses some of the problems and costs likely to be encountered in the use of teams, along with how the impact of these problems and costs can be reduced.

Sometimes the successful use of teams requires several attempts. For example, Allina, which runs seventeen nonprofit hospitals in the Midwest, tried for several years to form teams during the 1980s but failed because there were hostile relations with labor unions. Some of the hospital administrators who had worked at the hospital for over twenty years had never even met a union official. The unions were not blameless—a worker remembered that union officials taught that "*boss* spelled backward is a double SOB." Allina finally formed a team of management and union officials and gave it a charter to try and change the attitudes of all people concerning the union and the need for teams in the hospital. Allina has since created worker–management teams in a majority of its hospitals with "stunning results."[1]

---

[1] Brian Dumaine, "The Trouble with Teams," *Fortune*, September 5, 1994, pp. 86–92.

The use of teams can create potential problems in an organization—such as potential alienation of the staff support agencies. For example, the use of teams has caught on at the White House. Under the Clinton administration, teams of loosely defined clusters of friends and advisors represent an effort to cross established bureaucratic channels of command. Unhampered by the typical inertia of the government bureaucracy, these teams are able to cross bureaucratic entities and go where necessary to get the support needed to pull together initiatives for the President. There are, however, significant risks in that some of the bureaucrats who have been out of the decision process may be alienated, and gaining their commitment during the implementation of the strategies developed during the informal team deliberations will pose difficulties. The implementation of the North American Free Trade Agreement (NAFTA) and the emasculated health care initiative of the Clinton administration are two key examples. Sources close to the President say that the focus is on teamwork with the objective of tearing down the walls between agencies and allowing for more efficient government. When teams are used in the federal bureaucracy, who yields power is not as easily determined as under the well-defined bureaucratic way of doing things.[2]

REASONS FOR FAILURE

Inadequate Delineation of Authority

A common failure in the introduction of teams is inadequate delineation of the authority and responsibility of the teams, the team leaders, and the first-level supervisor. This failure can lead to a lack of understanding on the part of people regarding their legal authority in making and implementing decisions in the teams. Even if the people are able to assume considerable authority through influence, this is not enough. Failure to prescribe adequate stipulations of authority for everyone based on the work packages for which they are responsible will cause ambiguities in the relationships of people and decisions to be delayed, and there will be a high probability that some things will fall between the cracks during the team's work. If the team leader and team members are uncertain of what is expected of them, their morale and sense of well-being toward the team effort will be weakened.

Ruined Relationships with Subordinates

There is no question that the introduction of teams in an enterprise changes the traditional relationships between managers/supervisors and subordinates. If the existing relationships with subordinates have been one of command and control, the changed relationships will threaten supervisors, make them unsure of their influence over subordinates, and will give subordinates new

---

[2] Michael K. Frisby, "Power Switch," *Wall Street Journal,* March 26, 1993, p. A1.

freedom in building new relationships with their peers, associates, and stake-holders. If subordinates have been given authority to work closely with suppliers and customer representatives, their world of operation has been broadened, and they will take on added responsibilities that, from the perspective of a traditional supervisor, could be perceived as ruining the subordinate–supervisor relationships. Problems of this sort can be reduced by making sure that all subordinates and supervisors receive managerial and social training, understand what the new relationships mean, and then have time to develop new working relationships with their former subordinates.

The Concept is Great, but the Execution Is Troublesome

When people first hear of a strategy to introduce teams into the organizational design of an enterprise, their reaction is likely to be favorable—particularly if they believe, perhaps naively, that their work and authority–responsibility relations will not be changed. The trouble starts when they realize that the team strategies will change everything about the enterprise and everyone's work and interpersonal relationships. In theory, the use of teams sounds great, but the impact on the organization's culture and on people's careers will make for some anxious times until people are able to sort out what it all means in terms of a personal impact on them. It is important to take time at the front end of the introduction of teams to deal with likely problems and challenges. Visiting other organizations that are using teams to benchmark the challenges and difficulties that they faced during implementation of teams can be valuable in getting people to see that the introduction will be troublesome to some extent. Insight into how other companies have met these troubles will help in acclimating people to teams.

Negative Union Attitudes

Opposition from unions will arise if the leaders and key members of the union are not involved in the process of preparing for and using teams. A commonly perceived threat is potential alienation of union workers in companies that have decided to use company teams. Organizations that have successfully introduced and used teams have been careful to work with union officials in developing and implementing strategies for teams. If the unions use teams in their own organizational design, they will be more amenable to working with management in helping get the organization and the people prepared to accept and cooperate with the new team strategy. In the use of teams, the unions are key stakeholders.

"We Are Different"

Sometimes when the use of teams is suggested as a new organizational design strategy, the opinion will be voiced that "we are different—and teams aren't going to work here." In part this is true, because each organization tends to have its own unique culture, and that culture provides unusual challenges in the introduction and use of teams. However, when the "we are different" issue is raised, time should be taken to talk about the perceived differences in the enterprise that might inhibit the use of teams. A thorough search of the literature is likely to uncover some organizations that are similar to the company and have used teams successfully. A visit to those organizations can help reduce the mistaken perception.

Undercut the Manager Role

In the traditional organization, authority, responsibility, and accountability are delegated down through the organizational hierarchy. Any departure from this delegated vertical flow is viewed with suspicion by too many managers— particulary those that are traditional in their thinking about how organizations function. In an organization that has an authoritarian culture, the introduction of teams will cause some, if not all, of the supervisors and co-workers to lack enthusiasm for the new team design. Under teams, workers can become enthusiastic about the notion of participating and come up with ideas and suggestions. The supervisors no longer have the option of telling the workers to "knock it off and get back to work." In such circumstances, it is easy to visualize that the company will spiral into self-directed anarchy—particularly if time and effort have not been taken to spell out the authority and responsibil- ity of team members and leaders. Management hesitation concerning the role of the teams vis-à-vis traditional managers and supervisors can add to the confusion and doubt about the wisdom of using teams.

At one plant, a failure to define the responsibilities of teams, and the perceived failure of senior management to make a clear commitment to the use of teams, created difficulties. One of the key teams that had been appointed resorted to guerilla warfare. Managers had canceled its proposal to scrap the cards that engineers used to record the time spent on each job. A disheartened team arranged to collect the cards and stored them under a desk. Months elapsed before managers realized that the supposedly vital data was not being logged into the computer. A considerable cost was incurred to find the cards, sort them out, and put them into the computer before costs on a development project could be tracked. Another problem at this plant consisted of ideas submitted by workers that were never followed up by management. Workers felt that someone should have gotten back to them concerning the ideas that they had submitted. Again, workers perceived a managerial lack of interest in the use of teams. Older workers in the plant resisted pressure to learn several jobs on the team. Most confusing of all was the slowly dawning recognition that the chaos due to the poor introduction of teams had no end in sight, and that the introduction of teams into the plant required careful preparation and was not a one-shot effort—rather, it was a journey. The previous environment under the traditional manufacturing foremen was a culture of "Go to work and do what I tell you." A few training courses, the appointment of teams, and then back to a culture of "business as usual" was not enough to do the job. Time is simply needed for the traditional managers and supervisors to go through the rethinking and attitude changes needed to depart from the traditional supervisory roles.

Devalued Management

Managers and supervisors may feel that their roles have been lessened in the enterprise and that their status or stature has been reduced because teams are able to manage themselves. If managers and supervisors have been operating in a command-and-control mode, with a strong feeling of being in charge, any action taken to reduce their unilateral authority in managing the enterprise could be perceived as damaging to their ego. Team members who sense that they have new power in the enterprise can easily fall into a pattern of showing less respect and obedience to their supervisors. The likelihood of this can be lessened if a company is careful to acquaint both team members and supervisors with their new reciprocal roles.

Interpersonal Difficulties

People issues—such as clashing personalities, backgrounds, and values—become particularly challenging when team members come from different disciplines in the organization and may have been at each other's throats for years. Companies must train managers and team leaders and members to meet these differencies openly and frankly—talking about the issues until everyone appreciates the other person's views, prejudices, values, and predispositions.

Personnel Issues and Interpersonal Communication

Functional or disciplinary managers may find it difficult to handle personnel issues in a team-driven organization. As they try to support more teams and at the same time maintain a critical mass of personnel competencies, issues of priorities can arise. For example, selecting which people to assign to a particular team becomes a major issue due to the need to support other teams and to maintain the critical mass of people to support the functional entity. People likely to be assigned to teams will have questions concerning pay, promotions, individual/team reward systems, and how their careers will probably be affected.

Teams do not stumble or fail because of some strange esoteric reason. They fail because of a failure of people—a failure that ultimately can be traced to a manager who has oversight responsibility for the teams. One author claims that self-directed work teams have about a 50 percent failure rate caused by lack of management commitment to the team-driven organizational change process, management impatience, and the lack of required budget and time allocation of training for leaders and team members. The author further notes that even if implementation and support are impeccable, failures can occur due to faulty business basics, declining markets, or using the wrong technology.[3]

Simonds and Winch state that when something has gone wrong on a project, seven times out of ten the cause is a breakdown in communication—not a breakdown in technology.[4]

Lack of Empathy

Failure to understand the viewpoint of other members of the team can cause an individual team member to believe that the team is likely to be a failure. When teams are formed, members may often find themselves in adversarial relationships. Thus, when the team is formed it is important that processes be set up so the team members can get together and share their differences, prejudices, values, and viewpoints. An early airing of team members' views will give the members a feeling that their views have been heard and respected. This can help pave the way for decisions to be made nonadversarially.

Failure to prepare employees for the cultural shock of starting to work on self-managed teams can be threatening. People are used to doing things the way they've always done them and may go into shock when faced with a totally different nodus operandi. Practical suggestions for implementing the change to teams that will reduce cultural shock include getting the organization ready for the change, getting the right people involved, including team members, developing and executing the strategies for the change, and then implementing the change with planned strategies carried out in an artful way. One important strategy for successful change is to personalize the changes so every employee feels that he or she has a stake in the success of the change. Clearly, employees should be told in unequivocal terms why a change is necessary.

Lack of Forethought and Afterthought

There are a lot of challenges that face the introduction of teams in an enterprise. Teams can be high-performance organizational units, but there is a cost to maintaining them. A common trouble arises when companies rush out and form teams for the wrong kind of job—such as quality circles that are insufficiently empowered and are not accepted in the culture of the enterprise. Teams are often launched with little or no training or support, no changes in the design of work, little effort to establish the specific authority and responsibility of the teams, and no supporting systems (e.g., E-mail, to help communication between the teams). Another problem is trying to put loners on a team

---

[3] Fisher Kimball, *Leading Self-Directed Work Teams,* McGraw-Hill, New York, 1992.
[4] J. Simonds and M. Winch, "Human Side of Project Management," *pmNETwork,* February 1991, p. 24.

when they would best be utilized as individuals who are creative and dedicated but prefer to work alone. Such people are not necessarily better off on a team. Finally, teams should be used when the work requires that people interact with each other.

Questions about Pay and Rewards

A likely problem in the use of teams concerns how the teams will be paid. Some questions include the following:

- How will merit evaluations be done on the team—by individual evaluation or team evaluation?
- How will salaries and wages be paid—for individual performance or team performance?
- How will the star performers on the team feel about being paid based solely on the performance of the team?
- Will pay given strictly for individual performance encourage teamwork?
- Can teams work effectively in a sharing ambience and through their stakeholders and still be paid based solely on individual performance?

These questions should be dealt with up front in the development of team strategy. To delay discussions on these issues until problems arise will damage the culture of the team and raise questions concerning management's commitment to the use of teams.

When the issue of compensation comes up in the use of teams, challenging issues are raised. At Johnson and Johnson, after some experimentation, a concept called "broadbanding," which eliminated multiple salary grades in favor of just a few, was used. The primary purpose was to facilitate teamwork and movement by employees into different jobs. After one year, nearly a third of the company's affected employees complained. They did not like the lack of a clear upward career path and were unhappy about being lumped in a job band with people they had previously surpassed. At American Express, the use of reengineering teams changed the company's works processes to create products and services for customers more effectively. Reengineering eliminated layers of jobs and salaries, including the jobs and salaries that managers looked to as their next position. American Express was forced to make the remaining jobs more attractive for lateral movement through spelling out the skills likely to be gained by lateral movement and from where future promotion would come.[5]

Holding a team accountable is tough. Not many teams have been fired for doing a poor job. How many teams have been promoted for doing an outstanding job? If the decision is made to have the team leader held accountable for

[5] Fred R. Bleakley, "The Best Laid Plans," *Wall Street Journal,* July 6, 1992, p. B1.

the work of the team, then that individual should have the option to veto any member of the team and to decide work assignments on the team, including schedules and fund allocation. The rights to send performance and pay recommendations to the team member's functional manager and to initiate action for the removal of any member of the team are needed. Only one person can be assigned the ultimate accountability for a unit or a team. When co-leaders are used for the team, one of the leaders must be senior so the issue of leadership of the team is not obscured or evaded.[6]

How do you adequately judge the performance of someone who is constantly rotating from team to team? One study of the causes of failure for alternative reward programs found the following:

- Failure to articulate a clear work-team vision
- Lack of management commitment to make the rewards program work
- Absence of a champion to spearhead team development
- Inadequate communication of program goals, the development processes, etc.
- Insufficient employee involvement in program design
- Inability to overcome resistance to change
- Limited availability of training resources
- Poor planning and execution
- Unreasonable expectations of achieving a short-term payback
- Untimely initiation of a pay system change

The authors, following up on their research results, recommend that the rewards issue for team-based compensation be addressed later, after the work processes have been delineated, the team has been organized, implementation strategies have been developed, and general acceptance for the use of teams has been gained. They generalize about the obstacles likely to be encountered when developing any type of team rewards system:

1. Overcoming employee and supervisory resistance to change
2. Picking the right performance measurements methodology
3. Setting reasonable performance standards
4. Assigning accountability for work process and results
5. Rewarding individual contributions[7]

Failure to Plan and Implement Properly

Planning is necessary to enhance the chances of a team working effectively. The following planning failures should be avoided:

---

[6] Neil Carson, "The Trouble with Teams," *Training,* August 1992, pp. 38–40.
[7] Sam T. Johnson, "Work Teams: What's Ahead in Work Design and Rewards Management," *Compensation & Benefits Review,* March–April 1993, pp. 35–41.

- Managers take a hands-off approach, "order" the use of teams, and then leave the teams to their own destinies. This will result in little more than a waste of everyone's time.
- Managers do not hold the teams responsible and accountable, and they avoid regular reviews of the team's progress. If team deadlines are missed, or if their work is not of high quality, managers do nothing.
- Management fails to devise a strategy for handling conflicts among team members.
- Management tells the teams that they have all of the authority needed to do their job but fails to designate the specificity of that authority through appropriate documentation.
- Management fails to make the objectives and goals of the team clear, or fails to instruct the team to study probable and possible objectives and goals, clarify them, and seek management review of these.
- Management withholds or provides resources as a means of rewarding or punishing the team.

Teams can work well and avoid the aforementioned negatives if management understands that teams are like any other organizational unit—they must be actively managed through the appropriate process of planning, organization, motivation, direction, and control.

Teams can get into difficulty if there is a prevailing belief that teams are the end rather than a means to the end of improving organizational competitiveness. Another difficulty is for the teams and the senior management to become too enamored with the concept of self-management. While teams can be designed to be self-managed, such management must be done within the context of the strategic management philosophy of the enterprise, consistent with the leadership style desired by senior managers. To be self-managed does not mean to be independent—rather, the teams are building blocks in the organizational design of the enterprise and should play supporting roles in the design and execution of organizational strategies.

COSTS OF USING TEAMS

It costs resources to use teams. Experience has shown that the following team costs can be reduced but cannot be avoided:

- Maintenance costs for keeping the knowledge, skills, and attitudes of the team members current.
- Training and education costs for scheduling the team members' attendance at training and education sessions. When a team member is out for training, someone on the team has to pick up the absent member's duties.

- Costs of potential interference with the creative and innovative skills of the loner.
- Costs of management's role, which is not diminished but rather is changed as the responsibilities of facilitator, counselor, teacher, coach, and strategist take on new meaning and duties in working with teams.
- Costs of changing attitudes (i.e., resources and time). Changing people's attitudes is probably more difficult than having people affiliated with the teams learn new knowledge and develop new skills.
- Costs of properly training people to work on teams.
- Managerial costs if time has not been taken to develop an understanding of how managerial roles have changed vis-à-vis teams.
- Costs of reporting relationships. A manager may no longer have approval authority held previously under a command-and-control culture. For example, a concurrent engineering team will conduct an ongoing design review through the workings of the team. Having an engineering manager "sign off" on the design becomes superfluous considering that an ongoing design review has been carried out by the team.
- Costs of making decisions using teams. However, even though team decision making is costlier, the decisions that are made are more thoroughly analyzed and evaluated. More people are involved in the decision process, and there are opportunities for more in-depth evaluation. Once the decision has been made, the people are more likely to support the decision since they have had a part in making it.
- Costs of self-directed anarchy if the teams are not properly prepared, are not actively led and managed, and do not have ongoing evaluations of how well they are working as organizational units and the quality and quantity of the results they are producing.
- Costs of nonsupport. Any organization tends to have a base of institutional knowledge and memory. If the teams are not able to access this institutional know-how, their ability to produce meaningful results can be hampered.

One company that instituted the use of teams with inadequate preparation of the people or culture suffered major setbacks in its financial position because of lower-priced products from competitive companies. The teams were blamed for the company's difficulties—which was untrue, because the company would have suffered the setbacks without the use of teams. What happened to the teams in this company? Senior management took back from the teams whatever authority it had delegated to them. Cost cutting became a key corporate strategy. The culture became one in which criticism was not permitted. People fell into the habit of "not rocking the boat" and accepting the dictates that came from senior management, with little or no input from the working levels of the company. Senior management took on a "Rambo" management style.

Today, the company's survival is in serious question. Key people have left the company, a union is making good headway in organizing workers, and there is a general culture of distrust, lack of confidence, mixed loyalties, and uneasiness. The teams may well have been part of the problem this company faces. In other words, the use of teams, although improperly introduced, brought to the surface many shortcomings of the company that had remained hidden before teams were introduced.

KEY INGREDIENTS OF TEAMS

You cannot have teams that will reach their fullest potential without several key ingredients: trust, loyalty, conviction, and commitment. The following conditions must exist:

- *Trust:* The atmosphere in the organization among the team leader, team members, managers and supervisors, and stakeholders can be described as one in which there is firm reliance and trust in the integrity, ability, and character of all of the people. There is confidence and faith on the part of everyone that each person will do his or her job mindful of the high degree of interdependence among team members as well as other supporting personnel of the enterprise.
- *Loyalty:* There is devoted attachment to other members of the team and to organizational purpose. People support each other, particularly in periods of adversity or major challenges. The organizational purpose becomes the overriding intention toward which the teams are functioning. Information is shared, and decisions are made through careful and diligent coordination and cooperation of everyone. Even though hearty debate will be carried out by the team members regarding team strategies, when the decision is made to pursue a particular strategy, team members will support that strategy in a loyal and heartfelt manner.
- *Conviction:* There is a fixed and strong belief that the use of teams makes sense and is the way to go in the design and implementation of organizational strategies. People have an explicit belief and unshaken confidence that teams can and will produce productive and profitable results for the enterprise. When questions arise concerning the wisdom of team strategies or team results, members of the teams are quick to explain and defend the use of teams. The discussions of team strategies are likely to be spirited, with honest differences of opinion. Once the decision is made, the team members have strong and vocal convictions that the best decision has been made and will fully support that decision.
- *Commitment:* People are strongly committed to the teams' work and purposes. People are entrusted with the authority to do what is necessary to make the teams work effectively and efficiently. Team members are

pledged to commit their knowledge, skills, and attitudes toward the optimum performance of the team in working with all of the stakeholders involved. People are bound both intellectually and emotionally to the teams and their purposes.

SUMMARY

This chapter discussed some of the negatives associated with the use of teams. Teams are not a cure-all, and the introduction of teams can uncover problems and shortcomings that have previously remained hidden. Part of the strategy for introducing teams should be to examine both the probable benefits and costs of using teams—including the likely problems and negatives arising out of their use. Benchmarking organizations that have had successes and failures in using teams can be a valuable learning process for leaders who wish to move an enterprise to a team-driven culture.

Senior managers have a clear responsibility and obligation to see that teams are properly introduced into an enterprise. Once a strategy for introducing teams has been formulated, senior managers must maintain oversight of the effectiveness with which that strategy is executed. Senior managers are role models—a part they should play based on a careful, quality-driven strategy.

This chapter also discussed the following:

- Teams usually fail because of poor preparation of the people and culture for the use of teams.
- Traditional supervisors sometimes feel that the use of teams will destroy their relationships with subordinates.
- Unions are key stakeholders when teams are used. They must be involved early and deeply in the development and execution of a strategy for using teams.
- Each organization is different, as is each organization's culture. Careful analysis of the culture of the enterprise can provide insight into some of the likely negatives and the problems to be encountered in the use of teams.
- Managers can easily fall into an attitude that teams undercut their role, devalue management, and will blur the authority–responsibility patterns in the enterprise.
- Pay and performance evaluations are key issues that need to be considered when teams are introduced. How the pay increases will be allocated to individuals vis-à-vis teams, is a major question that needs to be dealt with in a forthright manner.
- Teams are not the end—rather, they are a means for focusing the use of resources to deliver value to the enterprise and its stakeholders.

- There are obvious as well as subtle costs to using teams. Appreciating these costs can be useful in developing and executing a meaningful and successful strategy for the use of teams.
- Trust, loyalty, conviction, and commitment are key ingredients in a culture in which successful teams deliver successful results tuned to both the operational and strategic initiatives of the enterprise.

In the final chapter a summary of the positive side of teams will be presented.

____14
TEAM RESULTS

The results separate the winners from the also-rans.

This book has described how alternative teams are used in the design and execution of organizational strategies. It has provided many examples of the use of teams and the consequences they have wrought. Organizations that have used teams have found that favorable results have been realized when teams are planned for properly and used effectively. A few examples have been reported in the literature of teams that have not produced the results that were expected. In some cases, these teams have failed and have been replaced by traditional organizational designs for the development and execution of strategies. The reader will note that some of these results have been reported in a different context elsewhere in the book.

This chapter presents the results that have been reported by organizations using teams. These results have been reported in the management, business, and engineering literature. The author of this book has gained insight through his consulting work into how teams produce consequences for the organization. There have been only a few research studies that have documented the results that teams have produced. The findings of a few of these research studies are reported in this chapter.

In chapter 13 the negative results that teams produce is described. As would be expected, the reporting of negative results has been much less than the positive results. Managers, and others are much less likely to report bad news. This is probably why there is a scarcity of negative results in the use of teams. Nevertheless some poor results have been reported—as is presented in chapter 13.

The improvements gained from the use of teams are impressive. A word of caution, however: The use of teams alone was not solely responsible for the reported improvements. Rather, the use of teams aided, facilitated, and increased the probability that improvements would come forth. The use of teams set in motion a series of organizational improvements that would likely not have come forth without using teams. Improvements in workflow, the organization of work, new production methods, quality initiatives, and the development of a culture that emphasized continuous improvement all contributed to the overall improvements realized by those enterprises that used teams. It is difficult to separate the sole impact of teams on organizational improvements from other changes that occurred as a result of the use of teams and a growing awareness of everyone—even those people who were not on the teams—of the opportunity for improvement. In other words, the use of teams facilitated an organizational culture in which creativity and innovation flourished, people participated more fully in those matters that affected their work, and a high degree of people's ownership of products, services, and processes set a new tone for the motivation of people in the enterprise.

It is difficult to ignore the potential improvements that are associated with the use of teams. These teams change the way people work, give team members an enhanced feeling of ownership and individual accountability, and engender an empowerment that tends to bring out the best in both individual and team performance. As the team is successful, team members have an enhanced self-image of their worth to the team and the enterprise and put forth their best efforts so the team continues its winning strategy and so team members are recognized as winners in the culture of the enterprise. For those people who have experienced the pleasure of being on a winning team, there is a feeling of power, status, and well-being due to associating with winners.

Overall, the record in the use of teams has been impressive, with favorable results being reported by the users of teams. These results have been direct—such as through productivity and quality improvements—and indirect—through enhancements of the culture and development of new insights into leadership.

The bottom line about teams is simply that their use stands an excellent chance of producing favorable results. When teams are used, direct results are produced—such as improvements in productivity and quality. In addition, the use of teams sets in motion trigger effects, which cause changes throughout an enterprise. Sometimes it is difficult to distinguish between the direct and indirect results. Some of the indirect results that are produced by teams include subtle changes in the culture and employees' improved use of knowledge and skills. Another indirect but valuable result is positive changes in employees' attitudes, such as a greater sense of well-being, a greater feeling of belonging, and improved work satisfaction.

INGERSOLL REDUCES LEAD TIME FROM DAYS TO HOURS[1]

This section discusses how one firm has benefited from implementating a cross-functional team; how this firm reduced its order processing time for a line of products from almost two weeks to a few hours; and how, as a result of this improvement, its sales for that line of products tripled within a year.

Based in Rockford, Illinois, Ingersoll Cutting Tool Corporation (ICTC) is a manufacturer of cutting tools and inserts. In 1992, ICTC management became concerned with the amount of time it was taking to process and manufacture orders for a line of products called modified standard cutters. In an effort to understand how to reduce this time, ICTC joined the Center for Quick Response Manufacturing at the University of Wisconsin–Madison (UW) and decided to sponsor a project by UW graduate student David Johns.

Johns's task was to analyze and recommend ways to reduce time in the order processing portion of the total lead time for modified standard cutters. Johns was supervised and advised in his project jointly by Mike Wayman, team leader for steel products at ICTC, and Professor Rajan Suri, Director of the UW Center for Quick Response Manufacturing.

The specific goals of Johns's project were threefold: to understand the steps involved in the current order processing system; to identify specific sources of delay and recommend ways to eliminate them; and to provide recommendations for reducing order processing lead time by at least 60 percent. (Although the goal of 60 percent reduction may appear aggressive, the final results actually exceeded this initial target.)

Johns found that there were up to twelve areas an order might pass through. These ranged from inside sales, estimating, accounting and design, to purchasing, manufacturing, and shipping. Johns studied each of these areas to determine the steps involved and to estimate the lead time for the steps. It took Johns several months to understand the whole process. The result of his study was a flow chart (Figure 14–1) that had over eighty steps and spanned three pages.

Managers at ICTC were amazed. Although each of them knew what was done in their own area, no one had ever analyzed the whole process. Johns also discovered that it often took ten working days or more to process an order before it reached manufacturing.

After this initial phase of the project, the next task was to identify and eliminate root sources of delays in order processing. Under advice from Suri, Johns applied the principles of quick response manufacturing[2] to arrive at three main recommendations. The first was to eliminate checking and return

---

[1] This is based on "Ingersoll Reduces Time from Days to Hours," by R. Suri, Technical Report, Center for Quick Response Manufacturing, University of Wisconsin–Madison, 1994.

[2] For a description of the main principles, see R. Suri, "Common Misconceptions and Blunders in Implementing Quick Response Manufacturing," *Proceedings of the AUTOFACT 1994 Conference,* SME Press, Dearborn, Michigan, 1994.

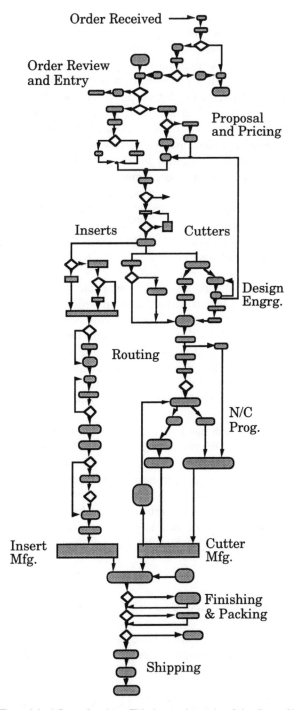

Figure 14–1. The original flow of orders. This is a schematic of the flow with details of the eighty steps omitted. (Reproduced with permission from Rajan Suri and the University of Wisconsin-Madison.)

steps through cross-training personnel. For instance, instead of a quality person checking and modifying the work of the routing department, or vice versa, one person would be trained to do both of these jobs in a single step. A second way in which delays could be reduced would be to share information across departments through a common database. Previously, folders would be shipped between departments for simple pieces of information. Having a database whereby everyone had access to the information would speed up this portion of the process. Implementation of this idea, however, would require tearing down organizational walls, since traditionally information that belonged to a department could only be accessed by that department.

The third and most significant recommendation that Johns made to ICTC was to form a team that had all of the people necessary to process an order in the same area. Forming such a closed-loop team is one of the core principles of quick response manufacturing. In addition to collocation, members of the team would be cross-trained in multiple functions and be given the ability to obtain all the information they needed locally. The flow for orders would be highly simplified.

Johns's project was well received by management, and in March of 1993 ICTC president Merle Clewett formed a team within the company to refine and implement the recommendations, using Johns's project as a starting point. The final recommendation by this team, shown in Figure 14–2, was accepted by the company president and implemented in the summer of 1993.

Since that time, ICTC has continued to hone its order procesing. It has reduced the processing time from over ten days to less than twenty-four hours for most modified standard orders, often processing an order in as little as four hours.

This lead-time reduction has had a significant impact on ICTC's business. According to team leader Wayman, orders for ICTC's modified standard line of cutters have increased threefold. "This is true for both the number of orders received and in terms of the sales dollars for this product," says Wayman.[3]

Wayman stresses that major changes like the ones at ICTC would not have been accomplished if the president of the company had not been so supportive. "Clewett championed the cause of implementing Quick Response Manufacturing," Wayman says, and "without his involvement, it would have stalled early on."

POSITIVE RESULTS OF TEAMS

The results discussed in this section have been reported in the literature, in company annual reports, through conversations and correspondence by the author with select company personnel, and by information provided to the

[3] Based on an interview published in *ManuFax,* vol. 3, no. 1, Manufacturing Systems Engineering Program, University of Wisconsin–Madison, 1994.

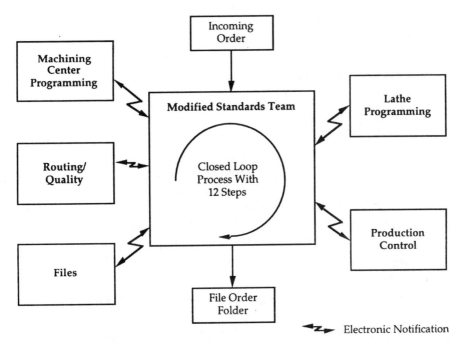

Figure 14–2. Revised flow of orders through a cell for modified standard cutters. (Reproduced with permission from Rajan Suri and the University of Wisconsin-Madison.)

author in his consulting work. In some cases, the results are specific; in other cases, the results are general, at times informal, and at times very brief. Some of the results have been highlighted by organizations; in other situations, the results have been gleaned out of both formal and informal information sources made available to the author. In citing the results from the use of teams in this chapter, care has been taken to express those results in a summary fashion and in the language used by those organizations that reported the results. Sometimes a company would report several benefits; in other situations, a company might only one or two improvements. Whatever the source, the results that have emerged have carried an important message: Working with teams does produce results that contribute to the well-being and competitiveness of an enterprise.

The results are given a preliminary classification as follows. The categories are then each briefly discussed.

1. Productivity increases
2. Quality improvements
3. Cost reductions
4. Earlier commercialization
5. Improved supplier relationships

6. Enhanced customer satisfaction
7. Changed management systems
8. Cultural enhancements
9. Employee satisfaction
10. Creativity and innovation
11. Strategic initiatives
12. Stakeholder image
13. After-sales service improvements
14. Development of management potential
15. Development of leadership potential
16. Reduction of parochialism and provincialism
17. Improved product, service, and process development
18. Greater use of knowledge, skills, and attitudes
19. Organizational design changes
20. Profitability increases
21. Ability of teams to make and execute managerial decisions

Productivity Increases: Gains have been realized in producing more output in products and services with fewer resources, thus reducing costs and improving efficiency and effectiveness in the use of organizational human and nonhuman resources. Productivity increases have taken the form of overall plant productivity, reduction of unit turnaround time, and improved production assembly time. One plant claimed to have increased productivity by over 70 percent in three years. Another company claimed that the use of self-managed production teams at one point increased productivity by 25 percent compared to other of their plants making the same products. An aircraft engine manufacturer using teams to invigorate its production capability realized productivity improvements of 20 percent—and in the process updated and streamlined its production assembly operations. An instruments manufacturer claims that the use of teams increased its output by 90 percent. A traditional plant in the food processing industry was shut down and a new automated factory was started up using self-managed production teams without reducing production rate.

Scores of service companies like Federal Express and Investor Diversified Services (IDS) have boosted productivity up to 40 percent by adopting self-managed work teams.[4]

In Salem, Ohio Keithly Instruments increased productivity by 90 percent, and lowered absenteeism by 76 percent, when it formed production teams. A team comprised of people from seven departments at Adolph Coors Company reduced by half the time it takes to develop and produce a new beer.[5]

[4] Brian Dumaine, "The Trouble with Teams." *Fortune,* September 5, 1994, pp. 86–92.
[5] Glenn M. Parker, "Team Players and Teamwork," *Soundview Executive Book Summaries* 13, no. 4, pt. 1 (April 1991): 13.

A key benefit of self-directed teams is that all elements of productivity tend to improve—quality, cost, scheduling, and decision making.[6]

Quality Improvement: Improved quality management philosophies and techniques have spawned an impressive track record of improvements in the quality of organizational products, services, and processes. These improvements have led to greater satisfaction of internal and external customers, enhanced attainment of organizational objectives, and quality leadership in markets. Reduction of service errors, reduction of factory defects, and overall higher quality of the performance of organizations have been reported in the literature. A few examples follow.

A truck manufacturer initiated a quality team to audit a vehicle's quality as it came off the production line, tracking down the cause of any quality defect, and implementing solutions. Since 1990, the average number of demerits has been reduced by nearly 80 percent, and warranty claims were reduced by 50 percent from three years ago.[7]

At Motorola, Total Customer Satisfaction teams have authority to make changes in production or other work procedures. Bonuses are paid for improved defect rates and cycle times. Teams compete with one another for gold medals in company-wide performance contests. Motorola spends $70 million teaching employees techniques for identifying and fixing problems.[8]

Cost Reduction: There have been decreases in the cost of products, services, and organizational processes leading to price advantage in the marketplace. Both direct and indirect costs have been reduced through better use of team-organized labor, materials, and capital equipment.

At an insurance company the use of teams reduced personnel needs, thus saving $250,000 per year, and at the same time increased the volume of work handled by over 35 percent. Workplace safety teams have been used to reduce accidents and lower workers' compensation costs. Cost reductions in product development are usually reported when concurrent engineering project teams are used to do simultaneous design of products and organizational processes. A global procurement project team was used to save over $100 million on an annualized basis for a company. Companies that have used teams to evaluate safety strategies have helped to provide input for the slashing of workers' compensation costs by as much as 40–60 percent. The reduction of direct costs have helped to reduce overhead and fringe benefit costs as well.

Some specific reductions achieved through the use of teams include: (1) warranty costs; (2) factory waste; (3) manufacturing costs; (4) costs of accidents, sickness, and absenteeism costs by as much as 50 percent; and (5) defect rates and manufacturing processing time.

[6] Nancy A. Hitchcock, "Can Managed Teams Boost Your Bottom Line?" *Modern Material Handling* 48, no. 2 (February 1993): 57–59.
[7] Elias Pascual, "Mack Learns the Error of False Pride,';' *Wall Street Journal,* Manager's Journal, July 11, 1994, p. 1.
[8] G. Christian Hill and Ken Yamada, "Staying Power," *Wall Street Journal,* December 12, 1992, p. 1.

Safety teams that included equal numbers of workers and managers, reduced accidents as well as lowered workers' compensation costs, sometimes sharply.[9]

Earlier Commercialization: Through the use of concurrent engineering techniques, the development of products and organizational processes is facilitated and the product or service goes to the marketplace sooner. Greater profitability, enhanced customer satisfaction, and more efficient use of resources result. In the automobile industry concurrent engineering has helped to make American manufacturers more competitive through earlier commercialization—matching and in some cases exceeding what the Japanese auto manufacturers have been able to do. Getting to the marketplace sooner enables a company to get a lead on capture of the market for the product or service. Companies that have realized earlier commercialization of their products have made concurrent engineering a key straegy in dealing with the competitive pressures of the marketplace. Earlier commercialization means earlier and more revenue flow. In industries where the state of the art is changing fast, earlier commercialization is a prerequisite to survival. A few specific examples of earlier commercialization through the use of teams follows.

Colgate has revised its new-product development process to use cross-functional teams on selected product ideas and to speed up global commercialization of the most promising products. Only about 20 percent of ideas make it to prototype, down from around 50 percent. Each product idea managed by a cross-functional team has to meet specific criteria at six different stages in its life cycle.[10]

Chrysler's Neon automobile was developed by a core concurrent engineering team that mobilized 600 engineers, 289 suppliers, and blue-collar workers in the campaign to deliver the new car model in a speedy 42 months, for a fraction of what any recent small car had cost. Part of the reason for the speedy development was an uncharacteristic willingness on the part of the team members to borrow from competitors.[11]

Improved Supplier Relationships: Through closer partnerships with a few select suppliers, improved vendor products and services are purchased more efficiently, with more timely delivery. Vendors join concurrent engineering teams and help develop Original Equipment Manufacturer (OEM) products as well as more suitable vendors' parts and components, which leads to greater satisfaction of both vendors and customers. By bringing suppliers onto the teams the vendors have a greater opportunity to design more appropriate parts for the OEMs. Improvements in vendor parts and better delivery schedules

[9] Brent Bowers, "Businesses Fall in Love with Workplace Safety Teams," *Wall Street Journal,* March 16, 1994, p. 1.

[10] Christopher Power "Flops," *Business Week,* August 16, 1991, pp. 80–82.

[11] "Chrysler's Neon: Is This the Small Car Detroit Couldn't Build?" *Business Week,* May 3, 1993, pp. 116–117.

resulted. Since the typical OEM spends somewhere between 40–55 cents of each dollar on parts and services, having the vendors serve on the team is essential. Members of self-directed production teams can deal directly with the vendor's personnel, thus removing the traditional requirement of going through purchasing. The long-term contrasts and team membership of vendors have resulted in significant cost savings through the reduction of inventories and reduced manufacturing waste.

At the H. J. Heinz company a team was appointed to find and work out partnerships with the most efficient suppliers around the world and consolidate purchasing across all of the company affiliates. It took less than four months from the launch of the team until contracts were signed with suppliers. As of the end of 1993 the team has saved Heinz $100 million on an annualized basis.[12]

Enhanced Customer Satisfaction: Both internal and external customers report satisfaction with the products and services that are delivered to them when teams are used. These products and services are of high quality and are delivered on a more timely basis. By having customer representatives on the teams, the OEM gains better insight into customer needs, leading to greater satisfaction by the customer. Also, the customer sees the work developing on the products; if they see something that needs to be changed, immediate corrective action or added enhancement to the product can be carried out. Sales teams composed of sales representatives, engineers, technicians, and production managers improve service to customers, helping significantly to win new accounts. Order cycle time is reduced, thereby getting the product to the customer sooner, along with invoices. The use of e-mail for invoicing has added to procurement efficiencies.

In a study of the use of self-directed work teams in the northeast region of the United States, the most frequently cited critical reasons for work-team introduction were to foster product-quality improvement and to enhance customer satisfaction. This was followed by the desire to improve productivity.[13]

Changed Management Systems: Traditional management systems are modified through changes in the manner in which planning, organizing, motivating, leading, monitoring and controlling of the organizational resources is carried out. Managerial work, design, and flow are modified. In companies using self-managed teams the role of the traditional supervisor has been eliminated, to be replaced with an individual who is a coach, teacher, mentor, or facilitator. Fewer managers and supervisors are required: those that remain perform different duties than under the traditional hierarchical organization. Teams handle the administrative portion of the work, do scheduling of their members, plan vacations, evaluate team member performance, and hire and select members for reassignment out of the team—or even recommend members for

[12] *1993 Annual Report,* "The Power of Change," The H. J. Heinz Company, p. 3.
[13] Sam T. Johnson, "Work Teams: What's Ahead in Work Design and Rewards Management?" *Compensation & Benefits Review,* March–April 1993, pp. 35–41.

discharge from the company. When teams are used, the advanatages and challenges of building and maintaining a participatory style of management and decision making are evident. Consensus decision making becomes the norm for the manner in which the teams handle their work. Sometimes "360-degree performance appraisal" routines are established in which peers and others above and below the employee evaluate his or her performance. Fewer, simpler job classificatons are needed.

The horizontal corporation that emerges when teams are used eliminates both hierarchy and functional/departmental boundaries. In its purest state it has a skeleton team of senior executives at the top that handles such traditional support functions as finance and human resources. Virtually everyone else in the organization works together in multidisciplinary teams that perform core processes such as production and product/service and process development.[14]

At AT&T cross-unit teams are used to encourage cooperation among otherwise independent businesses. A team that includes the heads of four major business groups runs the company from day to day. Other management innovations include the development of a set of company values called the "common bond" and new ties with unions, including having union representatives sit on planning committees at both the corporate and plant levels.[15]

Cultural Enhancements: The beliefs, customs, knowledge, practices, and conventionalized behavior of the organizational social groups are modified. The team organizational culture ties people together, giving them a different meaning, principles, and standards to live and work by. People tend to share problems and opportunities more widely, due to a greater sense of belonging. Some of the more distinct cultural characteristics that emerge include:

Greater participation

More empathy

Better communication

Greater sharing of information

Socially accepted adversary roles

Improved morale

More candid discussions

Broader thinking by team members

More shared interests

Greater trust, loyalty, commitment and respect

Greater sharing of information and viewpoints

Greater overall sense of cooperation

---

[14] John A. Bryne, "The Horitontal Corporation," *Business Week,* December 20, 1993, pp. 76–81.

[15] David Kirkpatrick, "Could AT&T Rule the World?" *Fortune,* May 17, 1993, pp. 55–66.

At one company workers had been called employees or subordinates. Now everyone is called a member of the company and managers are now referred to as coordinators or coaches.[16]

Employee Satisfaction: Employees find more meaning in their work as they become a peer team member in an organizational unit dedicated to improvement of work processes and work output. People find greater identification with a greater variety of work, learn new skills, find more challenges and greater rewards. By belonging to an effective, dedicated team, the members feel a greater sense of pride in their productivity. Other elements of employee satisfaction include:

Greater feeling of contribution
More self-destiny
Greater enjoyment of work
More outlet for creativity

The improvements in productivity that have been realized by companies are often accompanied by improved morale, greater pride, energizing of team members, and increased opportunities for the members to have greater visibility in their work and in the company. In most instances, team members are given the opportunity to conduct training and orientation sessions for new members. For many of these team members it has been the first opportunity they have had to do this kind of work—and be recognized for doing it.

Creativity & Innovation: Greater opportunities are available for suggesting improvements in both the technical aspects and management of the work of the organization. People feel that their opinions are valued, and they are encouraged by an enlightened management to bring forth ideas for continuous improvement of the organization and its work. Being creative and eager to suggest new ways of doing things becomes a standard of conduct in the enterprise.

Teams have been used to conceive and execute R&D projects, contracting out the technical work and details to commercial labs, and then working with these labs to evaluate performance on the R&D contracts. Companies have reported that most of the innovative ideas for new products flow from interdisciplinary teams that focus on specific product lines with success rates resulting in the ability to introduce new, innovative, and competitive products. The openness of the teams' work, coming out of cross-functional and cross-organizational relationships, has made new product development a major criterion for success in the enterprises.

---

[16] Ralph Stayer, "How I Learned to Let My Workers Lead," *Harvard Business Review*, November–December 1990, pp. 66–83.

At the Rubbermaid company most ideas for products flow from a single source: teams. Twenty teams, each made up of five to seven people from different functions of the company, focus on specific product lines. So successful has the use of teams been in coming up with ideas for new products—and managing the development of these products—that senior management at the company fear what would happen to the identification and development of new products without teams. Rubbermaid's success rate in introducing more than 365 new products a year seems incredible, considering that the company does no market testing.[17]

Teams of doctors, nurses, administrators, and even engineers are challenging every step involved in treating conditions ranging from heart disease to urinary tract infections. The aim is to root out steps that add costs without improving results. The potential savings could run to tens of billions of dollars a year.[18]

Strategic Initiatives: Since team members are given greater access to organizational performance information, they sense opportunities for both operational and strategic initiatives. Ideas for product and service improvements are sensed by the team members, and these ideas are then put into the mainstream of organizational discussions to determine their merit. The 3M company has a policy, "Thou shall not kill a product idea," that has become a way of life in the enterprise.

Workers serve on teams set up to benchmark the competitors, thus gaining an appreciation of the strategic challenges facing the enterprise. When workers serve on technology assessment teams, they bring valuable input and gain insight into how emerging technologies can impact the strategic direction of the organization. Enterprise managers recognize more than ever that ideas from workers—and everyone else in the enterprise—can help in setting the strategic direction.

At the General Motors Corporation part of the remedial strategies to improve the company's competitiveness involved the use of teams. Teamwork between designers and manufacturing personnel cut 33 percent of assembly time on the newest models of vehicles.[19]

At the Swiss Corporation for Microelectronics and Watchmaking remedial strategies have brought forth one of the most spectacular industrial comebacks in the world—the revitalization of the Swiss watch industry. Project teams were used to bring a focus to the revitalization of this industry.[20]

Stakeholder Image: The perceptions of teams and team members is broadened as they work with key stakeholders of the enterprise, such as unions,

---

[17] Alan Farnham, "America's Most Admired Company," *Fortune,* February 7, 1994, pp. 50–54.
[18] Ron Winslow, "Health-Care Providers Try Industrial Tactics to Reduce their Costs," *Wall Street Journal,* November 3, 1994, p. 1.
[19] Jerry Flint, "GM: Not Fixed Yet," *Business Week,* November 8, 1993, p. 46
[20] William Taylor, "Message and Muscle," *Harvard Business Review,* March–April 1993, pp. 99–110.

customers, suppliers, and local community groups. Employees realize that the success of the enterprise is tied inexorably to many stakeholders having different yet interdependent claims on the values created by the enterprises. Employees who have such perceptions work to enhance effective networks with organizational stakeholders. Enhanced ties with union officials, local community groups, and suppliers provide ample opportunity for the teams to support the enterprise's well-being.

Allina, which runs 17 nonprofit hospitals in Minnesota, had tried to form teams through the 1980s but always failed, in part because of hostile relations with unions. By forming a team of management and union officials and giving the team authority to negotiate union and management differences, successful teams were finally created in a majority of its hospitals, with remarkable results.[21]

After-Sales Service Improvement: Since the concurrent engineering teams participate in the planning for the logistical support of the product, the subsequent services provided to the customers are enhanced. When service and maintenance personnel become members of the concurrent engineering teams, they gain insight into the needs for support of the products when the customers take possession.

Development of Management Potential: The use of self-managed teams expands the exposure of all team members to the theory and practice of management. Team members develop new and enhanced capabilities in the knowledge, skills, and attitudes needed to manage themselves, the team, and the enterprise. Team members come to understand the challenges of the management functions of planning, organizing, motivating, directing, controlling of resources, and are offered the opportunity to carry these functions for the team. People that heretofore were never exposed to what managers do now have the opportunity to try their hands at being a manager. For many it is a unique and challenging experience—and can lead to their progression up the management ranks of the enterprise.

Reverberations from the use of teams include the shift of management from a traditional direct superior-subordinate relationship to one of facilitator, coach, mentor, advisor, teacher, trainer, counsel, consultant, guide, or some such role in which there is less giving direction and more providing of resources and creating an environment for people to work together with economic, social, and psychological satisfaction, as they create value for internal and external customers. A plant manager of Baldor Electric Company's Westville, Oklahoma facility notes there is a need to go through rethinking and attitude changes as the traditional managerial and supervisory roles change under the team-driven enterprise.[22]

---

[21] Brian Dumaine, "The Trouble With Teams," *Fortune,* September 5, 1994, pp. 86–92.

[22] Tracy E. Benson, "Empowerment: There's That Word Again," *Industry Week,* May 6, 1991, pp. 44–52.

Rapidly disappearing from the General Electric plant in Grove City, Pennsylvania are the old-line foremen. At this plant 600 nonunion hourly workers manage their own jobs by teams, facilitated by five nonsupervisory salaried workers. At GE's turn-of-the-century locomotive works in Erie, Pennsylvania, the foremen are gone, and assembly times on new locomotives have been cut in half since 1992. At GE's Appliance Park in Louisville, Kentucky, a close relationship with the local union has resulted in giving up lucrative piece-rate pay scales and the reduction of overtime. A no-foremen, work-team approach has been adopted at the plant. The plant has gone from a $47 million loss in 1992 to a projected $40 million profit in 1995.[23]

Development of Leadership Potential: Team members develop greater empathy for leadership roles and understanding of the key challenges to be met in performing leadership activities in the team and the enterprise. When team leadership is rotated among the members, they have the opportunity to try out first-hand their leadership capabilities and potential. As a result, there is a greater pool of potential leadership available to the enterprise. When team members become designated leaders of the team, their pride and sense of accomplishment is enhanced.

At the Goodyear company employees are empowered to make key process and product decisions. The company executives turned its corporate culture on its head when they decided to implement a team approach to process and product development and problem solving. Extensive training helped to prepare employees to serve on teams that work with suppliers, customers, and other employees. A flatter hierarchy resulted, and performance appraisals now focus on the ability of an individual to work as a team player, and decision making has been pushed down to the level where the information can be developed.[24]

Reduction of Parochialism/Provincialism: As team members work together interdependently with members from other disciplines and organizational units, they tend to see and appreciate the problems and challenges other organizational units face. A greater sense of appreciation for what other disciplines and organizational units must do to contribute to the larger whole of the organization is gained.

An example of organizational improvement through the use of self-managed teams is the Phelps Dodges Norenci copper mine in Arizona. Workers there are part of a flexible team, rather than cogs in the organizational machine. Team members are encouraged to cross-train in different jobs. Under the old "command and control" management philosophy workers were isolated, cut off from one another and from their supervisor. Under the team management approach they are allowed to express their own opinions more liberally—any

---

[23] James R. Norman, "A Very Nimble Elephant," *Forbes,* October 10, 1994, pp. 88–92.

[24] Frederick J. Kovac, "Goodyear Agility Focuses on Collaboration, Technology, and Empowerment," *Focus,* National Center for Manufacturing Sciences, Ann Arbor, Michigan, June 1991, pp. 2–3.

worker can go to the general foreman and talk to that individual. In the past decade Morenci's annual productivity has gone from 100,000 pounds of copper per employee to more than 300,000. Accidents have declined from 14 per million employee hours to fewer than two—the result to team work, smarter work, and an enhanced environment for people to do their best.[25]

Improved Product/Service/Process Development: Shorter development cycles, reduced costs, higher quality, earlier commercialization, and enhanced profitability result from the use of concurrent engineering teams. Team members gain a greater appreciation of what it takes to get the enterprise members to work together to prepare the enterprise for its competitive challenges. Some specific examples of improvements in product/service and process development follow.

A manufacturer using a team as the principal agent of change transformed the company's approach to manufacturing from a single facility to a focused factory dedicated to a narrow, newly developed product line. Teams helped to rethink every process from product development to distribution. As a result of the teams' deliberations, two layers of management were eliminated, product groups were given their own sales staff, and more time was spent up front defining products and organizational processes to build, market, and service these products. Teams were used to develop products faster than the company's previous formal product-development organization.

At Hewlett-Packard company small teams are used to develop products faster than the company's former formal product-development organization. Every employee is encouraged to rethink every process from product development to distribution. Two layers of management were eliminated, product groups have their own sales staffs, and more time is spent up front in defining products and organizational processes to build, market, and service those products.[26]

Greater Use of Knowledge, Skills, and Attitudes: Employees working on teams find more outlets for their abilities. They are challenged more fully through learning multiple skills, and they acquire greater knowledge in working as a specialist and contributing member of alternative teams. The likelihood that employees are not being used at their level of potential is reduced. In addition, they have opportunities for additional training to acquire more skills. In some cases the qualified workers train new workers—in classrooms and on-the-job. The opportunities for additional training include technical, social, management, and leadership training.

At one company, teams of workers were formed to resolve quality problems. The team gathered data, identified problems, and worked with suppliers and with other workers to develop and execute solutions. The teams took responsibility for measuring quality and then used those measurements to improve

---

[25] Myron Magnet, "The Truth About the American Worker," *Fortune,* May 4, 1992, pp. 48–65.
[26] Robert D. Hof, "From Dinosaur to Gazelle," *Business Week/Reinventing America,* 1991, p. 65.

production processes. The results were impressive, rejects fell from 5 percent to less than 0.5 percent.[27]

Organizational Design Changes: Teams play a role in downsizing and restructuring an enterprise, leading to fewer levels of hierarchy and the reengineering of organizational processes. Organizational designs are built around processes, in addition to the more traditional means of organizing resources, such as functional homogeneity and geographic alignments. Matrix organizational designs have emerged as the principal means for bringing a focus to teamwork in the enterprise. Less bureaucracy, more complex patterns of authority, responsibility, and accountability, greater empowerment, flatter organizational designs, and less vertical management are important. Many of the hierarchical and functional boundaries are reduced or even eliminated. Yet functional specialization has not been eliminated.

At the H. J. Heinz Company three task forces independent of the normal organizational structure were established in the areas of procurement. Results from these task forces include replacing a traditionally decentralized purchasing system with a centralized negotiation strategy. The company's suppliers are now being dealt with on a global basis.[28]

At the Ford Motor Company, global product teams will now design cars to be sold around the world.[29]

In Basilicata in southern Italy automaker Fiat recently opened a $2.9 billion plant that has an important objective: to shake off hidebound work practices. Fiat spent $64 million training workers and engineers to operate in independent, multiskilled teams. Factory workers and office staff work together under the same roof. Top-down decision making is dead—problems are solved by teams actually working on production.[30]

Allegheny Ludlum, a billion-dollar U.S. maker of specialty steel, gives its managers considerable freedom to operate within the broad boundaries set by the company. Each manager operates as part of a team-run business unit, with bonuses tied to the individual business unit goals and the overall performance of the unit.[31]

A public utility, Texas Electric Company uses teams to unify all organizations responsible for the completion of its nuclear power plant construction projects. The use of such teams has facilitated the completion of projects on time, within budget limits, and with the highest levels of quality and safety.[32]

[27] Ralph Stayer, "How I Learned to Let My Workers Lead," *Harvard Business Review,* November–December 1990, pp. 66–83.

[28] *The 1992 Annual Report,* H. J. Heinz Company, Pittsburgh, Pa., p. 1.

[29] Kathleen Kerwin, "Ford," Cover Story, *Business Week,* April 3, 1995, pp. 94–101.

[30] Jane A. Sasseen, Robert Neff, Shekar Hattengadi and Silvia Sansoni, "The Winds of Change Blow Everywhere," *Business Week,* October 17, 1994, pp. 92–93.

[31] "Briefings From the Editors," *Harvard Business Review,* May–June 1993, p. 10.

[32] Elizabeth A. Bretz, "Teamwork at Comanche Peak Takes on a Dimension," *Electric World* 206, no. 5 (May 1992): 53–56.

Profitability Increases: Measurable enhancement of profit performance is the final test of the efficacy of teams and of the performance of the enterprise in its marketplace. In a steel company, a team studied and recommended a $5 million capital investment to renovate an aging mill. The renovated mill paid off in profit, improved product quality, and reduction of overtime.

Teams have been the primary contributor to profitability at the Mack Corporation. Since 1990 the number of hours required to build a truck has been reduced by 41 percent, and inventories have been slashed in half as a percentage of net sales and break-even sales point. In 1993 the company increased its U.S. market share and posted a sales increase of 38 percent, outpacing a market that increased 32 percent.[33]

Ability of the Teams to Make/Execute Managerial Decisions: Teams make and execute managerial decisions previously reserved for managers and supervisors. As the teams carry out managerial fucntions, they are actively involved in making decisions: allocating resources, assigning people to jobs, evaluating individual and team performance, hiring new team members, dealing with nonperformers, and passing judgment on how well the organizational work is going. Teams are responsible for finding problems that inhibit effective performance, and then designing strategies to correct performance shortcomings. Sometimes teams design their own training manuals. Teams have been involved in plant location studies, design of financial strategies, and assessment of competitors' products. At an insurance company self-managed teams take care of all the activities for processing claims. These teams are also responsible for the traditional supervisory functions of hiring, work scheduling, overtime, and performance evaluation.

At the Motorola cellular equipment plant in Arlington Heights, Illinois, self-managed teams hire and fire their coworkers, help select their supervisors, and schedule their own work, in consultation with other teams. In 1993 the factory's 1,003 workers were organized into 168 special teams dedicated to improving quality, cutting costs, and reducing cycle time. Quality teams have come to the office at Motorola. A team of lawyers and engineers reduced the standard invention disclosure form from fifteen pages to two and reduced backlog without adding staff. The improved disclosure process saved the company the equivalent of 44 years of engineering time last year. The quality team won a gold medal at Motorola's annual Total Customer Service team competition, topping a field of 4,300 teams from eleven countries.[34]

Examples of modest investments of time and money in the use of teams has paid off dramatically at the Freudenberg-NOK auto parts factory in Ligoneir, Indiana. With other company plants going through a similar process by the end of 1995, it was estimated that a $2 million investment in teams and their suggestions would result in a direct payback of $12 million to $20 million.[35]

---

[33] Elias Pascual, "Mack Learns the Error of False Pride," *Wall Street Journal,* July 11, 1994, p. 1.
[34] Ronald Henkoff, "Keeping Motorola on the Roll," *Fortune,* April 18, 1994, pp. 67–68.
[35] James R. Treece, "Improving the Sound of an Old Macine," *Business Week,* October 25, 1991, pp. 134–136.

At Heinz, team-based quality and safety efforts have reduced workers' compensation costs by 60 percent and helped make the company the quality leader of the pet food industry. Evaluation teams are helping to streamline factory operations and improve quality, in some cases reducing overhead by as much as 40 percent. Teams develop their own plans, present them to coworkers and work to implement the changes with little direct intervention by management.[36]

SUMMARY

This chapter presented an overall profile of the likely results that are produced by teams.

The results realized in the use of teams are basically of two types: (1) specific and measurable direct accomplishments, such as improvements in productivity, quality, cost, or earlier commercialization of products and services; and (2) indirect results, such as increased employee satisfaction, enhanced culture, emergence of more creativity and innovation, and the development of leadership initiatives in the enterprise. The direct results are easier to recognize; the indirect results can be subtle yet can enhance the firm's ability to compete.

Leaders and managers who are considering the design and development of a strategy to use teams in their organizations will find that a perusal of this chapter will provide insight into what to expect. When teams are introduced into an enterprise, everything is affected. Teams can produce direct and measurable results and can set in motion a series of trigger effects that are likely to cause meaningful changes throughout the enterprise—ranging from its strategic management, to the workers who are working on production lines of whatever type, to the creation of value for customers.

After a company forms a new team, it would be useful for team members to read the material in this chapter and then discuss the material in the context of expected results. Discussing these results at initial team meetings can be worthwhile.

The following key messages were provided in this chapter:

- The positive results to be realized from the use of teams are impressive and should help motivate managers to try using teams to improve competitiveness.
- The results of teams that are reported in the chapter do not come from rigorous research—rather, they are a collection drawn from many sources.
- Teams change the way that people work and ultimately affect the cultural ambience of the enterprise.

[36] *The H. J. Heinz Company 1993 Annual Report,* "Working Smarter," p. 17.

- Both direct and indirect benefits result from using teams.
- Some of the direct results, such as productivity and quality improvmeents, cost reductions, and greater profitability, set in motion trigger effects, which affect the personal careers of people as well as the culture of an enterprise.
- Teams sometimes do not work and are disbanded. Lack of top management support is a major reason for the failure of teams.
- Overall, the results of using teams provide clear evidence of the wisdom of using teams in the strategic management of an enterprise.

INDEX